Unraveling the Bible
The Colonization of Earth and the Making of Mankind

Copyright © 2023 by Steven Machat

All rights reserved.

Permission to reproduce or transmit in any form or by any means, electronic or mechanical, including photocopying, photographic and recording audio or video, or by any information storage and retrieval system, must be obtained in writing from the author.

Unraveling the Bible is a registered trademark of Steven Machat.

To order additional copies of this title, or to contact the author, please e-mail, smachat@gmail.com

For more information about Steven Machat please visit: stevenemachat.com

First printing January 2023

Library of Congress Cataloging-in-Publication Data

Paperback ISBN: 9798374350838
Hardcover ISBN: 9798374350906

Machat, Steven

unraveling the bible: the colonization of earth and the making of mankind / by Steven Machat

Published by AR PRESS, an American Real Publishing Company

Roger L. Brooks, Publisher | roger@incubatemedia.us
americanrealpublishing.com

Edited by Debbie Machat
Stan Lee photograph by Gage Skidmore
Printed in the U.S.A.

The Truth is Finally Revealed

UNRAVELING THE BIBLE

The Colonization of Earth
and The Making of Mankind

STEVEN MACHAT
Gold Edition
The Book of Earth - Opus I The Epic Rock Opera

From the Author

Hi. My name is Steven Machat. I am today heading to my seventieth Earth birthday celebrating seventy full circles of Earth around the Sun.

I say "on Earth" as I am more than just my body. I am an energy with a consciousness that I got as a gift from my parents, who got a gift from their four parents to incarcerate them into a physical life here on Earth. And so on and so on.

But is life here a gift? Or is it a sentence? If a sentence, to do what and for whom?

When you study the other living beings on Earth, those beings—be they plants or animals and even fungi—all participate in the circle of life here on Earth. Life on Earth is sharing the elements of chemicals inside our Earth's atmosphere. All beings take and then give. We animals breathe in air and exhale carbon dioxide that plants use, and those plants give us air.

But we humans change Earth, and those changes take away life forces on Earth. Other beings do not change Earth. We make Earth an urban jungle. We believe Earth is ours for the taking. We do not understand the concept of living and sharing. We are an organism that takes and gives nothing back intentionally.

We kill Earth all for our own personal glory. We are really not here to make Earth life better for Earthlings. No, we are here to make

Earth the newest urban jungle of all the other planets that exist in the universes and galaxies of conscious existence.

We human beings are not from Earth. Our bodies may be from Earth, but our consciousness is not. We act like other beings in that we must eat substances from the Earth itself to exist living on Earth. We excrete what our bodies do not need and in so doing give Earth back what we did not need. What we give back is used by other Earth beings. When we physically die, our bodies are broken down by other lives, and those substances that made our bodies are returned to earth.

But we are a consciousness that has intelligence with wants and needs that will exist after our physical Earth life. So what are we—a consciousness—doing here on Earth?

Why were we physically created? How were we physically created? Whom does our lives on this planet benefit if not Earth?

We were created to serve something. This book gives you the answers to these questions. The answers are inside what we are taught is the word of the God. But what was that god, or God?

I unravel the Bible as I always knew it was based on something. And I found the sources many of us have of the Bible. They were buried in our sands of Earth time in the regions of what we call the Middle East, as well as everywhere the Nefilim lived and altered Earth for their wants and needs.

The head scientist of Nefilim's exploration of Earth named Enki kept a written record of what they did and why the Nefilim exploration team on Earth, called Anunnaki, did what they did.

These tablets and their translations into early civilized man's first written languages were discovered and torn apart to discover the meaning of those symbols and then put together by many an explorer searching for answers who came before me.

I just put together the timeline of what went on and why they did what they did—"they" being the aliens who came to Earth from planet Nibiru on their visit to colonize Earth and search for gold, which they needed to save their planet. And when they realized they needed living helpers who could obey orders as slaves and then serve the upper-class Nefilim in their urban cities of our ancient societies, they made mankind the two-legged animals in existence on Earth and gave them intelligence. They could follow orders.

You will now learn their story, which is how the Bible begins.

I share with you the unraveling of their written diaries, which were retold so mankind could understand despite mankind's limited intelligence at that time. Events that took place over hundreds of thousands of years were compressed into stories that began the day mankind learned how to write, which was about 6,000 Earth years ago. There are more stories, but not all are contained in what we call the Bible.

My goal is to do something to help start us on a path to end the divisions of mankind. My goal is to end the wars of whose god is the boss. My goal is to unite mankind so we can become a planet of one nation just like our aliens were a planet under one leadership called Nibiru.

I pray this book helps you take the blinders of superstition and fear of bodily death that are inbred into your minds from the day your parents and their surroundings—say you are a Jew or a Christian a Jan or a Buddhist, Hindu, or a member of the So religion and whatever else it is that your community prays to seeking a god that interferes in your life as this is what that god does for that god's living.

May we all unite as one race of collective consciousness that respects the individual consciousness we are here on Earth. United, we collectively agree to make this planet that has become our home a heaven we dream about here on physical Earth. A heaven created for all of us to be united custodians of the planet so others who come after us live a life of health and happiness.

Just to get you versed in what went on before mankind was in control of earth, I now will share with you these truths hidden in our sands of thoughts outside the current ruling societies' boundaries of knowledge and wisdom.

Unraveling the Bible Revelations

To understand the Bible, we must understand the meaning of symbols we call words and the letters of an alphabet we use to write those words at the moment in time when they were initially used. To understand what came before, we must go to that time of creation. We unfortunately do not do that, and we allow the past to control our present. We allow the superstitions of the past hidden in those words to control our present and shape our future.

When you see the word Bible, it makes you feel something. Does it not? What do you feel? You automatically think of god and you think of our creation. You may think it is truth or you may think it **is made of lies. But it does scare you.**

These sounds of words that change, depending on which language you are speaking using the same symbols of pronouncing words, are magical symbols trying to share the sacred meaning of what came before. The meaning of those symbols must again be seen in the light of their creation. Those symbols were created to show the future of what went on in the future's past. They were sometimes simply created to control the thoughts of those living in the future with the superstitions of the past.

A great term we use today to explain this phenomenon of the word is the word *talisman*. So I feel it is a must in order for one to unravel the Bible that we examine the phenomenon of what went on in the past. We have words and symbols that include letters of the words that we must reexamine to get the true story of who we were so we understand what we have become as a "thought-conscious" species living here on Mother Earth. And please understand that earth, the planet, is our mother for it is she whose body, we as a consciousness, live in and must learn to live with if we are to survive.

Let's start with the word phenomenon. What does this word mean? One good definition I feel is "a phenomenon is a fact or situation that is observed to exist or happen." The fact or situation that you observed is one whose cause or explanation is in question. You cannot explain it.

So what is normal for you to do is explain it with concepts reduced to an image you create by using magical words. An example is, "God did it." Or, "God told me to do it." Energy made something happen, and you cannot explain the energy, so you give the energy a source and that energy is god.

But what is god?

God is many things. But today many of us beings believe god is one visible identifiable being who made us. God is who we live for and why we carry on. God is to whom we return when we physically die. We believe in an afterlife, and all the major religions tell us what we must do while we are alive to return to god. And since it is hard to live a whole life the way the religions tell us, when we do wrong, the religions tell us how we can make up with god. Notice there is a third party who tells us what god wants and how we can make up with god.

We can pray to god for forgiveness. And these prayers are so the God or gods look on us and give us favors for our prayers.

Why is god written with a capital G so it becomes God? Some places write GOD, or in some religions, you will see G-D.

Are these not superstitions? Ask yourself what superstitions you are being sold. And then ask yourself why a society needs a god deity. What would we beings do if we did not have a deity that we talk with before we do what we do.

A deity is capitalized when there is only one. God, the only deity, is a hypothetical being we consider divine or sacred. This is also the definition one can find in the Oxford dictionary.

God is a term we used to explain the supernatural that we cannot explain.

In this book, I specifically write to show you that there was more than one deity in the development of our societies here on Earth. The deities were a tribe of alien beings who created mankind the physical being and gave us our societies. This tribe of beings called themselves the Nefilim. When mankind was a newer being, we called all of them tribe gods or used their name and called them what they called themselves, Nefilim.

Never are we taught the supernatural and how it happens let alone is an inquiry of the supernatural allowed so we can figure out collectively the metaphysical truths of how certain energies can make the phenomenon happen. It's magic to some, and to others it is very explainable.

Quantum physics was created by mankind's never-ending quest to explain what we cannot see and to discover how things unexplainable to the eye happen. Quantum physics is what I have studied nonstop for most of my life. I ask why and set out to discover how this happened.

Everything starts with a thought. Everything. The first thought is the absolute beginning of everything that comes alive. The first thought of everything is the Supreme Being, and we are all part of that first thought. We are all part of the Supreme Being as the energy source of everything that exists and more.

That first thought is the Big Bang that scientists talk about when they try to explain the phenomenon that created life. That first thought begets all subsequent thoughts the same way an atom of energy can divide or the way a physical cell does divide. Thought is how matter is made. That energy of thoughts creates the matrices we live in called universes and galaxies. And those matrices create the energy inside the matrices called planets inside those universes to give us our physical bodies that are taken from the planet's dense bodies' existence. Planets are alive, and we are the fruits in physical form of those planets. We will go over all this later.

Can you see the wind? Can you talk with the wind? Can the wind change our world order without ever speaking or showing itself to you? Is a thought the wind? Then does it even exist? Think why you believe something that you cannot prove exists. How do you prove love? What is love? Answers we will go over at another time.

Let's return to the concept of talisman and its twin, the concept of an amulet. We must understand the magic of an amulet or a talisman. Both are the same concept. An amulet is what we give to others to control their memories of events we wish them to remember when they look at the amulet. We can even give ourselves an amulet.

A talisman is what we leave for others to see when we wish for them to remember what we want them to know about what went on before in our time here on Earth.

The magical purpose of an amulet or talisman, an object either made by man or nature itself, is to put a spell on it that makes you, the observer, believe that object is endowed with special, magical, unseen powers to explain and protect or bring good fortune to the observer.

An amulet is something you can carry on your body or with your hands like a rose to show that you love the one you gave the rose to or even the box of chocolates. If it's about a third-party definable god, the amulet can be a necklace bearing a cross or an image of a man hanging on the cross or two triangles connecting as one, which means man and woman, but we call it the Star of David.

These objects of love or god can become talismans, such as paintings of roses or nature or statues of Jesus hanging on the cross or Christ dressed in his purple robes laced with gold to show you that Christ is watching over you. The Jews have no identifiable God image, just images of things to let all know your belief in that Jewish God.

An example of a powerful unexplained talisman of our current time are the pyramids of Memphis, Egypt. We see the pyramids on images around the world and allow others to tell us that they are 4,500 Earth years old when scientists have used radar to prove that they were built 13,000 Earth years ago. If it's 4,500 hundred years ago, it fits the narrative that humans built the pyramids. If they are 13,000 years old, then something else, not us humans, built those pyramids. The truth is obvious if we use reason, but because it goes against the conventional system's narrative, we ignore the obvious truth and follow falsities.

How about the statue of Buddha?

Well Buddha was the enlightened one, so we are taught. So you, looking at this talisman of Buddha with eyes closed sitting in a meditative pose, means that the person housing Buddha or the establishment housing Buddha, the image in physical form, are enlightened and live the Buddha laws. Laws of how to control your thoughts and how you must exist to achieve enlightenment in your living form on Earth.

A divine being is one who has supernatural powers. Supernatural powers are really today's comic book heroes. And these beings did exist, and they had a king who told the others what this community of supernatural beings can and cannot do in the community they ran of living beings. The king was the only God. The family was the prince and princes. In Christianity, you are taught of the power of the Holy Spirit that enables one to do more than the ordinary.

These comic book heroes were created from the stories of the Nefilim. I worked with Stan Lee himself, and he and I would discuss the Nefilim and their space-traveling Anunnaki crew.

In the initial text that the Bible came from in the first place, that text being the Book of Enki, we are introduced to the words Nefilim as well as Anunnaki and Nibiru.

Nefilim is defined and it does appear in the translations that appear in the Genesis part of our Bible as beings who "fell" to Earth or as the "fallen ones." This tribe is referred to in the Oxford accepted version of the Bible in Genesis 6:4 and Numbers 13:33.

The word Anunnaki (Anunnaki, Anukki, Enunaki) in the Oxford dictionary is described as the Sumerian deities of the old primordial time. Primordial is defined as meaning (1) existing at or from the beginning, (2) constituting an origin, and (3) of or relating to an early stage of development.

But the Bible is a put-together book of books that exists among many others that explain events referred to in the Bible. One simple example is the Book of Enoch. This book is still in existence and was actually accepted once by the Christian Church before the Vatican needed to vote it out of the biblical canon we called the Old Testament. The Vatican calls this Book of Enoch heresy as it tells the story of the Nefilim and those beings who fell to Earth.

The survival of this book is the underbelly of the marginal as well as heretical Christian groups such as the Manichaeans and the Cathars whom the Catholic Church had tried to erase in both physical and thought form. But as we have learned, you can never kill a thought. You can kill the physical body but not the thought. The Book of Enoch is very much a part of this book as I unravel the Bible, and these thoughts are still alive when you study the Zoroastrian-Iranian, Greek, Chaldean, and Egyptian talisman beliefs.

Today we use the interpretations of the words related to the Nefilim beings to describe god and gods. This is really the concept of god that we are forced by society to believe in. Our society is based on this being called god who, if we behave, will take care of us when we physically die. How did these thoughts of control begin in our conscious minds? Why do we give away our powers to satisfy those who say they speak to god for us?

It is the story of our creators called the Nefilim, and this book will explain to all the ruses played on us and our societies. And yes, these Nefilim beings, as you are about to learn, are the ones who locked our thoughts called consciousness inside this Earth body when our collective Earthling consciousness was traveling space looking for a home to become physical beings and this planet caught our eye as we saw the Dream Catchers, the Nefilim, set out to catch our thoughts and incarnated us into beings caught in this matrix of existence. We initially existed to serve their wants and needs. We can get out of this place, and that is book three of this three-opus series called *Books of Earth*.

And when the Nefilim were done here on earth, they left us with no explanation of who or what we are or why we are here. One of the Nefilim, the Earth commander at the time of his departure back to Nibiru, did give Moses his Ten Commandments. These commandments explained how the Nefilim ran their society on Nibiru. It is funny that after you read this book, you will see while they were on Earth, they ignored each and every commandment as they created the havoc that we live in and under.

The Bible is really a collection of the Nefilim king and his son Enki's recollection of why they did what they did here on Earth. Our bodies and our locked-up consciousness are their gifts to Earth.

We are a very immature race of beings who still believe that one talisman, as opposed to a collective energy of thoughts, exists in some space somewhere or anywhere that created everything we can see. This being watches over us, and if we cry loudly enough, will come back to Earth to take control of us and save us from what we did or will do to each other.

You are about to enter the world of Anunnaki creation. They, in this book, are those Nefilim who fell to Earth as the Nefilim space traveling team whose role was to colonize Earth and mine for the gold the planet Nibiru needed to fix and plug the holes of its atmosphere.

The word "Nibiru" is not defined in the Oxford dictionary. This I find very interesting. It does appear in mythological talismans of the existence of Earth and how Earth began as well as how it may end.

The Mayan calendar, an unexplained talisman that revolves around this planet Nibiru, we will learn about in this book. Nibiru is rotating around our same Sun and is supposed to once again come near Earth and cause physical collisions or super hurricanes from the beyond when those currents hit earth. And once hit, it will change the Earth that we know now.

However, if you study metaphysical thoughts, you will learn that we—you and I—are nothing more than a thought from the eternal energy source of everything and more. Thoughts of things we have not yet been able to quantify as well as qualify. And these astrological signs given to us by the Nefilim are warnings of a rock n' roll tour of energies about to hit planet Earth, as the moon is in the seventh house and Jupiter aligns with Mars, allowing for a clear landing passage of new thoughts to rule our existence here on Earth.

The Age of Aquarius is an age of peace because we have an understanding of the energies that came before and ruled our existence as a consciousness locked inside these dense bodies of ours. And if I go to a subsequent line of that song, you will read "and love will steer the stars" of our universe. And steering those stars we will live in a world of no more falsehoods or derisions. We will have golden living, not of gold but of the supreme color of visions. We will use mystic crystal-clear revelations, which are visions that will allow the eternal true physical liberation. A liberation that will happen when we shut down the body's machine mind to live in a planet of true liberation of understanding why are living here on Earth in our present incarnation not ruled by Talisman and those Amulets of our ancestors' past life experiences.

In this book, you will learn that Nibiru is a planet inside our universe. Nibiru rotates around the Sun. But unlike the other nine known planets of our universe, the orbit of Nibiru is a planet that circles our Sun once every 3,600 Earth years. Nibiru has an elliptical orbit that becomes an ecliptic orbit when it comes near the other planets that follow orderly rotating lanes circulating our Sun. Nibiru has its own lanes of travel different from the other nine, as we will learn about in this book.

I first learned of this planet when I was traveling on a rock and roll stage set on an Earth space ship touring the band the Electric Light Orchestra (ELO) back in 1978 reading a book called *The Twelfth Planet* by Zecharia Sitchin. That author was heavily engaged in reading the Sumerians Samaritan tablets that mankind found in the sands of time where those urban empires once existed. My friends and coworkers gave me looks I still see to this day as I shared with them the contents of the book, which I admit I did not understand and have searched for the meaning till this day.

I will now end this section on Revelations as if we are in a classroom together, and I will begin the narration of the story I have put together, which is book one of the three-book *Book of Earth* Series I call *Unraveling the Bible: Colonization of Earth and the Making and Civilizing of Mankind.*

    This book is dedicated with LOVE to everyone I know and will so know. You all gave me the strength and energy to carry on whether you know it or not. Love is the answer.

    And it is the love I live and the love I share with my editor and my wife, Debbie Machat, to whom I especially dedicate this book. As it was with Debbie's never-ending love and support as my editor (of the content and grammar) and my partner that we give birth to our child the *Book of Earth* Series.

    And without Debbie's love and support questioning everything so created, I never would have created let alone finished these writings.

Of all men's miseries the bittersweet is this: to know so much and to have control over nothing.

—Herodotus

TABLE OF CONTENTS

ACT ONE: COLONIZING EARTH 1

   Act One, Scene One: In the Beginning. Prior Times The Creation of Our Current Solar System..3

   Act One, Scene Two: The Birth of Earth and Earth's Moon...........11

   Act One, Scene Three: The Nefilim Decision of Colonizing Earth for the Gold 17

   Act One, Scene Four: The Actual Acts of Nibiru Colonizing Earth and Now Mars for the Gold 27

1)	Planning the Voyage	29
2)	The Trip to Earth	29
3)	Colonizing Earth. Setting Up the First Campgrounds	31
4)	The First Gold Rush in The Waters Near Edin	34
5)	Transportation of The Gold Back to Nibiru	36
6)	The Gold in Nibiru	38
7)	Back on Earth: Looking for More Gold Reserves on Earth	39
8)	Colonizing Mars to Help Transport the Gold Reserves from Earth to Nibiru	41
9)	Colonizing Abzu in Southern Africa to Mine the Gold Found in the Hills	42
10)	Back to Edin: Building the First Urban Anunnaki Workers' Communities	43
11)	Back On Nibiru: Next Trip to Earth and Mars	44
12)	Back to Earth: New Anunnaki Team Get Their New Homes and Jobs	47

13) Earth: Princes of Nibiru Doing Their Work 50
14) The First Nefilim-Anunnaki Royal Court and Their Workers 53
15) The Igigi's Mutiny on Mars 56
16) Back to Abzu and the Earth Gold Mines 58

Act One, Scene Five: The Earth's First Workers' Revolt 61

Act One, Scene Six: Making Lulu, the Primitive Worker 63

ACT TWO: THE MAKING OF MANKIND 67

Act Two, Scene One: The Creation of Mankind Prototype One: Lulu Mankind's First Male and Then Female Prototypes 69

Act Two, Scene Two: The Second Model of Mankind 77

Intermission 81

A Whole New World 83

ACT THREE: POPULATING EARTH WITH MANKIND 87

Act three, Scene One: Creating the Upper World White-Skinned Servants 89

Act three, Scene Two: Mankind Mold Three—The New and Improved White Team 93

Act three, Scene Three: Nefilim Life as a Member of the Anunnaki Earth Colony 95

Act three, Scene Four: Update on the Igigi Living on Mars and a Visit to the Moon 99

Act Three, Scene Five: A Visit to the Moon 101

Act Three, Scene Six: The County of Edin and Its City States 105

Act Three, Scene Seven: And Now Round Four of Mankind Models 109

Act Three, Scene Eight: Ka-in and Abel The Story 113

ACT FOUR THE SEEDS OF MANKIND'S RELIGIONS AND WORSHIP TO A SKY GOD **117**

   Act Four, Scene One: The Genesis of Mankind Religion 119

   Act Four, Scene Two: The Birth of Priesthood 129

   Act Four, Scene Three: Marduk and the Nefilim Igigi on Earth ... 133

   Act Four, Scene Four: Earthlings in the New World 135

   Act Four, Scene Five: Edin Before the Great Flood 139

ACT FIVE THE GREAT FLOOD **141**

   Act Five, Scene One: The Great Flood, a.k.a., The Crossing

   The Background 143

   Intermission 149

   Act Five, Scene Two: Earth after the Great Flood 151

   Act Five, Scene Three: Back to Earth Thirteen Thousand Years Ago 157

   Act Five, Scene Four: A New Physical Order on Edin: Abzu, South Africa, and the Andes Mountains 163

ACT FIVE, PART TWO THE ANDES MOUNTAINS **165**

   Act Five, Part Two, Scene One: The Incas 167

   Act Five, Part Two, Scene Two: The Story of the Rules and the Societal Controls of This Incan Community Who Call Themselves Quechua 171

ACT FIVE, PART THREE THE AGE OF LEO **177**

   Act Five, Part Three Scene One: The Giza Pyramids of Egypt 179

   Act Five, Part Three Scene One (b): Dividing the Lands of the Nefilim Colonies on Earth The Age of Cancer 187

Act Five, Part Three, Scene Two: What Do We Do with the Children's Children of the Nefilim Royal Retinue Who Colonized Earth? 189

Act Five, Part Three, Scene Three: The Need for a Smarter Mankind Model 197

ACT FIVE, PART FOUR THE AGE OF CANCER 201

Act Five, Part Four, Scene One: The First Royal Family Civil War 203

Act Five, Part Four, Scene Two: The Peace Treaty 211

ACT SIX THE CREATION OF THE EARTHLING CIVILIZATIONS IN EDIN, EGYPT, AND ELSEWHERE 213

Act Six, Scene One: The Visit of the Nefilim Royals King Anu and Queen Antu 215

Act Six, Scene Two: The Coming Age of Taurus. Maybe 7,200 Earth Years Ago The Creation of Imperial Religions The Creation of Imperial Governments 221

Act Six, Scene Three: The Bible Era Mankind from Above Is Given the Nefilim Rules to Govern Themselves and Have a Predictable Resulting Order That Will Run Earth for The Nefilim 227

The Beginning of Mankind's Kingship 233

Act Six, Scene Four: The Tower of Babylon and Marduk's Run to Egypt 235

Act Six, Scene Five: Egypt and Central America in the Age of Taurus. 237

Act Six, Scene Six: The Epic of Gilgamesh A Demi-God 243

Act Six, Scene Seven: Marduk and His Games of Playing Tug-of-War with His Dominions in Egypt and Babylon 251

Act Six, Scene Eight: Mankind Checkers versus Nefilim Chess An Overview 255

Act Six, Scene Nine: Civil WAR—Marduk (Ram) versus Enlil (Bull) 261

Act Six, Scene Ten: Abraham 267

Act Six, Scene Eleven: Moses 275

ACT SEVEN THE ERA OF ARIES 291

Marduk In Control and Earthlings Creating New Societies On Earth Act Seven, Scene One: Israel And Judea 293

Act Seven, Scene Two: The Aryans and the Creation of the Hindu Religion 297

Act Seven, Scene Three: China and Their Mandate from Heaven 303

Act Seven, Scene Four: Zoroaster 305

Act Seven, Scene Five: Marduk's Egypt (The Ra, Now the Amun) 307

Act Seven, Scene Six: The Assyrians and Persians and Babylonians 309

Act Seven, Scene Seven: Speculation of the Neanderthal 313

Act Seven, Scene Eight: The Balkans 317

Act Seven, Scene Nine: Alexander 321

Act Seven, Scene Ten: The Aftermath of Alexander the Great. The End of The Age of Aries 335

Toll the Bells 343

Act One: Colonizing Earth

Act One, Scene One: In The Beginning. Prior Times the Creation of Our Current Solar System

Let's begin with the universe. We exist so we are part of existence living in some physical form. Yes, we can live as a consciousness like a gas or a liquid or a physical dense being, depending on the stage of our existence.

A universe is all existing matter and space considered as a whole. We are taught there is only one by our scientists. I personally disagree with this, as I believe existence is everything we can comprehend and even more. We are taught that a universe is everything that exists, but exists using our concepts of matter moving in space and matter is gases and liquids too, as we defined those subjects by our comprehension of those terms. So therefore a universe is everything we can comprehend. Everything. So with that definition, when we learn something else exists, it becomes part of our physical definition of the universe. So a universe becomes a physical object of gas or liquid and dense body parts. All three are needed to exist. They are a team of beings.

The universe as material objects in space and time is made up of the following objects that our minds can comprehend:
1. Galaxies—A Galaxy is in simple terms a huge collection of gas and dust. Inside a galaxy, one will find billions of stars and those stars' solar systems. The galaxy is held together by gravity; in our case, we are part of the Milky Way galaxy. And we are taught that the Milky Way galaxy is spiral shaped from our view of the galaxy here on Earth. Spiral, like our DNA body codes are shaped. And that spiral shape is why we call it the Milky Way as it gives us the milk of substance we need to have a physical life on some of our planets and their moons. Also, in the middle of our Milky Way, we have discovered a black hole. The galaxies of our universe get their shapes, it is taught today, by an invisible magnetic field that attracts energies to come together to create a gravitational system that will create the energy to create the substances needed to create thought conscious life in all its forms that we know and one day will discover.
2. Solar System—This is made up of planets that circle the same Sun or Suns, which are the energetic sources of the planets. A solar system orbits around their galaxies, but the opposite way the planets orbit around their Sun. There are billions of stars in our Milky Way galaxy. And we are not alone as thought conscious beings living in this galaxy.
3. Star—The head energy of that particular solar system.
4. Planets—The energies that circle the solar system in gas or liquid and solid forms.
5. Moons—The energies that are seemingly attached as if they are space islands to a particular planet and they share the same gas, liquids, or dense body forms as their planet which they rotate

with as the second hands to the planet being the minute hand of that planet's watch of existence.
6. Asteroids—These are the most ancient objects that get physical shape in a solar system. They orbit the Sun and do come down from the sky when the object comes too close to another planet's gravitational force.
7. Comets—The simple answer is that they are frozen leftovers from the formation of the solar system composed of dust, rock, and ice. They can range from a few miles long to tens of miles wide. As they are drawn to the Sun of a solar system, they heat up and spew gases and dust into a glowing head that can be larger than a planet, and some call the tail of the comet the brightest.

Prior Times refers to the time that Earth did not yet exist anywhere in time and space. This now comes directly from the tablets of the Nefilim who inhabit the planet Nibiru in our solar system, as they repeat what they report to have observed once upon a time when they on Nibiru got in-between the planets Jupiter and Tiamut.

In Prior Times, the solar system we live in was ten planets. Nine planets have the same elliptical path of rotation around the same Sun. The planets get a path as if they are the hands of a watch that rotates around a clock whose energy is the center of that watch that makes the second and minute hands as well as the hour hand work together to have the energy to carry on and keep that solar system's energy alive. Each planet has its own designated slot to rotate. Those nine planets in their rotating order from the view of one who enters our solar system from the furthest point from our Sun are the following:

1. Pluto, who we learn is considered once part of Mars and is a female planet. A female planet has a womb that can bear life.
2. Neptune, a female planet.
3. Uranus, neuter planet.

4. Saturn, a male planet.
5. Jupiter, a male planet.
6. Tiamut, female planet.
7. Mars, female planet.
8. Venus, female planet.
9. Mercury, neuter planet.

Life on planets in our solar system is nothing more than experiences the living live through on a planet with those experiences being the seasons of weather and its seasonal changes as the planet lives and does it yearly run of laps without stopping for a rest around the Sun. The Sun being the center, the heart center of the solar system of energy that makes the whole system work.

Each lap on that planet becomes your physical year of existence. All laps of the ten planets are not equal in our Earth time. But time is relative, and in actual time, each year equals one complete spin around that planet's Sun as measured in that planet's concept of time.

And each lap created an aging of your planet's body machine, which is different on each planet where you were physically created, not just from where you may now reside. This means if your DNA for your physical body design is from Earth, your body's machine of physical wear-and-tear time is different than say if your body were from planet Neptune—another feminine planet like Earth. We are about to discover what these really mean in physical forms.

Again, each full rotation becomes a year on that planet. Actual understanding of what time means differs on each planet. Again, I must repeat that time is relative and is calculated on the physical time it takes to conclude a full rotation around the Sun on the planet that the one who calculates that planet's time is focused on. Our Earth day and year is different than say a day and year on Mercury.

And now we learn of Nibiru. The Tenth Planet.

What is Nibiru? We learn it is a planet. Is it male or female? It must be female as it carries living, physical, made-in-Nibiru beings.

What is the rotation around the Sun of Nibiru? It cuts our solar system in two. The outer planets to Nibiru's view of rotation are Jupiter, Saturn, Neptune, Uranus, and Pluto. The inner planets are Mars, Earth, Venus, and Mercury. My thought, and I have no answer, is the following: Is Nibiru a living planet or just a planet now dead that has become a traveling spaceship of living energies created by advanced physical thought beings to run our solar system or galaxy and even our universe as the warlords of the universe?

Know this as fact, each solar system's planets' rotations do affect your physical life here on Earth. We live on a balance of a universal metaphysical energy inside our solar system and the galaxy that houses our solar system.

The vibrational frequency of a universe's energies give the universe and its galaxies and their solar systems their vibrational ups and downs. The vibrations are really a song of those ups and downs as if they are notes on a celestial piano. It is the key to life in your universe, which is nothing more than a concert hall of existence.

And yes, I use *universes* as opposed to *universe,* as I personally believe there is more than one universe. And my belief is that each universe consists of its own gravitational forces that make up what is called sacred geometry of each universe and creates the matrix that we beings live inside.

Then to complicate matters in our simple minds, the galaxy spinning the unique way it does creates an effect on our whole universe, which does affect our planet's balance. Know that truth, please. The truth of existence will get easier to follow and more beautiful as we continue.

I now share with you that Earth was not always part of this group. Earth came from another planet of the universe in this Prior Time. A planet that was a member of the exclusive team that circled the Sun, which our mankind makers—yes, our makers—you will soon discover called Tiamut, a female planet, meaning it could bear beings in physical form.

Tiamut's orbit was placed between Jupiter and Mars, so their story goes. The story was written by the living beings of a planet they called Nibiru. According to the Nefilim diary, which I call a text and written here on Earth as a tablet, the Book of Enki outlined their personal history of Earth. Their planet Nibiru's moon crashed into Tiamut, millions of what we now call Earth years ago. This crash took out Tiamut. It created a substitute player and a new lineup circling around the Sun in this universe. Copies of these Nefilim texts were found in different languages of different eras all over our Earth, but mostly in our Middle East region.

Nibiru has an elliptical orbit, which means it is an oval orbit that rotates around the Sun in a 360-degree manner. But Nibiru does not have the same orbit as the other planets that circle our Sun. These nine planets circle our sun in the same orbit lineup on the same track in the same place in the same lineups. This planet Nibiru has its own track orbit. The orbit is 360 degrees, but it is more like a comet that comes in close and then goes out far. Their orbit, when it gets near our orbit, becomes an eclipse, and this eclipse changes our sea of space and our atmosphere's air that gives us the relief that everything should be the same. Nibiru, on its elliptical run but different track orbit than ours around the Sun, intersects with our known planets when Nibiru passes the outer and then nears the inner. This eclipse causes a supernatural energy on the planets it passes close to as Nibiru goes around the Sun. This crossing occurs when Nibiru comes close to our Sun and then ends when Nibiru spins back into outer space outside the inner planets' rotational orbit. Nibiru leaves back into outer universe space for a set period of time, finishing its own unique orbit, only to come back like a clock's hands do again in its orbit of our planets and our Sun.

The time this planet Nibiru takes to have a complete circle of its solar system orbit around the Sun is 3,600 Earth years. This yearly circle on that planet Nibiru is called a Shar.

All orbits are 360 degrees, but not all orbits have 360 equal days or equal divisions of their 360 degree circle. Our day here on Earth we time at twenty-four Earth hours. They too have a day of twenty-four Nibiru hours. The Nefilim are those who gave us their system of counting time. It is all based on six. And twenty-four allows us to divide each day by four to give us two six hours of the concept of day and night. And six is the magic number that makes it easier to use in your computer's mind to figure out where you are in your 360-degree orbit of the Sun.

Maybe on Nibiru each day of their orbit run is different depending on where that day falls on Nibiru's special track around our Sun. Just a thought I now share. But for us on Earth to circle the Sun in full each calendar year we take 365.25 days. This gap we account for by adding a day to our 365-day year every fourth year. We call that year a leap year.

We are told in these tablets of a specific time that Nibiru comes in close to our Sun, crossing first the outer planets then entering into the orbital space of Mars and the asteroid belt, which back in Prior Time before Earth's beginning was the slot on the universe's circular racetrack reserved for Tiamut. Tiamut had a circle orbit around the same planets we now do of equal moments in that planet's time.

Well, this one particular time Nibiru's circuit run, as it entered our known planets' circuit run, did not go well for our universe's track team, the planets and their moons. Here is the story as seen and recorded by the beings living on Nibiru millions of Earth timeline years ago. This story comes straight out of the tablets we found buried in our sands of Earth's time.

Act One, Scene Two: The Birth of Earth and Earth's Moon

So again, please visualize a racetrack that has two different races using the same centerpiece our Sun. Nibiru crossing at one time in our solar system space was when Nibiru's orbit around the Sun crossed all the five outer planets plus Tiamut. There was no asteroid belt yet. Nibiru crossing occurs when Nibiru gets inside and crosses the outer planets on their orbit around our Sun. The crossing creates an image of an X.

Then after the crossing Nibiru shoots back into space as the other planets stay on their same course. In fact, Nibiru's crossing is just like a comet. The rotation of these comets is sometimes thousands of Earth years in duration. Nibiru's year around the Sun takes 3,600 Earth years. So when it leaves our vision, it is somewhere between three to five times as far away as Pluto is today from our Sun.

The Samaritan tablets, the first Earthling-written inscription of the Nefilim diaries that we know about to date, call Nibiru the planet of the crossing. The cross, the X. The planet of the crossing because it crosses the paths of the outer five planets and the inner planets and their same slot/order circular orbit of the Sun.

The tablets further share the following description of Tiamut. The planet was bigger than Earth. The planet's fixed orbit was where our asteroid belt is today. Our solar system is part of the galaxy we call the Milky Way. "Milky" as its name, because when we on Earth gaze into our galaxy, we see images that look like milk. And in fact it is the womb that gives birth to all the chemical planet material needed to start a planet that comes alive as a womb and that can allow beings to live on in physical body form of materials made from the womb that each planet becomes when it appears to outsiders to be a dense living form.

From these building substances and energized Suns of our Milky Way comes our planet's creator, which you must know is female. The planet again is a living womb that gives birth to life. The Milky Way is the womb of our solar system planet creations energized by the Suns inside each galaxy of birth. This galaxy has the substance we call mother's milk, which is needed to carry on our own planet's growth and continue lives in our beginning.

So as witnessed by the living on Nibiru, Nibiru started to really wobble due to other planets' and galaxies' energies on one of its trips around the Sun, as it came in closer to the Sun. The wobbling got Nibiru off its charted path. The planet Nibiru, we are told, had seven moons, and one of those seven smacked into Tiamut. The transcripts say, "The moons attacked Tiamut, ripping into her body and splitting the planet Tiamut into two not equal parts."

When the moon hit Tiamut, the inhabitants of Nibiru saw in their forms of space labs of planet Nibiru that split and witnessed the split. They had advanced equipment that allowed them to see and discover firsthand the articles of physical materials and were able to investigate and make solid hypotheses of what comprised Tiamut. Nibiruians felt they discovered the compounds of chemical metal groups inside

Tiamut's core. One of those substances that would be needed by Nibiru many eons later was gold.

The tablets' story goes like this. Nibiru's big moon called the North Wind hits Tiamut, and the top half of Tiamut is dislodged. The top half goes off into space and causes Tiamut's moon, which they call Kingu, to follow this top half into its new spot beyond Mars and on its way to Venus. This top half of Tiamut becomes our Earth and Kingu, the moon of Tiamut, becomes our current moon.

When Nibiru's moon, the North Wind, hit Tiamut and caused the split at the same moment, it dropped off on the new planet its bacteria and primal life forms. These life forms grew and allowed Earth the new planet to obtain and have the same basic life structures Nibiru's world had at that time. This is important to know as this becomes the reason the Nefilim believed they could survive in physical form colonizing Earth.

Earth went through many changes as life came to be on Earth, but the basic compounds of Nibiru had the needed horizontal connection so its life that existed in bacterial form on its northern moon was able to be transferred to Earth. This was now going on according to the tablets as a team of chemicals with a life force, maybe fungi, which I believe is the building block of life's creation of forms here on Earth as well as building an atmosphere for a planet to live and create other living forms.

Now, you ask, what happened to the other half of Tiamut? Well, that becomes our asteroid belt that lives and breathes, which is located before Mars and outside Jupiter. The asteroid belt is where the floating particles of different physical masses appear to interfere with the coming exploration ships of Nibiru on Nibiru's space travels to land on Earth and Earth's moon and Mars. The belt is also where our known science fiction writers have the battles of moving pieces interfering with their intergalactic missions. We only are told of one Tiamut moon, and that moon survived as it is now our moon chasing our orbit as it used to chase Tiamut's.

The Samaritan tablets in addition to Enki's Tablets refer to our asteroid belt as the Hammered Bracelet. And these wobbling but still rotating material pieces are the meteoroids that do crash into Earth as well as Mars and Jupiter and our Moon.

Everything you just read becomes relevant as our story of life on Nibiru continues. The true tale that caused the living inhabitants of Nibiru, called Nefilim, to land its citizens who the Nefilim, sometimes spelled Nifilim or Nefilim, called Anunnaki. Anunnaki are the space traveling team for those who leave their Heaven, a.k.a. Nibiru, to come and colonize Earth. Remember the Apollo team? Same game. We sent that team to the moon to see if the moon today could be colonized by mankind. It was that simple.

Nibiruians referred to their land as Heaven. We will learn that to return to Heaven by spaceship one had to go to the spaceport, which they called Heaven, and they have eternal life compared to us Earthlings as those from Nibiru lived Nibiru years not Earth years, and that means thousands of Earth years for each Nibiru years.

Nibiru, we learn, had a system of rules and order that is so similar to our past development of mankind's civilized societies. These rules and resulting order are where we experienced the concept of "the few may rule the many." Nibiru, who referred to its leading royal citizens as gods and lords, sent their Apollo crew with certain gods and lords to explore Earth to then see what they could get from Earth to help keep their planet breathing and capable of perpetuating Nibiru beings. The planet needed gold, so they needed to come to Earth and see exactly what was created when Tiamut split in two.

Once here, as we shall soon discover, they tested the gold they found and decided this metal could save their planet. This is Earth's first gold rush. But their rush was to get the gold out of Earth's lands and riverbanks and take it home to their Heaven called Nibiru. To get the gold, they would discover they had to colonize Earth. Why gold again? They needed gold to fix the leaks in their atmosphere.

Why did Nibiru need gold? Because it is the only substance they knew of that can be melted down and in melted form be hurled into the air of an atmosphere, once it is placed in the atmosphere in liquid form then made to stay put inside the atmosphere's gravitational force.

Nibiru's atmosphere was leaking, and the heat was coming in and going out depending on the current location of Nibiru's run around our Sun. Gold was used to stop the leaks of a planet's atmosphere. Gold is a soft metal. Gold has many uses in a machine-run world. It does not just need to simply glitter and be worn to show you have money or taste or style.

This colonization of Earth for our gold found here on Earth is why we the creations of Nibiru have such an obsession for gold. We were initially cloned and created with their essences, meaning their consciousness trained us to get the gold as the physical laborers of the Anunnaki team of creatures from Nibiru. The naked truth.

Act One, Scene Three: The Nefilim Decision of Colonizing Earth For the Gold

Colonization of Earth? Yep, you read right. Earth was invaded and then colonized.
Your questions should now be the following: Where did it begin and by whom and for what purpose? Three questions that I will now answer.

Did you ever wonder how primitive men built the wonders of the ancient world? Where do the prehistoric discs and stone carvings come from? Were these discs both drawings and language that tell a story about Earth before man?

Even the unexplained stone carvings found throughout our world—did you ever question where did they come from? Who did this? How come our languages began and are many and not just one? How did this happen? How do we have different gods when we say and believe God is one? How did temples appear that no man could actually build? Is it the same for our pyramids? Our laws come from where? Our priests, rabbis, and religious controllers of all religions respond to God, or one of the gods? Is our food alien to Earth? Are our domestic animals and plants from Earth's natural—if anything is actually natural—evolution or from some other creation? Our rainforests were created by whom? How did this Earth become what we see and live in now?

Well sit tight for here is the story of our conquistadors. And they were not pure and it's their impurity here today that makes us behave in such a vampiric manner.

This Nibiruian space conquistador ship crew can be called the Christopher Columbus of their era. They sailed the ship across the solar system to plunder and steal everything they could from Earth. However, they stayed for a while and made the civilization of mankind.

Many hundreds of thousands of Earth years ago, Nibiru had its "civil war." It was the battle of their Roses. The planet was ruled as a one-world order. A King An, whom they called god, but not the God of creation, ruled Nibiru. The ruling gods' descendants were princes and princesses also called gods as well as lords. They were the lesser gods. A pecking order to rule the many by the descendants of the chosen one. Now you can see the creation of our mythology in different societies with gods and goddesses all reporting to the ruler and his queen. These man-made myths are based on reality.

We the people called mankind were about to be created to be the slaves of these physical creators from Nibiru. Yes, we are a race created to be a slave race. We were made to serve our creating gods, and this is that story up until they maybe left Earth around our time we call 500 BC. We will get there as we follow in order the game we all played, called "life on Earth."

The Civil Nibiruian War began when the King An died. There was a physical fight for who was the next in line to become the new king and take over the leadership of the planet and her six moons. Our own history has many such stories.

The planet Nibiru needed gold to fix its atmosphere. The atmosphere was leaking the self-generated heat from the core of its center. The Nefilim Tablets describe how they sent spaceships out from their planet into the universe to locate gold but also set in motion nuclear explosions on their planet hoping to free the gold that was buried inside the core of their planet. Nothing worked. Nibiru's time was running short. In our time that time is hundreds of thousands of Earth years. The King An was dead, and war, the planet's elders realized, war was not the answer. The answer for the planet, the elders cried, was to find the gold.

Alalu, a citizen of Nibiru, was thought to be the next successor of the "great" and now deceased King An. Alalu had the required bloodline to the throne by being the oldest male whose mother was the half-sister of the previous King An. This means Alalu had the same blood as An from their mother, a requirement to be the new king.

Yes, this is where Egypt got its pharaoh inheritance rules with their priestly controllers. The pharaohs had to have the same blood of the mother of the previous pharaoh's bloodline. When the game of inheriting the throne in Egypt first began, the pharaohs were the Nefilim space Earth team called Anunnaki, as we shall soon learn.

But before Alalu's reign could be ordained as the new King of the Planet Nibiru, a young prince named Anu presented himself claiming he was the real direct descendant of the great King An. Now what does this land ruled by the royal bloodline do? The elders called together their court of Justice, which is called a parliament, and voted on a resolution to serve the Nefilim as a whole, not just the individuals competing for the position of absolute power watched over by the elders who are selected to oversee their government.

The Coalition Parliament, really an executive branch of elders, had a problem, which was now how to figure out how the law was supposed to be interpreted. Elders decided Anu was found to be the real king according to their Laws of Seed and Succession. But parliament did not feel Anu was ready, so they ruled that Alalu would become king and Anu would be the cupbearer. The cupbearer was the next king in line. Anu's family, no matter what, would be the bloodline thereafter.

The goal in this peace was to bring back abundance and have the planet of one nation Nibiru prosper once again. Again, for whom, we never learn. But my hunch is for the few who ruled the land.

The final solution of Nibiru became "let's go to Earth" and "take their gold and fix our Nibiru atmosphere." The answer was simple. We shall fly and land our ship on their water passages and go to land. Get the gold and using alchemy make the matter gas and then let it settle in liquid. Then transport it back to Nibiru.

But first to get the gold they had to travel to Earth. Traveling required space travel. And this travel required flying in and through our asteroid belt, a.k.a. the Hammered Bracelet. Their goal was to get past the Hammered Bracelet area and reach Earth alive and obtain the gold.

Remember from the earlier scene that the Nefilim knew of Earth's creation. They set sail in space to reach Earth but could not get it done under King An. They then tried under their new King Alalu, which did not work as King Alalu had been fired.

These earlier attempts ended up in the space area where previous spaceships go to die. They were lost in the black holes of space. The ships just could not get past the Hammered Bracelet. Now the beings of Nibiru became concerned. The heat was leaving their atmosphere, and things were looking very gloomy. It was time for a change. After nine Shars since Alalu began service as King, in Nibiru years, Anu the cupholder challenged Alalu to hand-to-hand combat. This was the required means to settle this type of dispute. Anu wanted to be the savior, and this was apparently the dual of their era. Anu won and got the throne.

Alalu, still alive but no longer the crown king, decided that he would save the planet himself. He went to the number one hub of all spaceships on Nibiru and into the area where they housed what they called the Celestial Chariot. There, without any authority, he decided to stay in a smaller spaceship. Once in and feeling okay with the ship's panel board, he stole the ship.

This ship had all the bells and whistles as this one was a missile thrower. The tablets say, "Into a missile thrower Alalu goes." He sat in the captain's seat, which shows through a navigation system the way up and out. He turned on the fire, which is the rocket ship's takeoff power. Powering on and through the takeoff noise-like music, Alalu escaped Nibiru's atmosphere. Also, this escape set off alarms notifying the authorities of Nibiru what just happened.

Alalu set his stolen ship's course for Earth. Why Earth? Again, as their books and records claim that when their northern moon collided with Tiamut, the people on Nibiru who were studying space saw the gold color veins that were part of the new resulting planet Earth. They knew those veins to be gold.

Thoughts? I have plenty. My first question was how did Alalu plan to survive in space after leaving his atmosphere not knowing that his lungs could breathe in the space? Then if the physical living body of planet Nibiru left the Nibiru atmosphere and went out further in space, how did the living organisms survive without necessities of life such as food and water as the distance from the Sun increases each passing Nibiru day?

Planets are living ecosystems of their own cosmopolitan territory. Planets are the living organisms. We are the living metaphysical consciousness that lives in their space and inside their planet-living physical suits. Here on Earth we have physical suits called Earth bodies from our Mother Earth.

When our new spaceman Alalu escaped Nibiru, his bet was that the planet Earth and Mars and our moon, as we will soon discover, had the nectar needed for these Nefilim, as they described themselves, to live and operate in these distance globes. Meaning the necessities of life with air, food, and water would exist.

It may sound like a *Star Wars* motion picture, but Alalu was getting to Earth and getting the gold so Alalu could hold his planet Nibiru as hostage. Is the ex-king the villain or the hero? All sinners are saints in reality. Why? Because he took the risk and smashed through the Hammered Bracelet to get the gold. But he did it for whom? His planet, or himself?

When Earth was first created, life outside of microforms, one-celled beings, life as we beings are, could not sustain itself at that time. But the Nefilim Tablets describe how Earth was stabilized. Gravitational and centrifugal forces made the planet dense so life could grow and prosper as Earth became a living womb for life to be created and to then become complex living organisms. The tablets refer to this era as the Prior Times. And so shall I.

The tablets describe Alalu's description of his trip. Alalu broadcasted his flight back to Nibiru to be the hero who saved his planet. This was not an oral transfer of stories. Alalu had a radio frequency that he transmitted from his ship to the planet.

Today, we as a race are beginning to do what the Nefilim did on their home planet. They knew a lot. Like how to domesticate animals as well as clone species, as we shall soon see, and how to travel through space without losing too much time. They bent space somehow. Plus, they could communicate, as I just wrote, back to their planet. They had FaceTime, which we are still learning how to do when we have no satellites connecting our primitive dots. The Nibiruians did it by breaking the code of the matrix of existence. They did not need physical forms to send their messages. They did need physical forms to receive the messages.

Think for a moment with me. These Samaritan written texts are around 6,000 or more Earth years old. Plus, we have the even older artifact tablets in pieces and some whole maybe hundreds of thousands of years old that we have discovered all over the sands and waters of Earth.

The Nefilim texts describe the outer planets—planets our eyes still cannot see without human aids. The texts tell of the beauty of Neptune and Uranus as well as Jupiter and Saturn. The beauty is so vividly described. However, they are not dense like Earth and therefore are not yet ready to be a physical mother of beings made up of more than one cell.

Then comes the *Star Wars* or *Battlestar Galactica* part of this journey, from Nibiru space to Earth. Our hero or villain destroyed the meteoroids that got into his way as Alalu tried to get past the Hammered Bracelet. For the first time we learned he used water to move the meteorites when they came near.

After the bracelet, Alalu saw the Red Planet, the planet we call Mars. Then Alalu saw Earth. Alalu says Earth is white on the top and bottom with a middle of blue, green, and brown. Alalu goes on to say Earth has a gravitational force weaker than Nibiru.

Alalu used his magic wand, a laser beam that took pictures and transmitted these picture bits to his home team. Alalu then shot the laser down to Earth and discovered, as the laser confirmed, there was gold. So, he landed. A rough landing it was. He says he opened his eyes and was happy to be alive. "We space sailors on Nibiru watched the telecast of the landing, then wept with tears of joy," I heard as I write this.

There is no discussion that I know of regarding air and Earth, but he does say he had his Eagle Helmet on. He was amazed to find out that he could breathe. He did not need his space fish suit.

Sounds romantic? Yes, but do understand this man was all alone. Now Alalu describes what he found on Earth. Alalu tells the viewer and us the reader about the trees with fruits, the marshes of green water, the dark-hued soil, and his quest for drinking water that he obviously found. Alalu also describes the short days.

Alalu, it is written, then broadcast his location to his Nibiru planet. He says, "On another planet I am, the gold of salvation I have found. The fate of Nibiru is now in my hands."

I find how Alalu proved it was gold fascinating. The distance between the planet and our traveler was so far away, yet they were able to substantiate the discovery. Alalu shot them by crystal transmission the images of what he found on Earth. This is what was written at least four hundred thousand years or more ago.

To be specific, Alalu transmitted the proof of the find through a maneuver of their technological machine. The machine was called the Tester. Alalu took the crystal innards out of the machine. From the Sampler, the crystal heart he took out. Into the speakers he inserted the crystals. This machine holding crystal and the information as if it were a computer of our era allowed Alalu to transmit his findings so both he and his planet could see and know the composition of the metal we call gold.

By the way, there are references to water on the spaceship. Not to drink but to use as a sword or a shield in space. Attacking meteorites were stopped and sent away by shooting the water as a weapon. The references say water helped their chariot in space. We apparently in this century are starting to use water the same way. To get into and out of space as well as keep foreign materials from colliding into our ships. And yes, as well as keep the traveling team lubricated and alive. No salty dogs would they become as they sailed the seas of space.

The new Earth world was about to begin. Traveling Nibiru ships would soon be filled with space beings called Anunnaki on their way to Earth, the moon, and Mars.

The first reason for the mission was to find the gold. And then when they discovered the gold, the Anunnaki began the process of collecting and refining and transporting the gold. Doing these three chores would take time, so the Anunnaki came to colonize a Nibiru outpost in space to support and sustain the Nibiru beings' life on Earth, Mars, and our moon while the mission carried on their wayward space travel ways.

ACT ONE, SCENE FOUR: THE ACTUAL ACTS OF NIBIRU COLONIZING EARTH AND NOW MARS FOR THE GOLD

How did life originally get to be here on Earth? Life, I must add, which we now can all learn resembled life on Nibiru. When one of the moons of Nibiru collided with Tiamut, the planet, the collision created a new planet that was soon to be full of land with water. The new version of the older planet Tiamut colliding with the moon of Nibiru created an explosion that, when its dust and atomic fire had settled, created an atmosphere that kept the new planet we call Earth together as one moving mass. The collision set the planet off into space where the universe's gravitational force caught the planet and got it to lock in and follow the Sun in a new circular motion in space closer to the Sun than Tiamut was before. Earth was now this solar system's inner planet and the third planet from the Sun.

This celestial collision's spare pieces not part of Earth or a moon became what we call meteorites. These meteorites, made up of the dislodged pieces of the old planet Tiamat, and now called the Hammered Bracelet, in time started landing on Earth as well as Mars, Earth's moon, and Jupiter. Once on Earth this fall from the sky sent then living microorganisms such as bacteria and fungi as well as viruses on the meteorites to our planet Earth. These microorganisms are able to withstand the radiation of the fall to Earth. This we have learned from our own space shuttles that return to Earth from space do survive the ride into space, as well as the traveling in space and the return visit to Earth without any protection other than their outer living layer of their cell. Straight up viruses are the building blocks of life, be it a plant or an animal of land and sea.

The organisms grew and became more elaborate than just one-celled living organisms. But again, all life begins with a cell, we are taught. I believe it begins with a virus that creates the cells as a virus does not have a nucleus membrane and therefore its DNA is not stored inside a cell. The cells of living organisms store the blueprint we call DNA that gives life its body and its biological reason to exist. Cells combined and evolution, as Darwinism explains, started taking place. The cells combined and first became plants. Plants photosynthesize and create the way for animals to form and use oxygen, not carbon, as the fuel that feeds its animal moving living machine. Plants to sea creatures to land-based animals we call reptiles then mammals. This is the path of the linear line of creation and its evolution.

In fact, the astrological signs that most of you know and are aware of explain the Nefilim understanding of creation. They explain creation by following the original names of each sign named after the circle of life as it was created. Water signs and Earth signs made with fire and air.

However, we shall soon see how our creation as Homo sapiens with our gifts of understanding and the ability to use our hands with our minds and communication skills were cloned by the Nefilim. We were cloned when the Nefilim were living here on Earth. The Nefilim on Earth referred to themselves as the Anunnaki in much the same way that our astronauts from Earth who went to the moon referred to themselves as the Apollo mission.

Here is the timeline of the Nefilim beginning their colonizing of Earth.

Alalu's trip to Earth and the proof that gold was on Earth excited the Nefilim. Plans of Nefilim travel were being put in order by King Anu and his cabinet of Elders of Nibiru. Earth was going to have its first gold rush.

1) Planning the Voyage

King Anu had two male children. Enki (Ea) was Anu's first born. Enlil was the second son. However, Enlil by way of birth seed (mom) and ordained succession had higher rank because his mother was Anu's half sister. This means the child had his father's bloodline as Anu and his sister both had their mother's blood. The concept of Earth's mother bloodline to determine inheritance rules of the next generation was first created here in Nibiru.

Anu did not know which son should lead the voyage to Earth. After much deliberation, due to the fact that Enki was the exceptional scientist between the two, it was Enki who was chosen to go to Earth to lead this first expedition.

2) The Trip to Earth

The trip was reported to be smooth sailing till the passing of Jupiter. Then the bracelet pieces appeared. To get through these asteroids, water that was stored inside the space ship was used as a weapon to blow away the material bodies that were crossing the ship's path. The captain of the ship shot the water as a cannon at the moving pieces of the old planet Tiamut, now traveling in broken pieces as the Hammer Bracelet from the collision with Nibiru's moon that collided earlier in space time. It is said that this Space Chariot with its fifty conquistadors was the biggest one the planet Nibiru ever made and used. Water was stored inside the ship and became their weapon of choice when necessary.

And now the explorers had a problem. The problem the ship had to deal with was by using the water to remove the material obstacles in their traveling path, they depleted the ship's water supply. Luckily, when the ship came near what they called Lahmu, our Mars, the travelers noticed the reflection of the Sun from Mars in the sky. They knew this was water. Yes, water on Mars.

The captain decided to land on Mars to get the water. The tablets go on to say that the gravitational pull was less on Mars than it was on Earth as the trip is reviewed. Enki, after landing by a Lahmu lake, writes in his Book of Knowledge that the water was great to drink but the air was not quite right to breathe, so the crew had to keep their Eagle Helmets on to breathe.

The scholars who translated the Book of Knowledge to the human tablets did not mention how long it took to actually travel from Nibiru to Earth. But the scholars determined the trip took a few Earth weeks at most to get from Nibiru to Mars. Mars to Earth we learn was no more than using the Nefilim space travel equipment for four Earth days. This ship was moving at speeds unknown to us now.

The Chariot now heading to Earth had to slow down before landing on the Earth's atmosphere. If not, the Chariot would perish due to the energy of friction. The ship would cause landing on Earth as it came through the atmosphere that protects Earth from invasion of objects traveling through space and that get stuck in the gravitational pull of Earth.

The pilot of the Chariot was known as Anzu. Anzu would soon be the Anunnaki in charge of the Earth's Nibiru spaceport and all Nibiru's spaceships that would be coming and leaving Earth.

I must again say that the planet Nibiru referred to its Earth colony beings as Anunnaki. The Nefilim who colonized Mars and then came to Earth were to be known as the Iggis. This story now really gets going.

The Earth's gravitational pull was too much to land on land, so they had to land on the sea. I believe the sea they chose is today called the Persian Gulf. Alalu Nibiru's ex-king and now astronaut was waiting for the explorers to come ashore. Alalu never went back to Nibiru after he discovered gold. He wanted to be in charge of the gold rush and stayed as he would then be in control of the astronauts chosen to come to Earth (Anunnaki). Alalu immediately got in contact with them. This he did by radio transmission.

This landing took place 443,000 Earth years ago. As I write this, I hear the song "2,000 Light Years from Home." Music was and still is my guide. The messages are placed in our space for me to connect the dots and relive this story in this time and place. I see this as I write this to you. I hear the Rolling Stones playing their song "2,000 Light Years from Home."

I find it funny that it is written in the Nefilim records that travelers created and then chanted in their new theme song with words written by Enki. "On a life-or-death mission we have come, in our hands is Nibiru's fate." Sounds like the US Marine war song that says "From the Halls of Montezuma to the Shores of Tripoli." You will see as I have discovered we are very similar now to what this species was back then when they came to Earth and colonized her.

Destiny for the moment was on the Nibiruians' side. The planet Earth would, because of these Anunnaki, survive, and Earth by fate would in time have its new human race. A race, I repeat, made to serve their creators who called themselves gods. A small g, which is different than the One Creator of all. The big G.

3) Colonizing Earth. Setting Up the First Campgrounds

Now the fifty-one explorers (fifty plus Alalu) on Earth needed to get to work so Enki, whose Nibiru name is Ea, contacted his dad Anu the King to get permission to create the chores that would help the Anunnaki survive. Alalu was supposed to be, in theory, a subordinate to the new King Anu.

Now I will repeat the chores the beings of Nibiru called work on Nibiru and now even on Earth must be approved by the governing board of Nibiru Elders, which the Nibiru text also refer to as the Parliament. Here you, as I do, will see the germ of creation that we here on our mankind Earth time have blown up into the imperial governments that rule we the people.

I must add the more I write and review and search for answers I do not see many Nefilim beings in their world order. I see a traveling planet of few beings who are totally controlled as if they were no different than an ant colony.

These Nibiru Elders are appointed to make up the rules and the order that others will follow, thereby serving the whole living group of Nibiruians. After selecting the chores, Enki now needed his dad's, the King's, authorization to assign the tasks to the individuals picked to perform the jobs so created. Blue collar workers' rules and regulations right from the start of building the colony as authorized by the white-collar Elders and their robed king and his queen.

The land Earth itself was given the name Eridu. Enki in his writings referred to Eridu as where he first landed. Edin, which is referred to in the Bible, would soon become the first urban community on Earth. Today the original location of the first urban community of Edin is very near the city we call Basra. Basra is off the coast of our Persian Gulf. Basra is also the land Iraq used for their Highway of Death when they took over Kuwait back in our 1990. Iraq wanted a seaport. Britain, the creator of nations in the Middle East under a League of

Nations Mandate in our twentieth century, promised this land to the new nation of Iraq when the time was right. Iraq got tired of waiting and just invaded.

The Samaritan Pentateuch text says that over the next six Earth days, God performed miracles. Get the six days of work as written in the Bible? Remember God meant Nefilim and Nefilim can be singular or plural. And as we shall learn, the Nefilim had instruments that were anti-gravitational and still to this day are unknown to common man. They had instruments that could part seas and lift rock and blow up cities with nuclear precision like cities such as Sodom and Gomorrah.

What were the miracles of these six Earth days? The miracles performed were the building of the community so they could all live and survive their time here on Earth. This community was built out of nothing at all.

The work tasks needed to survive were the following:
1. Create a source of drinking water.
2. They made bricks from clay to build their settlement.
3. They built their campgrounds.
4. They examined the plants and the fruits nearby to determine which were edible. The records show these plants with fruit were abundant and found all over the region.
5. They documented the animals they called creatures they found in the air or on the sea and land.
6. They built fences to keep the fierce creatures they discovered out of their camps. They even brought out of their ship the weapon they named the Beam that Kills to the camp to protect themselves from the creatures.
7. They built water ships to explore the rivers and seas as well as oceans. The local boats I envision were just like the airboats one can now ride in the Everglades I feel.

The first six Earth days, the Anunnaki discovered rain and thunder with its lightning. It frightened them as this was not what they expected, which makes me question if it rained on Nibiru. No answer did I find as my readings continued. But with an atmospheric shield to keep the universe energy out, they had to manufacture the water. It makes me feel that this race probably landed on Nibiru and closed off the planet and made it their own living creation. I now see the movie *The Truman Show*.

The moonlight fascinated them, as did the short days and corresponding nights. The moon's full orbit, which they called a month, was approximately twenty-seven Earth days plus seven hours and forty-three minutes.

On Earth's seventh day, Enki gathered them together and had what was to become Earth's first Sabbath. Their weekly day of rest. We are not told whose day or whose year. Is the day an Earth day or a Nibiru day? The same for the year. Whose year? Earth's or Nibiru's? Remember that Nibiru's year equals 3,600 Earth years. So just try to imagine what six Earth days meant in the Nibiru's concept of time. This is real jet lag.

They called Earth Eridu, and in slang, Ki. And as I wrote earlier, the first urban settlement was known as Edin, which translates to "us at home in the faraway."

4) The First Gold Rush in The Waters Near Edin

Now it was time to begin their Earth gold rush. This era in their books is referred to again as the Prior Times. Prior Times because they had not yet created their slave and servant race. The slave and servant race we call mankind.

The first Anunnaki sources of gold were found in the marshes, rivers, and shores of the oceans of Earth. Not inside the rocks or inside the land. The crew was looking for alluvial gold. Alluvial gold is gold dust. Gold nuggets would also do. At the end of the week, they went through their finds and discovered all kinds of metals. Metals like iron and copper. They found gold, but it was the least of all the metals in quantity they got in their first hunt. This went on for a year. Not sure what year.

Also understand, as we shall learn, the Nefilim were obsessed with astrology as well as astronomy. The difference between the two sciences (*I really believe they are the same*) is from which point of view one studies the skies as well as the view of the planets and stars from what point. Astronomy is studying the skies say from your particular point of view. So say your view of the skies is from here on Earth. Astrology is the study of space from no particular point; it is the study of the skies and the energies flying around in the sky. I say this because what I can surmise of the Nefilim is that they knew well before they landed on Earth what an Earth's day, as well as an Earth's year, meant.

The Nefilim also understood the act of creation and the need of metaphysical energies to keep the physical creation alive. In their studies of energy, which included air and the dynamics of energies through air and steam (the metaphysical elements), they studied space and motion through time to see the coming hurricanes and tornadoes of air as the air came into the galaxies. I assume they would be coming to the solar system that Earth resides in, which would interfere with the clean sailing orbit around the Sun that you would expect of a lake, as opposed to the waves of an upset ocean.

This aging physical process is hard for me to understand. So I tell myself the aging of the physical body is planet-based. The rotation around your energy source is how bodies age. Physical age is controlled in our DNA. We have Earth-based DNA, they had Nibiru-based DNA. Eventually, the DNAs were mixed, and that is how biblical Earthlings lived longer than we do. Some had the blood of the Nefilim from planet

Nibiru. That is different from Nefilim from the blood of Earth. You will soon understand this distinction. The demigod's race.

The more Earth-based your DNA, the shorter your life-span. But saying that, I believe your DNA can be manipulated to give you longer physical life-spans. So did the Nefilim believe it, and actually, as we shall soon discover, the Nefilim adjusted it for their new living pets and domesticated beasts of their burdens. Mankind—the beast of the Anunnaki's burdens.

5) Transportation of The Gold Back to Nibiru

Now with the first crop of gold ready to go, how do they move it to its retail Nefilim outlet? The tablets said they hesitated. The crew decided that since Nibiru was about to cross their orbit into Earth's orbit run on Nibiru's way around the Sun, they would not yet send this alluvial gold to Nibiru. They would wait until Nibiru had rotated out of their Earth travel to Nibiru ships travel plans. Why? The Nefilim wanted clear sailing home and did not wish to have any wakes left by Nibiru on its Chariot's voyage back to Nibiru.

To make this time worthwhile, we are told the Sky Chamber (SC) was taken out of the ship and put into use. This SC allowed them to go fly around Earth and locate the best spots that had gold in the veins of its local Earth.

The pilots of this Sky Chamber were Enki and an Anunnaki called Abgal. They flew over the mountains and valleys as well as rivers and oceans on Earth. The ships did not need gas. They flew on nuclear energy, apparently; I am being told as I write this.

They made a good record of their findings. In fact, this may be the creation of the Nazca Lines I saw when I was in our current Earth's Sky Chamber called an airplane flying over today's Peru. It was then where I finally woke up from my Earthling incarnate dream back in 1996. Over these lines I discovered that the word Peru meant *misty*. It is a Chinese word. More on this later in the upcoming Act 8. But here the relevance is these lines, which were obviously drawn by a laser from the sky, to show all what living beast existed on these lands. And if you dive deeper on this trail, you can see the remains of the ancient landing strips where something from the air landed here on Earth.

We are told that Enki in the Chariot brought the seven (7) deadly weapons to Earth from Nibiru. On this first SC flight, Enki hid the weapons somewhere on Earth. These two pilots were the only ones who knew where the deadly weapons were stored.

What were the deadly weapons? We shall soon find out—at least some of them.

Alalu, the first explorer and one-time king of Nibiru, was furious that the weapons were removed from the Chariot. As he, Alalu, wanted to bring the gold back to Nibiru with the weapons. Alalu wanted different things than Anu's son Enki did. We are going to have a showdown.

Also know the controller of the weapons controlled the fate of those then living on Earth.

So Alalu needed to manipulate events so he could gain control. And he needed to do it by tricking the others to believe his intentions were pure and good.

To persuade the others to agree to let Alalu get possession of the weapons, he needed to blast his way through the Hammer Bracelet, a.k.a. the asteroid belt. This occurred as Alalu was planning on taking his stolen ship back to Nibiru. Why the trip alone? He obviously thought he would get a hero's welcome and get his crown back.

Enki explained to Alalu that Abzu the sky pilot knew his way through the belt and Abzu would pilot the ship the Celestial Chariot back without the weapons. Abzu had blasted his way through the belt to get to Earth, so a path out of Earth's region to go back to Nibiru now existed.

Alalu was not going home alone was the message. Alalu will be the copilot.

King Anu was getting tired of waiting for the gold. Anu instructed his son that during this orbit rendezvous, gold must be brought to planet Nibiru. It was essential to test the gold dispersion technique to restore the atmosphere. Time was moving and things must be checked out to see if this gold was the answer to their prayers to save the planet.

King Anu made his point and Enki did as he was told. The Nefilim's wish was to be granted. Soon they would be able to touch and see from a sample what the gold could and would not do when put to use in Nibiru. The gold and other sample materials were loaded into Alalu's stolen ship and not the Celestial Chariot, as originally planned by Enki. Now loaded, the smaller ship was sent back to Nibiru with its first take of Earth's gold and other trinkets from Earth.

The tales of the trip were recorded. What fascinates me is their recorded use of crystals to find the path through the belt that Alalu had created. The trip also tells how Nibiru was located by its crimson/red glow in space. The radiant planet they called home, we are told.

Once home on Nibiru, a hero's welcome the two men Alalu and Abzu received. Then came the time to test the gold.

6) The Gold in Nibiru

Guess what? It worked. The gold would save the planet Nibiru. The story tells how they mixed the gold in their version of a petri dish. Then it is said how the gold powder mixture worked to save Nibiru. It worked, and in enough quantity, it would make the leak in the atmosphere closure permanent until the next wear and tear issue arose.

So now the thought process of the Nefilim on Nibiru was for them to make it permanent, so the next step was to get their endless supply of gold. Earth would be their colony. It was a game-changing moment not just for the Nefilim but also for Earth. The space invaders would now really colonize Earth.

You may ask, how did the gold get into the atmosphere? The gold was shot into the air with their version of drones that dispersed the powder, which I will label gold dust premium, into the Nibiru atmosphere with crystal beams moving the powder into its required place in their atmospheric space.

7) Back on Earth: Looking for More Gold Reserves on Earth

Enki and his crew kept getting the gold from the water, but then suddenly that well of gold began to go dry. Another Shar passed and then there was not enough loose gold to fix the Nibiru atmosphere problem. So, Enki goes up, up, and away in his beautiful helicopter type of Earth-exploring device, a balloon looking for the real gold payday. He finds this in what today we call South Africa. As he says in the texts, "Looking down from the air, golden veins from Earth's innards were abundant."

King Anu, upon receiving this information, instructed his son Enki to stop the gold water looking and go into the veins of Earth and get the gold. "Now how do you do this?" was the question asked by the Earth-based Nefilim-Anunnaki when Enki told his team of the new instructions.

Enki SOSs his dad, King Anu. Dad realizes his son Enki needs help with both the command as well as management of the Earth space station. So, Enlil the son who is the heir apparent Prince of Nibiru with the right blood mother to inherit and run the kingdom is sent to Earth with a new Nibiru crew. This colonizing work would require more Anunnaki power. Physical and machine work was then needed. We know and call this sport of work mining.

Since the work was to take place on a distant part of Earth from their command posts in today's Levant region, it was time to divide the work. The command was divided. Enki would take the mines, and Enlil would manage the command posts. This division of the command was decided by Anu, who came himself to Earth on his first royal visit to see what was going on. There was a lot to decide—a very common trait among us even today.

The big three, father and sons, huddled. Decisions were made. Enlil was now in charge of the spaceport, which they call Nibru, meaning the place one goes to go back to their Heaven called Nibiru. I am starting to understand what this race did with language to communicate. They changed meanings with vowels as in Nibru and Nibiru.

The gold would now be more plentiful, so more ships were needed to transport the gold to their home on Nibiru. Meaning they needed a spaceport.

Lots, as if they were straws, would determine which son would stay and who would go. Enki thought that since he was the first one on Earth it was he who should stay and build their home. The homes for the "upright ones," as they now called themselves. This meant that they could stand on two legs as the other beings living on Earth that they saw before they started altering creatures could not stand on their two feet as we now do. At some point those two-legged beings in time would fall and move around on their four appendages. The home base to go to and from Nibiru was now forever to be called Edin. And to get to Nibiru you go to Nibru.

Dad did not agree with Enki's logic. The father as the King of Nibiru did a good job and persuaded Enki to accept his fate. It was decided that the two princes, as I said, would draw lots to see who did what. This way fate would be determined by drawing the lots to see who would do what. Plus, apparently, Enki as the oldest drew the lot first, so his fate was actually determined. Enki was sent to Abzu, South Africa.

Dad promised that Enki would be forever known as Earth's Master. Enlil was to be known as Lord of the Command.

Question for you readers or listeners: Are you starting to see where titles of names and resulting attitudes we have today came from? Dukes, barons, generals, and on and on. It gets better as this story develops.

Now, as I said, we focus on both Alalu and Anu who traveled to Earth from Nibiru.

Alalu publicly decides he wants his crown, and therefore, his throne back. So he and Anu engaged in a wrestling match as the rules of Nibiru provide when elders collide in their wants and needs. Anu won. Alalu, a poor loser, lashed out at the crotch of Anu and succeeded in biting off and eating Anu's testicles. "Mike Tyson," I hear a spirit say in my ear.

This was a huge blow for the planet Nibiru and their Earth colony. How can Alalu be so bad? After much deliberation and contemplation with the elders on their FaceTime devices from Earth to Nibiru, it was decided not to execute Alalu but to banish him to Mars. And, I must add, Mars alone.

Anzu, the sky pilot of this team, volunteered to stay with Alalu till his sickness devoured him. Apparently, the testicles and flesh of the Nefilim are not ripe for them to eat of each other. They are not cannibals of the skin of each other. However, your organs? Your blood? It does not say. Maybe some biologists and historians believe this is higher DNA than we have now. A DNA that evolves and stops cannibalism. Just someone's thoughts I share with you here. Me, I believe anything is possible.

8) Colonizing Mars to Help Transport the Gold Reserves from Earth to Nibiru.

We now learn the Nibiru tale of Mars. And in fact begin to understand our Earth's obsession of discovering previous life on Mars. Here is this story.

Mars becomes the place the Nefilim decided to transport the gold from Earth to in small quantities. Then from Mars they would use a bigger ship for a larger load to fly back to Nibiru, their home. Why Mars? Because there was thirty-eight percent less gravity on Mars than Earth. It was an easier takeoff to do with heavy loads. These are numbers I have discovered in the cuneiform tablets, which are records left in Earth's sands before mankind was taught how to read and write, around six thousand Earth years ago. Then mankind wrote their version of the tablets about our creation in their own hand and created The Samaritan Texts, which were also found in Earth's sands of time.

These thoughts made into this story were first written in mankind's scripts over 6,000 Earth years ago. The actual stories are so much older. Fascinating that this knowledge is known and withheld from the consciousness of our masses.

Why? So we the sheep people believe the system that owns and controls our current lives with its belief in a god who watches only over Earth from the sky.

9) Colonizing Abzu in Southern Africa to Mine the Gold Found in the Hills

Let's leave Mars and flash back to Earth. We go to the south of our planet to the continent of Africa. Here in our time machine we shall enter Enki's Earth laboratory.

First, we see how Enki now goes to work creating the machinery necessary to the Anunnaki mining gold. Enki beams his designs (blueprints) to Nibiru. Once received, the Nefilim start creating the devices. You see, Enki is the creator of ideas and then the one who makes the designs. A true idealist.

Here let's gaze on one device, which he called "Earth Splitter." The tablets call this design special and new as it is: (1) that which crashed into the wall as well as (2) one which crunches what comes down after the crash. Crash and crunch is the concept.

Do you wonder how sites like the Egyptian pyramids or the Temple at Baalbek were created? The tablets discuss the technology used to excavate and cut rocks to perfect size and then lift those rocks to sites so the structures could be made. The masons who pretend to have this sacred knowledge, which I believe is not complete, call this movement of stone Rosslynn, or floating stones. It is really an anti-gravitational source that lifts rock without any aid of other machines or man.

10) Back to Edin: Building the First Urban Anunnaki Workers' Communities

Enlil chose to build his Earth home in the northern side of Edin in the snow-covered hills of today's Lebanon. So now that his home is his permanent location on Earth, Enlil now builds a landing site for the alternative site for spaceships. This today is the site we call the Roman Temple of Jupiter. This is located in what we today call Baalbek.

The Nefilim were white skinned—very white, apparently. As I said, they had a temperate climate back on Nibiru. The atmosphere kept the heat of the Sun out. There was no humidity and probably no rain. They lived in Nibiru off the radiating heat from the center of their planet. That heat did not color their skin. And all their needs were grown in a laboratory. As I see images developing in my mind, the Nefilim is a race of beings who got command of a floating object in our universe that was traveling in our solar system and used it to create living beings who they needed to amuse themselves and keep their planet, Nibiru, a scientific-controlled laboratory, floating. I even see the story of Superman, then known as Kal-El, as his parents sent him to Earth before Krypton blew up. Superman was my personal favorite comic book.

When these Nefilim came to Earth, many did not like the heat found on Earth. Their planet, Nibiru, again radiated internal heat. The

Nefilim did not have the Sun to directly heat their bodies. Nibiru's atmosphere protected their bodies living by keeping the heat from the Sun out. Again, I repeat, they needed Earth's gold to keep the Nibiru atmosphere's insulation working. This insulation was able to keep the scorching heat of the Sun's rays out as the planet Nibiru traveled its orbit around our shared Sun. So many Nefilim travelers being Anunnaki, as well as the Igigis now knowing the heat of the Sun, chose to live in a temperate Earth climate, one where the heat was moderate most of the day and night.

This is why the Earth Nefilim settlers, again referred to as Anunnaki or Igigis, settled in the regions by mountains and valleys. They wanted a temperate climate. We shall discover this truth as Earth's colonization development continues.

11) Back On Nibiru: Next Trip to Earth and Mars

We now flash back to Nibiru. With their newest inventions ready to come to Earth, the Nefilim got the newest Celestial Chariot ready for the trip to Earth. "All aboard!" was the cry.

Fifty new passengers were chosen to become part of the Nefilim-Anunnaki team, and these select few were placed on the ship. This group had a female, meaning a Nefilim with a womb, nurse named Ninmah in it. Ninmah is a central character in the creation of mankind.

I write this now to show you that what we are doing on Earth right now may be history repeating itself. Our planet Earth's atmosphere has sprung a leak. We will need to fix it sooner than later, I assume. We may be just like the Nefilim at an earlier stage of their development living on Planet Nibiru. The living planet had sprung a leak from wear and rotation moving around the Sun and needing repairs. Maybe just this thought shows you what we will end up doing as we too will colonize material moving objects in the empty space of our universe or the galaxies.

The truth is we, mankind, are a new addition to the players of higher consciousness of thought-producing, physical beings.

Back to the Nefilim version of our Cape Canaveral. The Celestial Chariot ship is sent to sail the skies of our common universe from the Nibiru folks' point of view.

Ninmah, who was on this ship, was the half-sister of Enlil and Enki. Same dad, meaning King Anu. The mother was different, and this means a different bloodline, but Nefilim just the same. This will become important as time goes by in the creation of us Earthlings.

Ninmah was a nurse, we learn. A nurse to them was one who was a medical expert and one who could and did resurrect the dead. This is what we read she did when the new ship landed first on Mars. Anzu was found dead.

We learn how Ninmah resurrects Anzu. She used a Pulser and Emitter. What the names of these items are, we do not know. But we are told the following: "From her pouch she took out the Pulser; upon Anzu's heart pulsing she directed . . . she took out the Emitter, its crystal's life giving emissions on his body she directed." Guess what? After repeating this apparent life charge a few times, Anzu opened his eyes and was now alive. His consciousness was brought back into his body.

We then learn that Ninmah gave Anzu the "Food of Life" and the "Water of Life." Revived, Anzu told the traveling crew what happened to Alalu in his sentence to banishment to live alone on Mars.

The new Nefilim pilgrims ended up creating a brand-new space station on Mars. This Mars colony was set up to box Earth's liquid gold and then put it on the ship to transport the gold juice back home to Nibiru.

We now learn of the different fleet of spaceships that the Nefilim had for this travel.

Ship one was a Celestial Chariot ship. This was the largest of the fleet and was used to take travelers from Nibiru to Earth and Mars. Mars was about to become the landing hub to take the gold back to Nibiru in larger quantities.

Ship two is the rocket ship. This was used for short trips. Like a short travel to the moon or Mars from Earth and vice versa.

Ship three was the Sky Chamber (SC). This ship was used to travel around the Earth, and I assume first used to fly around Nibiru for domestic planet flights or the other celestial planets that the Nefilim visited while traveling space. This is what Alalu stole on his trip to Earth. The takeoff and landing strip for the Sky Chamber may in fact have been what today we call the Temple of Jupiter.

The Sky Chamber was also used to descend from large celestial ships to the surface of the planets. Doing this, I assume, makes the weight load easier to land the apparently apartment-building-sized Celestial Chariot Ship. Why? Because after the living leave and the total weight load of the traveling ship load is reduced, it is easier to land.

Now with Anzu again back in top living shape, Ninmah declared Anzu the commander of Mars as her father Anu had asked her to do. Anzu was told that there would be hundreds of settlers soon, who we now learn were to be called the Igigi. The Igigi means settlers of Mars as opposed to Anunnaki, the settlers of Earth. At this stage of their colonization game, twenty of the fifty passengers on this ship became settlers on Mars.

Ninmah was in charge of domesticating life for the inhabitants of both Mars and Earth. With her on this first journey, we discover, are mysterious seeds of a bush from Nibiru. This bush would grow and bear fruits and flowers that are an elixir. A potion that would give the Anunnaki and Igigi physical strength, cure their living space bodies of bacterial or viral diseases, and keep their moods happy. I believe one of these bushes is the grandparent of our hemp weeds as well as coca plant. And I believe it is when we discover the true potential of hemp, we will be able to cure disease and keep and maintain our strength. In addition, when one digests the flower, one's mood does, in some manner, change accordingly.

We will soon discover that the Nefilim-Anunnaki planted Earth with these crops and created for food and pleasure the domesticated animals of our world. Some animals were created to eat and other animals, like cats and dogs, were for our own enjoyment. The cats I believe are a little bit more evolved than dogs. Cats are captured spirits from beyond our solar system and watch us evolve. But watch us for whom? This is just a thought.

12) Back to Earth: New Anunnaki Team Get Their New Homes and Jobs

Ninmah goes to Earth with the remaining travelers. There Ninmah tells her half-brother Enlil they have a son together whom she calls Ninurta. The parents agree to bring the boy to Earth. He was named Ninurta because he was the blood of these half siblings and became the highest on the list of succession of his generation.

Spaceships became a common occurrence here landing and leaving Earth. The volunteers who went to colonize Earth were heroes back in Nibiru. And they became plentiful here on Earth. But after their chores, what did they do for fun? Causing trouble by looking for something to do is what all creations do.

Enlil has a master housing plan. Enlil will build a five-star community of the Anunnaki. Five-star like we are. Two arms, two legs, and one head is what makes us a five-star animal. Not all animals have five stars. A snake is one linear line. We resemble a Sun. We have a north and south, which are the legs. And we have an east and west, which are the arms. And we have our center, called a head, which moves maybe

210 degrees as it needs to move to do what our head, the computer of our body, tells us physical beings what to do.

Stretch those five points like stars and you will understand the communities build in their Levant, which they call collectively, "Edin." Edin was away from Nibru, the first command post of Earth back then. Nibru was a special spot that no one except the chosen few could go near. It had the secrets that were not to get into the wrong hands. Folks, Nibru is the Sinai Peninsula. That is why Sinai is so important in our thought process.

Now the community of the Anunnaki started building their land community base. Up first, the Anunnaki built the new command post without hidden weapons that was called Laana. Then they built city two, and this is called Lagash. The third city is Shurubak, or the Heaven City. The third city is between city one and two. The fourth city is Nibru-ki. Nibru-ki, it is said, that Enlil proclaimed, as it is written, said, "a bond heaven" (Nibiru) and Earth, or Ki, which means, "In it I shall establish."

The fifth city is not yet named. But it is said that the fifth city shall be the new landing post to allow spaceships to go freely between Earth and Nibiru. Enlil was not a fan of the base on Mars. Enlil was a control freak. Enlil wanted control of all the colonies as he was the future king of Nibiru.

Here in the scriptures we learn that Nibru refers to The Heaven and Ki refers to Earth. Now follow me. From this Heaven on Earth space, you went back to be with the other gods (Nefilim) on their planet called Nibiru. The space shuttle between Earth and Nibiru leaving Nibru in the Sinai Peninsula was the trip we humans envision in our minds and is reinforced by religions as the shuttle to Heaven. The Heaven being where we sit with the Nefilim-gods and do what our Earthling-created religions says we do when we get to heaven.

Now we Earthlings knew but really never got to understand the game of Nibiru and their team of Nefilim living on Earth as a space-traveling team called the Anunnaki. Anunnaki, who are Nefilim, which in their language means "gods." These gods would leave Earth from Earth's Heaven station and go back to Nibiru.

We are not told the stories of life on Nibiru. We have this information as the journal of what Enki and his Anunnaki, as well as the Igigi crew, did on Earth. Our experience with Nibiru is we know where the orders came from. Orders to tell the Anunnaki how to build Earth so it would serve the Nibiru goals. And of course, we know how they were carried out. Nowhere do we learn how the Nefilim spent their days living this so-called eternal life. Eternal, because their life-span was so much more than our Earthling timelines. But their bodies just like ours did eventually die. Physical death just depended on what model your physical DNA was and which beings' DNA you were made from. You could be made from Nibiru or Earth or a half breed, meaning a combination of both.

Understand anything that has a beginning will have an end. Anything made from spirit living in a three-dimensional body is temporary. Spirit outside a body is eternal. Energy that does not end until it goes back to its source. Our energy source is your choice Creator of All, GOD, or the Supreme Source.

The Nefilim in their bodies will die, and they too will go back to the matrix of their creation or ascend. And if they can ascend and reach absolute zero where energy goes to eternal sleep, they will have reached Nirvana, which is the utopia of everything and more. No wants nor needs just a state of being. No energy of thoughts anymore.

Before we continue, here are some thoughts to share about the Nefilim. What did these creatures do for pleasure? Or was life just work and no play for the community run by their king and royal families? Did they have organized sports? What was their music? How about theater? What about boutiques to have new clothing and create new ideas, or department stores of approved clothing for the workers to wear? Uniforms? What was life like in Nibiru with everlasting life? What did they do in between meals and before sleep? Did they sleep? Religions as they were created by us Earthlings worshiping these Nefilim gods do not fill in that void. We are not taught what the people who created the religions to their god thought or heard of what life back with the gods on Nibiru would be like.

13) Earth: Princes of Nibiru Doing Their Work.

Enlil, who was not a fan of the Mars move, decided he would build a new landing post in what would become the fifth city beyond Edin, which he called the Chariot Palace. The name is also Nibru again as this place replaces the early version of Nibru in the Sinai Peninsula. The old spot would now be where the secret weapons and other sacred creations of Nibiru would be hidden from others. Nibru again means "Earth's Heaven," and is not Nibiru, which is "The Heaven." Nibru was built so the spaceships could come and unload directly from Nibiru to the royal retinues directly at the palace. And most importantly, Enlil is in charge of what the traveling load is made up of and who is registered back on Nibiru to receive the load—the import and export business of that time.

Enki the Nefilim, idealist or genius and apparent mad scientist of colonizing Earth, builds his castle in Earth's sand on our southern land mass, which we today call the Great Zimbabwe ruins. These ruins are where Enki managed the mining of the gold. It is also where Enki started experimenting with cloning and splicing DNA to make different beings. I believe it is here we can learn the making of the mammals we see today on Earth, which never would have survived without some angel of sorts protecting these species from the wildlife of nature.

Just think how some of our tame and now domestic animals survived. Think how these domesticated animals survived wolves and lions and tigers too, to name but a few. Enki was a living Victor Frankenstein. We shall learn more soon.

If you're hungry for more info, look up a 1700s alchemist named Johann Konrad Dippel. He lived in the region we today call Germany. This man explored in his Earth-based life many unconventional thought ideas. He is who a few credit with being the inspiration of the novel character called Dr. Frankenstein.

Enlil had the Upper World and his Edin. Enki then had his Lower World. The Lower World was called Abzu, not hell, which many scholars apparently confuse as being the same.

Now Anu back on Nibiru had his FaceTime with the explorers as a community visitation by again their FaceTime machines. He tells the six hundred on Earth they shall be called Anunnaki, which means, "Those Who from Heaven [Nibiru] came to Earth-Eridu [Ki]."

The three hundred then on Lahmu (Mars) he named the Igigi. The Igigi meaning "those who observe and see." The Watchers, as they are referred to later in the Egyptian tale soon to be shared herein. Plus, these few Igigi, who do multiply and play a crucial role in creating the Aryan civilization here on Earth, which I do share in the coming tales. It gets really deep. It makes you understand where all the hate and division comes from that is so embedded in our living DNA. By sharing this, I pray we can change.

The Nefilim did not have a word for marriage. For a permanent relationship to build a house and raise the traditional family, they had the concept *espousal*, which was the concept of having a permanent relationship to procreate and make their heirs. And it is here we discover the tradition of the female spouse adopting their male partner's name.

The bloodline is the mother, but the living family name is the father. Get it?

Both Enlil and Enki did just this—get a spouse and procreate. They both realized on Earth they are stuck for a period of time. So, they needed their spouse to run their home. However, understand that these relationships were not exclusive. They both slept and reproduced with many, including their half-sister Ninmah. What went on here? Sleeping and creating offspring with Ninmah was done not so they would have an heir to the throne of Nibiru. It was done to make sure their offspring would have a place in the royal retinue. By having this spot, they would be able to rule in the overseas territories. Those territories being Earth, Mars, and the moon, as well as other spaceports, which these scriptures do not share. You just instinctively feel that Earth was not their only colony.

Enki took Ninmah his half-sister to Abzu and tried to have a male heir. Ninmah, we learn, only bore him daughters, not just one, but a few.

They would not be covered in these scriptures. However, before coming to Earth, Enki did play around and conceive a son whom they called Marduk with his Nibiru princess known as Damkina. Marduk means "one in a pure place born." This was the coming dynasty family feud of half-brothers and offspring. Enlil versus his half-nephew Marduk as the Fight Bill of spiritual watchers of planet Earth are about to see.

Marduk came to Earth with his mother later. The mother's name is changed to Ninki, to show to all the living on Earth her relationship with Enki. These Nefilim had more than one relationship. It is where the Mormons and Arabs and African tribes, as well as the Bible's David and Solomon, learned it was okay. In their minds, it was okay to have more than one wife or husband as it was in Heaven-Nibiru.

Marduk would soon fill our world with his twisted, evil ways. And if you reverse evil, my friends, you and all can live with free will, not the will of those in control of your thoughts. The games of today are explained from birth in these tablets I share with you as I come to understand our translations of the epic story of the creation of our Earth today and how we got here and why we got here.

Let's flash to Edin. Enlil, who wanted an Earth-born son, seduced a young Anunnaki female named Sud. She bore the child whom they named Nannar (Sin). Sud changed her name, and it became Nenlil.

We then learn that these two controlled rulers of Earth, Enlil and Enki, started producing babies with more than one Anunnaki female here on Earth. These offspring would grow and confuse greatly the orderly structure of life and who controls what here on Earth. Each new child wanted their place in the Sun of family royalty. Also know each new generation had their own court ready and able to move up to the next level when one above their court should pass on or leave the system.

14) The First Nefilim-Anunnaki Royal Court and Their Workers

So, let me now introduce you to the first Nefilim Royal court and their heirs. These small gods, Enki and Enlil with Ninmah, become the royal court serving their ruler of Nibiru in their Earth colony. This is where the twelve-seat table of the legend of King Arthur or Zeus and his Mount Olympus palaces of power concept begins.

Enki had five sons from his spouse Ninki. Those children were Nergal, Gibil, Ninagal, Ningishzidda, and Dumuzi. Enlil had three with his spouse Nenlil. Those three were Ninurta, Nannar, and Inanna, totaling eight. So now we have the magic of eight. We have the big three, who were Enlil and Enki with Ninmah. You have the eight offspring of Enki and Enlil with their two Anunnaki spouses. And the twelfth is Marduk. Those are the first twelve of the Nefilim Royal Earth family.

Life on Earth with a family who needs something to do starts to get very complex. There was social disorder of inheritance and rule. It was a social disorder as we have learned. This is the seed of our community of equal destruction. Control by rules and force to make sure those rulers of their family are kept in their ruling place with something to do.

Life on Earth then was an assembly line triangle. One angle was to mine the gold. Angle two was then to transport the gold from Anzu to Edin so they could melt the gold down into liquid form. The third angle then was to get the liquid gold to Mars and prepare for the final trip to Nibiru. And in Mars, business was simple. All they had to do on Mars was accumulate the Earth's liquid gold and then place this load on the ship to Nibiru. Also, they had to check the paperwork to see what they were transporting and to whom. Our first customs checkpoint.

Enlil was one character who thought of life as a chessboard of sorts. It was you versus him. Enlil would strategize his moves to make you move where he wanted you to move so he controlled your game of life. These moves were all motivated by fear of Enlil losing control and not being able to protect his territory. Enlil trusted no one, not even his own children.

Enlil was paranoid. Well, we see in others what we will do ourselves. He made sure his abode, the command post, was protected with the finest of weapons. He had searchlights called beams. And these beams became a radar type of light. They picked up movements in the dark as well as light. Think of the sweeping border patrol of our US-Mexican borders. See the similarity. Ours is still more primitive, I feel.

The system was created by the Nefilim's ME. ME translates to The Tablets of Wisdom. The ME on Earth controlled the first Iron Dome of its sort. An Iron Dome is a defense system in this case for attacks on the land as well as in the air.

The Nefilim, as we are learning, had a society with one absolute ruler. That ruler in this time space was Anu. And his children followed his rule, which was run and enforced by their ME computer system.

These Nefilim (gods, as they referred to themselves) had artificial intelligence run the administration of their one world order. As I continue to write, it fascinates me how we are just catching up to where our body designers were before.

Can you imagine their mankind creations when first created watching these chariots in the sky move? Imagine when they heard or saw the thunder and lightning in the sky. Imagine today what our pets and our beasts of burden think and feel when our planes, trains, and cars, as well as trucks, come into contact with these creatures. I say that so you see that we were the Anunnaki's pets too. And boy did they control our thoughts by inducing fears to own and control our time here on Earth.

Just imagine the shakings on Earth as spaceships came and went. You can see the creation of our different cultures' myths really being descriptions of the Anu family dynasty game being played before the new model beings,' called mankind, living eyes. Yes, I repeat, again, we are a created species.

The ME would become a problem later in time. That problem occurred when the ME fell into the wrong hands. Then the ME would give a solution. Really, an eye in the sky. One that can read your minds. For if an attack was needed, this was the machine that set their drones in motion. A force to kill and destroy anything that got into its radar. Hand-to-hand combat only occurred for those who wished to be king.

The ME would also give technical solutions to needs and desires, which are called problems here on Earth. One could and did ask the ME to give the Nefilim ideas on how to build what was needed to survive and thrive as the few Anunnaki-Nefilim colonized Earth. Then this think tank machine would help the Nefilim build the coming civilizations needed to keep mankind alive.

Soon these gods (Nefilim) would have their new creature soldiers to fight hand to hand. We are those tin soldiers of our ancestors. And the

Anunnaki space travelers would sit on their chariots of fire and be amused as mankind killed each other to make the Anunnaki happy. Remember the Bible, as translated, refers to gods, not God. And these gods could be very mean when they did not get their way. They taught mankind how to maim and kill others in human bodies as justified behavior when those others (them) upset the god of those (us) lands.

Life on Earth, I will repeat, was a problem for the Anunnaki. It was a military sentence in essence. The Anunnaki were sentenced to Earth for a duration of time and then allowed to go back home. Home to be celebrated as heroes. The short Earth days, we are told, started bothering most of them. So many who were just soldiers did not want to stay. But the gods who ruled where having a blast making a new world just like the Catholic Church did when they invaded the Western Hemisphere with their conquistadors in 1492. They did it for their god who is not the Supreme Source no matter what the Vatican says.

15) The Igigi's Mutiny on Mars

The residents of Mars were a little bit more restless. Their leader Anzu was constantly informing the big three of Enlil and Enki on Earth and Anu in Nibiru via their FaceTime that the Igigis wanted their own place on Earth.

Enlil tried to pacify them, but it did not work. Anzu and Enlil would soon become enemies.

When the moment was right, the Igigi planned a mutiny. This moment did occur. Here is that story.

To have a mutiny, it is good to have force ready to stop those who you are revolting against from stopping the mutiny in its tracks. Weapons would do. And so the Igigi decided among themselves how to fight the king and his team. Anzu became the volunteer to get the weapons.

Anzu went to Earth and stole the ME. He went to the spaceport where he knew the weapons were hidden, as he and Enki put them there.

At the scene of the crime, some Igigis lay in wait for Anzu, and with their support, Anzu did escape with the ME.

Enlil flipped out and needed his Samson. One Nefilim-Anunnaki volunteer to do the job. The new hero is from the royal Nefilim family line. This was one job that required one to be very strong, as the ME was power. For the possession of the ME made the mutiny few invincible, so it had to be taken back. Enlil's oldest son Ninurta came to the rescue. An aerial battle ensued. Just imagine the first airplane fights in WWI.

With the vocal aid of FaceTime types of phones, Ninurta communicated with Enlil. Enlil the quarterback coach gave Ninurta the path to tackling the enemy and getting back the football called the ME. The play worked. Anzu was captured and executed. Marduk, Enki's eldest son, was ordered to take the body back to Mars where Anzu was buried. Marduk was then appointed the ruler of Mars. See how the brothers, the sons of Anu, get their family involved?

The tablets say Anzu was judged and convicted. But judged by whom and under what set of rules we do not know. There was a judicial system in place.

So now we see the Nefilim had an executive branch called King and his Royal Court of Elders. And now we learn of a judicial system. A system that can order death. My questions are what about an army, and what about a police force? I don't have those answers yet, but what about a three-tier system to have law and order? Does the population as individuals have a say?

We can figure out when this mutiny and execution occurred, for the tablets say this occurred in the twenty-fifth Shar. Remember, each Shar is 3,600 Earth years. A Shar is one Nibiru year. Please be aware I will start interchanging Nibiru for Heaven, as this is the Nefilim's language and where the magic word Heaven came from.

So, to get the Earth date of when the Igigi mutiny occurred, multiply 3,600 by twenty-five. The number you get is 90,000. The 90,000 is how many Earth years have passed since the Anunnaki roamed Earth. We know that they came to Earth, as they write in their tablets, 443,000 Earth years ago. So, this mutiny took place in our time 353,000 Earth years ago.

As I said when this section began, we humans live Earth years. That is the season of existence our DNA blueprint creates for our living bodies. The Anunnaki, full-blooded Nefilim, have Nibiru-womb-created DNA and therefore have a physical body that was created to live Nibiru years.

16) Back to Abzu and the Earth Gold Mines

Now down under in Abzu, Enki was playing God the creator. Enki was toying with the then living Earth creatures making his new creations. Enki would put his research into the computer we called ME and then tinker to tailor new creations of animals, plants, and material. The lad was bored, yes? But what a mind of creation Enki apparently had.

Enki's partner in creation was his son Ningishzidda. They fed information to ME to unravel new theories so they could make discoveries. This is how we mankind were soon to be created.

One of the creatures the tablets discuss is the tall, two-legged creature that lived among the trees. Their front legs were hands that they used to move things around. This is the first mention of the Homo Erectus species that lived in Africa. It is also where they got the prototype to create mankind.

This is in the clay tablets. Our school systems teach that Homo sapiens miraculously evolved around three hundred thousand years ago. These are non-truths as the sapiens were created in a laboratory. Truth in theory is Darwinism. It's true maybe, but evolution takes time. The

Nefilim living on Earth and playing gods sped up evolution by creating the new mankind. Yes, more than one, as we shall soon see.

Act One, Scene Five: The Earth's First Workers' Revolt

Now in the tablets we learn about the uprising in Abzu by the Anunnaki mining crew. This uprising took place in the land we today call South Africa. The Anunnaki workers revolted and refused to continue their mining. Enlil had to help his half-brother Enki out.

In Edin, Enlil's house was surrounded by the workers from Abzu who left Abzu and brought the revolt to the land of the elite ruling class of the Nefilim. Travel for even the miners was easy in those early days. Remember, they had the Space Chariots and power boats that look like submarines for long domestic rides. For short distances they had boats that looked like the airboats of the Everglades.

The mining workers wanted out of their mining gig on Earth. We now learn of the experience of global warming during their tenure on Earth. The weather, they noticed, was changing. The ice caps were melting. It was hotter down in Abzu than when they started more than ninety thousand Earth years ago. So, a solution was needed. The Anunnaki's spare time was not being fulfilled. There was nothing to do but just mine. Mine and then eat and try to go to sleep when Earth's night took over the sky. Something had to give. They needed free time and hobbies to pass their nonwork moments. And they did not want to do the manual labor of mining anymore.

The workers said to get a hold of the ME and get machines to do this labor of mining the caves of these lands looking for the gold in the Earth. They would not do it anymore. They felt as if they had no life. "This is not work made for us Nefilim. Create machines!" was the cry.

What will the elite rulers of Nibiru do?

The brothers Enki and Enlil got a hold of King Anu by their then FaceTime. The three of them decided to create a Primitive Worker, what they called a Lulu, which was the nickname for the Primitive Worker. A quote from the tablets: "Let the Being so to be created be the toil of the Anunnaki carry on his back." The first mankind slave. A slave made to dig and extract gold in the mines of South Africa.

Act One, Scene Six: Making Lulu, The Primitive Worker

What a blast this would be to see with remote viewing—looking back in time as a witness watching an energy motion picture show. Not one who becomes the energy as a physical being then living as such in that time or era. Yes, I know this time travel remote viewing can be done. And there are two types of time travel. One you enter by dropping into that dimension of time as it's a frequency and you change your atoms to enter that frequency. Not easy to do. The second is you concentrate to the frequency of time and enter that into your astro-travel abilities and tune in and watch or hear the show you requested, but you are in a picture show of sorts. You are not taking part where you can make change. As a witness, a voyeur of sorts, this is very possible. And I am not the only one who knows this can be done.

Now we learn how mankind the species without Darwin's evolution theories of nature, and without intervention, theories began.

The tablets share the following story:

No one in Edin knew of Enki's experiments on the living beings down under in his Abzu land in the region we call Great Zimbabwe. Enki was splicing up living beings and seeing what he could clone and or change into new forms of existing life on Earth. He had cages for his experiments that are ruins that still exist down there in Abzu so all can see. And as he was bored, this was his hobby until there was a need to create the Lulu, the Primitive Workers.

The tablets say in our translated words, "Upon discovering what Enki did with his free time, the Elders of Nibiru were angry." "How do we do this?" was the question the elders on FaceTime in Nibiru asked the brothers Enki and Enlil in Edin, here on Earth. It's important to understand that the Nefilim apparently acted as a unit when decisions were taken. Really, like bees, when the queen bee who lives longer than the worker bees makes a decision that all follow.

This was quite a culture shock to the Nefilim. Even the brother's half-sister Ninmah is shocked. She says to Enki, "You cannot make a new species and play with the creator's selection of existing beings. Who are you to change destiny of living species here on Earth. How can you do this? You are not the Creator of life."

As an aside, even though they called themselves gods, with a small "g," to them they were not what we here on Earth believe God, the word, means. The tablets let you know they believed in a Supreme Being. This being is the source that is in control of the energies that exist inside the universe and the galaxies and our solar system, which creates the conditions needed for life in physical form to exist. This is the metaphysical explanation of our human existence. This Nefilim species spent time examining what they could perceive in their planet Nibiru's run around our solar system and the galaxy, and for all I know, the universe that their machines could pick up the energies that exist in those spaces. The Supreme Being energy is beyond everything we can fathom inside our energy's awareness. We are only a loose particle of energy of that Supreme Being force. This you will understand, as my third book of this series, *We've Got to Get Out of This Place!*, shares.

Now Enki and his son Ningishzidda (Ning), who helped dad play with living Earth creatures as their source of enjoyment, must tell what they have done while living alone in Abzu. They actually captured species of life and created their own scientific laboratory as if this were the prequel to the movie of our lifetime *The Island of Dr. Moreau*. The movie where a "mad scientist" makes half-human beings. The father and son confessed to tinkering with the beings of Earth.

Now the elders realize they must create the Primitive Worker. They asked their mad scientist, "What do you feel we should allow you to do? Where do we get the body to make this living prototype primitive worker?"

Enki and Ning decided to use this animal that played and swung in the Abzu plants we call trees as their prototype. The tablets go on to say, "In their image, create a primitive worker." Sounds like the Bible. The Gods created man in their image.

The tablets go on to say they must give this creature the essence of the Nefilim (gods). The being was created in the image of the Nefilim (gods)—the Nefilim Enki as well as his half-sister Ninmah.

We also learn that the Nefilim did understand the moral dilemma of creating a new species with their knowledge. To create a living creature, a slave to them, was specifically prohibited in their authorized charter to explore Earth, which lets you know that this thought was not new to them.

Enlil was against it at first. Enlil is actually quoted as saying, "Creation in the hands of the Father of All beginning is held." They too believe as I do in the one creation force—again, the force that I call the Supreme Being.

Enki created a worker's crew to help create new life, the Primitive Being to his scientific chambers, which he called the House of Life. Remember, travel from Edin to Abzu then was quick and easy in the Sky Chamber (SC). In cages on Enki's House of Life, one could see the caged experiments he was making to create new creatures from the old. Again, one can see ruins of these grounds if you travel to Great Zimbabwe in real time or view in reel time.

Finally, Enlil gave in, and they agreed to let the program begin. But here are the seeds of dissent between the two brothers who were the gods (one the master and the other the Lord of Command) of Earth in the Bible. For Enlil becomes the god who wants to keep mankind primitive, ignorant, obedient, and fearful. All so the species knows its place. This Enlil becomes the angry god of the Hebrew Bible who wishes to let mankind drown in what we call the Great Flood. Enki is the benevolent Nefilim-god who keeps mankind alive in the Bible story of the flood. And Enki's son Marduk, as a coming attraction, becomes the god of hellfire who, when he gets upset, will teach us to burn each other for Marduk's amusement, as we shall soon learn.

ACT TWO: THE MAKING OF MANKIND

Well, my friend, here is the act of mankind's creation. This is our story of how we, mankind, were physically created. At first a Primitive Worker who would do the work for the Nefilim and their space travelers, who were called the Anunnaki space team for Earth. The Nefilim needed a thinking being working for them as their slave. So back to the drawing board went Enki. And here is what happened. And know that this story takes place hundreds of thousands of Earth years ago. This marries perfectly what our scientists say is when our version of mankind first appeared on Earth and the stages of our development as a race and species into what we are now from what we were then, as we started as a Lulu.

MANKIND IN A PHYSICAL BODY, SOME WITH THE WOMB OF ENTRY. THE WOMB IS THE DOOR OF THE MATRIX OF PHYSICAL LIFE. JUST MEN WITH THE FIRE THAT IGNITES THE PHYSICAL SEED SET LOOSE INSIDE THE FEMALE MATRIX OF PHYSICAL EXISTENCE HERE IN OUR DIMENSION WE CALL EARTH.

THE SEED ONCE FERTILIZED IS THE PROGRAMMED DNA THAT ALLOWS OUR CONSCIOUSNESS TO EXPLORE AND GROW IN A LOCKED-UP PHYSICAL BODY. OUR DNA IS FROM WHOM? THIS IS THE CRIME. WE ARE LIMITED BY OUR

PHYSICAL DNA. WE ARE ENERGY FROM A SUPREME SOURCE YOU MAY CALL GOD. BUT THERE IS NO IDENTIFIABLE PHYSICAL GOD.

My friends, those capitalized words are not from me, for I just channeled those words and did as my energy told me to do. We are not from Nibiru nor are we Nefilim. I believe we are a collective consciousness, a tribe, that broke into individual forms, who used and allowed the Nefilim energy with their dream catchers to lure us, as a collective consciousness, to enter this matrix called Earth and its locked atmosphere. Once locked in this Earth dimension, we leave the collective consciousness of thought beings as an individual drop. And as an individual thought being fall into this body that we currently reside in while we live here in and on Earth as a physical being with our locked consciousnesses following the computer-like orders of our brains and doing what the brain as opposed to our higher consciousness says we should do. We become caged beasts of burden for our dream-catching creators.

Act Two, Scene One: The Creation of Mankind Prototype One: Lulu Mankind's First Male and Then Female Prototypes

Okay, ready for the magic moment? Here we go.

Sitting around the laboratory, the two, Enlil and Enki with a few others who are not individually named, then in control on Earth, say among themselves as reported inside the tablets, the following:

1. Should we with wisdom new tools fashion, now new beings create?

2. What knowledge we possess to use cannot be prevented.

3. Is this fate what we are about to do? Or is it the destiny of Earth we are about to create?

4. How do we control, or do we not control what we are about to create?

The Earth-based crew said, "Let's ask the elders of our community back on Nibiru what we should do." The so-called elders got together and by a vote among themselves, we are told, Anu got permission for his children to create a new species.

But this species was to be for slave work. To serve the creatures of Nibiru living on Earth as the Anunnaki team. Living on Earth to get their home planet Nibiru the Earth gold needed so that the Nefilim beings could fix Nibiru's atmosphere, and so life on Nibiru could survive.

So, the original game plan of mankind's creation was for mankind to be limited by design in the beginning of its creation, to be nothing more than a Primitive Worker.

The father of this creation was chosen to be Enki. The son of this creation is Enki's son Ningishzidda (Ning). The holy ghost of spirit, the life force that would enter the matrix, a.k.a. as the womb, is Enki's half sister Ninmah.

At first these three Nefilim beings now in charge go to the location where Ning was experimenting with the living species of Earth. These Model T species were without the essence of consciousness. They were machines that could not improvise. The game of Primitive Worker creation was to get limited consciousness (thought) of a planned Primitive Worker to actually be able to stay put and work as if they were a machine with physical animal capabilities. To actually work as a slave with the ability to understand commands and the physical strength to work in the gold mines. In essence, to do what the Anunnaki did and no longer wished to do. The Anunnaki team were done with the physical aspect of mining and collecting the gold itself. They would now oversee the slaves they would call Primitive Workers.

Why did they not create a machine to do this work? Why they felt that they needed a being that could process commands and redo and do as they were told is not mentioned at all. My instinct is you would need hands that could work individually as well as collectively and respond to nature as nature responds to being ripped apart. These Nefilim scientists understood that a machine would be limited, and so a being that could use its hands, which can be used as individual fingers and collective forces, was much more valuable for the job that needed to be performed.

The creatures created by Ning were caged and wild. I believe that it is here the deer and the others like moose and Santa's reindeer with trees growing from inside their heads were created. I believe that these creations were not capable of using their antlers to move the dirt and get the gold. Good try, but no go.

However, the animals so created were beautiful and graceful. They were perfected so they could reproduce and live in the wild as animals of Earth's forests and grasslands. The creations were not good for the mining but were allowed to roam free. I see in my awareness the Anunnaki moving these species around Africa, where they could play and reproduce as long as they had food.

Just sharing an image now with thoughts I now see. A bone is really a tree. It lives like a tree. Does it not? It is also the last part of our Earth bodies to go back to Earth just like trees when we die. The trees lasts longer than their leaves. And the bark of the tree is the tree's skin. What this means is there is a higher symmetry in our living beings' physical bodies, be you plant or animal.

So, you few who say the antlers are the bones of trees may be correct. As I do believe our bones are the trees and branches of our bodies here on Earth. Then the rest of our parts get to live and be protected by our trees' bark that we call skin. We are plants that can move, and because we are mobile without help from others, we can do more than stationary trees as we move around Earth.

Back at the home Abzu laboratory.

In this caged area, we read how the animals in these cages had "four parts of one kind. They had hind parts of another creature they possessed. . . . Creatures of two kinds by their essence combined." Ning showed these creatures to Ninmah, and she flipped out.

The game of creation did not happen immediately. No, it took time, Earth time, to find the perfect DNA combination, it is written, and for the fertile egg to hatch in the womb that would give the egg life.

I believe that the kangaroos too were a failed experiment to make a Primitive Worker. Also, many of the animals on the island that one can see in Madagascar must have begun with the factory of Enki. My thoughts I share on the failed experiments of making the perfect Primitive Worker. Plus, this makes for a great explanation of creation of what now exists.

We now learn that the scientist in the lab used the female creatures as the surrogate mothers. The eggs of creation (fertile eggs) were placed into these wombs. The surrogate mothers took time.

One can read the following in these scriptures: "In a crystal vessel, Ninmah the admixture was preparing, the oval of a female two legged she gently placed. With ME Nefilim seed containing, she the oval impregnated . . . the oval back into the womb of the two-legged female she inserted."

The first two-legged creations did not work. We are told they were born deformed. They were deaf, hairy, had short arms, and were blind to name a few defects. Plus, they were only creating males. Just like I once thought that mules were somehow created from donkeys. A donkey, we are told in our biology courses, is a combination of two separate species of the African Ass. A mule is the offspring of a male donkey (jack) and a female horse (mare). I have learned researching this book that a mule can be male or female, but because of the odd number of chromosomes, they cannot reproduce.

The animal instincts of these creations were stronger than a machines side. The creators did not behave. Finally, Enki, our Dr.

Frankenstein, said to his half sister Ninmah, "We need a Nefilim female to insert the egg into. How about you?" Enki asks.

And Ninmah answers, "Yes, let's do it." And my friends, the first human male as a Primitive Worker was created.

This male prototype is blackhead, they write. The lines transcribed are the following: "Shaggy like the wild ones he was not. Dark black his hair was . . . like dark red blood was its color . . . like the clay of the Abzu was its hue."

Let's put this all into our systems of what schools of controlled learning teach us here in the Christian Western world.

One, we are told that Homo sapiens emerged around three hundred thousand Earth years ago. We know this by studying the mitochondrial DNA (mothers) and the Y-chromosomes (male) of the fossils we discovered. The trees of man called bones is where this information we store is found. The fossils, as in many we discover, really mean the creatures were in abundance.

Two, it is now widely accepted by our thought-controlled system that the first "cabbage patch" is to be found in Southern Africa. This is where mankind began. And it was not Lucy the Ape, it was Ninmah the daughter of Anu, who created mankind. Our physical creator was female.

This story does match our timeline of mankind's development. But finally, we can learn the how and why it happened. And yes, that still leaves the question to be answered: How did the first beings arrive? The answer I see is that they opened a hole to the physical world—the eternal matrix—and escaped inside this matrix where bodies are formed from the mother womb. This womb is the source that you fall into when you incarnate inside the external physical existence of a universe. We, locked inside this universe as a consciousness, then fall into a body as we did here on Earth, and this body is mankind. Other consciousnesses choose other forms to live and balance their wants and needs. Why? Too much to philosophically explain. It all deals with karma. Another book in another time.

While Enki examined the newborn boy, it is written that Enki noticed a flap of skin on the boy's penis. Nefilim did not have this flap. This would be the tracker, we will learn, or how one could know if the soon-to-be-populated Earthlings were Nefilim or not.

It is also why Abraham was told by his Nefilim-god, not the one Supreme Source, who we will learn was Enlil, to circumcise himself so the Anunnaki-Nefilim would know that he and his followers were chosen by Enlil to survive. For soon the family feud of Enki's Nibiru son Marduk and Enlil would become the Judeo-Christian and Islamic biblical history of Earth.

Seeing that this firstborn was more than a creature, Enki gave the child a name. He called the boy "Adamu." Adamu means in their Nefilim tongue, "one who like Earth clay is."

Now the new issue. How do we multiply this baby boy? Easy. Let's get some volunteers to let us use their wombs. We will put our eggs that are fertilized inside their wombs so that oven can bake our creatures into physical existence.

There were approximately three hundred female Nefilim on Earth. The casting call went out. For this new game of life, they needed seven volunteers. Why seven? Who knows, but do remember on the voyage of the Nefilim-Anunnaki to Earth, Earth is the seventh planet, so as to reach Earth, the ship must pass the six outer planets we discussed earlier. So maybe this was just their magic number of inspiration or some thought very similar.

These seven females who gave their wombs up as experiments to create Primitive Workers became the new Nefilim heroines. Through their wombs the Primitive Workers were created and perpetuated as a new species here on Earth.

Ever study the Hindu story of creation? Check out their version of creation. Interesting how the Vedic poems of creation worship the seven women of creation.

In this first trial of the seven, it does not work. These seven created males. Now what?

So, with the blood of Adamu and his DNA as the base admixture for fertilization, Enki talked his spouse Ninki into being the surrogate actual oven mother. Remember these Nefilim had plenty of Earth time to spare as their lives were so much longer than ours, so what's nine Earth months here and there to explore and experiment creating a new species?

This is important to see and remember as this story continues. Ninki was Marduk's father's spouse. His mother in Nefilim law. Marduk believed that this oven, called a womb, was his by birthright as all the creation of the races legally were related to him. He believed the children, offspring from this act, were his inheritance.

In time the first mankind female was produced. We learn of the difference in her skin color from that of Adamu. Yes, she had the smooth Nefilim skin with the white color. She was different then Adamu. It is here that the blood distinction of your mother was created. For we all get our mothers body bloodline. Sorry guys.

Now they needed a name for this female. The name they chose was Ti-Amat. The name means "mother of life." Combine the two and you get Tiamat. Tiamat, the Nibiru name of the planet, which produced Earth when she was hit and split into two halves back in our universe time.

Enki, his sister Ninmah, his son Ning, and his spouse Ninki went on to create another seven female Earthlings. These were created from the same seven birth mothers who tried before, but the same way that Ti-Amat was created.

It was time to be rabbits and reproduce quickly. And these seven males and females were created from the prototypes of Adamu and Ti-Amat. These seven couples were caged in Abzu. They were watched, and they copulated among themselves.

Enki brought the first two prototypes to the upper world. He proceeded to show his prototype creations off. Like a model's runway show this was. Enki needed to protect their DNA, so it was decided they would stay in Edin. They were allowed to move around freely and be observed by the Anunnaki under these circumstances of free movement. They lived in Edin, unaware of their surroundings. Earth's first true freak show. And also the Bible's story of the Garden of Eden.

What amazed everyone in the upper world was that these two could follow commands and perform simple tasks. But they were not clothed nor were they housed. And they did not question anything. No inquiry as they just did what they were told to do. Obedient pets who wished only to be fed and probably pet.

But in the lower world there was a problem. The seven couples could not reproduce. They were made up of twenty-two chromosomes. The X and the Y combination as one were missing, we are told.

The tablets go on to say, "Like two entwined serpents Ningishzidda the essence separated.... Arranged like twenty-two branches on a Tree of Life were the essence.... The ability to procreate they did not include." Now we read about the rib so stated in our Bible. Each chromosome was given a sex gene. and what this means is only one is selected to be the sex. We call the X female and the Y the selected male.

Act Two, Scene Two: The Second Model of Mankind

Now the time came when the Nefilim need to fix the kinks in their mankind DNA. They knew they could do better.

Ning sedated both Enki and Ninmah. From each he went to their "ribs." I am not sure exactly what this means, but I know it is not the ribs that we know the word ribs to mean. Ning, it is said, extracted from both of the models their sex essence of boy for Y and X now for girls, which is in each cell we have, implanting into Adamu and Ti-Amat this sex essence as part of their DNA Tree of Life. "Tree of Life" is a very powerful image to explain the way life is programmed to physically grow. A tree that reminds me of the vines that grow grapes and produce, as they age, the nectar we call wine for the children of mankind to be first happy or become mean.

Enki now had two creatures roaming around Edin. Since they were his offspring, he did not want them to be Primitive Workers who could not use their intelligence. So Enki, whose symbol was a serpent, taught them what he felt they should know. This symbol of a serpent, our first medical doctor here on Earth, is still used today as a medical symbol. But the two serpents are also the symbol of the male and female chromosomes given to the creation by mom and dad, the parents of the new one.

Enlil was upset that these two creatures could reproduce. This meant a population of beings on their own impulses would now begin. Not one that is created on an as-needed basis like robots. That was not what was authorized to happen by the Elders of Nibiru. Ning then, we read, explained to his uncle Enlil that these creatures were not given the gift of Nibiru life. This meat that they would not live as long as the Nefilim. They would die on the Earth's timeline for physical beings.

So here we learn that we mankind was not given everlasting Nefilim long life, and this was deliberate. It is also what we seek when we are told behave and God will get you into Heaven for the immortal life if you behave and follow God's rules while you are here on Earth. You are misled into believing that if you behave, god, a.k.a. Nefilim, will take you home to the Heaven they call Nibiru. You will live an endless life according to mankind's understanding of life not the understanding of a Nefilim. Everything is relative. We measure one versus the other, but only what we know and understand can be used as the measurement.

Please try to understand what you are reading or hearing and start to see so you can begin to accept the truth. It is hard to do, but once you are willing to go there and see the possibilities of this truth, the story of creation will unfold right before you outside your mind as you will leave the portal through the escape hatch, which many today call the bodies as opposed to the mind's third eye. Or at least mine did. You as an energy never die. You just shapeshift when you choose to reincarnate in other physical lives in all dimensions and their galaxies and universes and corresponding solar systems' planets. Not just this one.

To get out of a universe, you must go to that universe's source of energy we call the sun. Then where? The answer is in Act Eighteen of this series of books. But simply stated now, you ascend to another universe or galaxy or go straight back to the Supreme Being of Everything and more. You are now in bliss. Without wants or needs of any kind.

Saying this, I now imagine that the species called Earthlings was constantly modified. We were modified because the Nefilim did reproduce with female Earthlings, and this created new genetic brands. Modified, as we will discover, because in our beginning, these half Earth-Nefilim beings did have longer lives. We are also missing the genetic links that prevent us from getting sick and cause us to die quicker than the Nefilim. And if the Nefilim end for some reason is too early, they can be revived from the premature dying of the body before your body's true timeline.

Would you want to live forever in your Earth body? Would you not want to die and be able to come back and learn another way of being? Can you really live on after all your generation of beings are dead and gone in that body form? These questions are the philosophical peaks of existence. Who are we, and what are we here to do?

Understand this truth too. Enki is the creature that created the Earthlings. He gave them knowledge, and he was the serpent. Enlil the Anunnaki, who was against their creation, and when it was created was against their procreation, wanted them to be kept on an as-needed basis to fill the need for slaves and servants, revolted when he saw the two primitives, one male named Adamu and the female named Ti-Amat, starting to act just like him. So, he banished the two from his Garden of Edin. The two were thrown back to the underworld of Abzu.

The Bible combines the acts of Enki and Enlil as one god. They are half-brothers from different mothers. The bloodline is what?

Now down under in Abzu, our new creatures start serving and reproducing at their own desires. A race of mankind is perpetuated. But one with knowledge being able to understand what they were taught and without wisdom as they did not understand they were not taught how to see beyond the limits of what they were taught to be true. The created mankind did not learn the wisdom of life. To learn and become wise without elders is very hard to do. But you can. Just explore and learn to see beyond the forest of your mind and its blinders of fear and ignorance, which your mind cannot navigate as your mind is a computer, and as a computer, it is there to make you do what you are told by the system you must do to physically survive. I get very deep into this truth later in this series of books.

INTERMISSION

My thoughts, which I need to share.

Something goes on here, and the Nefilim create a new physical being for them to control and use as a slave to their rhythm, be it physical labor or domesticated service. How did they catch our essence, our consciousness, and get us locked in these physical bodies, which they created as if we were nothing but a car that they get to move and swerve in their physical bodies without any spiritual wants and needs?

Birth begins as a collective consciousness of thoughts that separate from the Supreme Being, the energy of everything, including the consciousness that allows our individual streams to dream in no physical time or place. This is until we dream of living inside a physical body machine and leave the team pool of consciousness where we come from.

We were initially born free. Hearing a song from my past, I will use those lyrics to explain what my thoughts are before you get incarnated into physical form of the matrix that gives life to the metaphysical energies that exist outside your body. The song is called "Born Free."

You as a consciousness are born free. You are born free and can watch grass grow. You are born free to follow your dreams. You are born free as a thought to follow your energy and surround yourself with beauty or darkness. You are born free, as free as the wind blows. Your dreams still astound you. You can watch the energies of stars being created as you gaze upon the creations of stars and the resulting matrix that physical star now controls.

The game is to stay free where no matrix of physical substance can divide you from the whole you. In body form you have rules of physical limitations that take away your ability to stay free. In life forms you are not a roaring tide. You end up needing a physical place to hide.

You end to ask yourself if this physical incarnation isn't worth giving up your ability to be born free. Because you're born to be free.

What is the real cost of life with your agreement to be caught by these Dream Catchers who promise you a life in a heaven that they control saying next time you can live in your own physical utopia.

Think about this as I share with all the creation of a thought machine from somewhere outside Earth's matrix now stuck here in this matrix of servitude for the few who have a set system in which they rule over you.

A Whole New World

Where did it all start?
Who are we?
No, what are we?
Why did we become these bodies?
What was our purpose here
And how did we come to be?

So let's begin the tale. . . .

The atmosphere on Planet Nibiru
Was about to disappear
Only gold could seal the holes
So the Nefilim went in search
Of the only source
They could use for that repair

So the Nefilim/Annunaki spaceships
Sped through the Universe
In their desperate quest
For a planet they could quickly find
Which could serve and pass the test

"Lo, down there!" the pilot cried to all

STEVEN MACHAT

"It looks like veins of glitter"
"Let's land our ships below
On Earth so we can see
Did we find the gold or is it useless litter"

And so the Nefilim sent
The Annunaki's down to Earth
And found their perfect place for gold
Nibiru would be saved
From certain death
Or so the story's told

But who would it be
To mine the ore
They had to figure out
So Enki designed a type of Beings
That wouldn't even question
What they were all about

He tinkered with the bodies
And made them bow to gods
Devoid of any higher thought
Control of these Earthlings
And sending home the gold
Is the only thing they sought

But those Aliens liked their "Humans"
So with them began to mate
Creating a brand new species
Changing the Earth forever

With a New World Order
Would be this Planet's fate

So finally, when the Nefilim left
For home to live a long life
And back to their old ways
They left us with a legacy
So the worshipping of "demigods"
Still remain with us today

—Debbie Veltri Machat

ACT THREE: POPULATING EARTH WITH MANKIND

Act Three, Scene One: Creating the Upper World White-Skinned Servants

So now with Primitive Man working for the Anunnaki, what was life like here on Earth? This is what I see. This is what I feel.

Before the creation of the Primitive Worker, the living ruling colonial system for the Anunnaki was a commune. There was no talk of money or exchange. There were no material goods to acquire. There were no celebrities to worship, nor gods and goddesses. Just the royal uncontested hierarchy of Nibiru telling their Nefilim Earth-based Anunnaki team what they must do on Earth for the planet Nibiru—exploring and getting the materials needed for Nibiru to survive.

Then the Nefilim created the Primitive Worker, a black-skinned creature that could do the slave work in the mines. Prototype Two was able to serve the urban areas of the Nefilim-Anunnaki up in the Upper World. There was a problem. The Nefilim did not want the black workers. They wanted white-skinned workers. They as a culture were not used to seeing black-skinned workers, as there was no evolutionary reason for nature to make black-skinned Nefilim, as there was no Sun exposure as we have here on Earth. The beings born on Earth did have a reason to be colored dark, as these beings needed to be protected from the intense Sun rays in Africa.

So soon we will witness the creation of the white-skinned Earthlings who were manipulated in their DNA to come out white-skinned. To the Upper World went their servants and slaves too. A society was being created.

Now what type of community? Not a commune. Nope, it was the beginning of the Imperial Rules of Feudalism ruled by the few kings with princes and princesses and lords from another land called Nibiru, who inherited from this land their so-called right to rule these Earth colonies of Nibiru.

Everyone not a slave or servant worked for the common good of all for the benefit of Nibiru. Life was dependable and so predictable. But life was getting easy as the Nefilim had their black-skinned slaves to do the physical work and the white-skinned servants to serve the Anunnaki. Life was boring.

What do we do, we humans, when we have too much time left unaccounted for? We cause chaos. We do things. We see black holes that we try to fill in with our wants and needs.

What did the Nefilim-Anunnaki do? Well, they caused trouble too. Here is their story, here on Earth.

I feel like a messenger of truth. I study people and places. I study why we do what we do. I study how we are controlled. Who made up our rules, and why do we believe them to be true? It all begins here in Earth's first urban centers.

We set the scene. Look beyond your minds as you read or hear this story.

We are now in approximately year 240,000 of Nefilim lives on Earth. The Nefilim who were cast as Anunnaki to live on Earth were also reproducing here on Earth. Now we have citizens of this Upper World outpost who have never been on Nibiru. These really native Anunnaki Earthlings had their life-spans sped up. They aged and died on a timeline different from the Nefilim but longer than Earth time. It was still much longer than our current life-spans, but was shorter than the Anunnaki who were born and raised first on Nibiru first.

Back on this Anunnaki Earth time, a middle class is developed. I now visualize *The Jetsons* cartoon series of my youth. Get it?

It's time for a middle-class lifestyle. And what do these middle-class Nibiru DNA created folks here on Earth want? They want their own domesticated servant. One who can do what they are asked to do but without question and future wants. Like a robot with a machine that needs a heart to work, not feel.

The problem is those north of the Earth's equator Anunnaki folks wanted white-skinned servants. Not black-skinned servants. So, what did our mad scientist Enki do?

Enki came to the rescue and created what we call the Homo sapiens.

Act Three, Scene Two: Mankind Mold Three—The New and Improved White Team

Really the third version of mankind. White mankind, Aryans, can think and do civilized chores for the few, not just slave manual machine labor. A domestic trained civilization to serve the middle and upper classes of Nefilim-Anunnaki as well as the Nefilim who live on Nibiru when they visit their Earth colonies.

This new species would end up all over Earth, except what they call dark Africa. The land between the Tropic of Cancer and Capricorn. This White Aryan race does become part of all non-dark African societies as mankind does not live on an island or in a valley like it did when each prototype, now called a race, began. The DNA is totally cross-pollinated, and so we will be one mixed race of DNA mankind.

Act Three, Scene Three: Nefilim Life as a Member of the Anunnaki Earth Colony

Here I am picking scenes we can see as these tablets do have teachings of what beings and planets do when the elements change and new world order begins.

Start with family. Now let's visit the new ruling grandchildren. Enki has two. One is a boy, Utu. The other is a girl, who we know as Ishtar.

Utu, a.k.a. Shamash, is known as the Mesopotamian Sumerian God of Justice. Very important energy in the coming myths of this era on Earth.

Ishtar gets mixed up with Inanna, who is Enlil's granddaughter. You now have two similar energies running around beating the Earthlings and saying they are the goddess of love and sexuality, but are never the Mother Goddess. Imagine being alive then and watching these Nefilim-gods just beat their beasts of burden.

These two born here on Earth are an example of what happens when the young do not replace the old. The young have nothing to do but again cause trouble. And trouble of dividing and hating others they will do. And at all times these gods are picking on the Earthlings created to serve and be the slaves to the Nefilim rulers and their second-class

Nefilim-Anunnaki team who are doing their work on Earth for planet Nibiru.

And life on Earth is about to get more crowded with Earthlings of all mankind races, once called prototypes. People like to copulate just as apparently the Nefilim and all beings without higher consciousness do.

Earth's consistent climate, we learn, does not exist over time. A comet we read about in the tablets of Enki crossed the path of our solar system. Apparently, it came close to the big three: Earth, the moon, and Mars. All three masses were affected by this cosmic disturbance. The energy that these planets create, as they do their kundalini twirl around the Sun, is upset by a retrograde of energy caused by the comet.

As we continue our awareness of life on Earth back then, let's look in on the geography. In these tablets, which are really Enki's diary, we learn how the polar caps of what today we call Antarctica began to melt back then. This melting caused oceans to rise and lands to change. Global warming and cooling are not new, unique things. We may be speeding it up, but we do not cause it. Learn that truth. And we must learn to be aware of the coming disaster. We need to protect ourselves from internal and external events that we can forecast by studying space, as the Nefilim learned to do, and not just have to see to believe. This is the ice age syndrome, which repeats over time with hot and cold weather changes of the atmosphere here on Earth from Earth's conditions as well as conditions of energies in our atmosphere and our solar system and galaxies.

The Nefilim let the stars and their movement forecast the future as opposed to us who still believe our Earth is the center of the universe, not just the solar system. The Nefilim planned for the coming future as dictated by the stars and their movements in the skies. A new land and water order was taking place here on Earth. But it did stabilize for a while, and both South Africa and Edin remained basically the same. These were the two home territories of the Anunnaki, Nefilim's Earth travelers back then on Earth.

Act Three, Scene Four: Update on the Igigi Living on Mars and A Visit to the Moon

Mars does start to go bye-bye as a place to live. This is normal, although we believe it's not. We judge things by our short life-spans in this physical form. In 1994 we saw a comet hit Jupiter. It means we today see that comets do hit planets. Well, this comet I spoke about above back then hit Mars, and the leftover tailpiece in time hit the moon.

Mars began to lose its atmosphere and eventually dried up. Mars could not support Nefilim life; even in their fish tanks we talked about earlier as the hit causes a huge leak, and their atmosphere, as if it's in a tub, goes down the so-called drain back to space. It may take time to disappear, but know the Nefilim see this happen, and as we will learn, they will start taking care of this issue.

Now what this means is the Nefilim Watchers called Igigi now have to come to Earth. But come on their timeline, not ours, meaning thousands of Earth years. Because they had long lives, the Nefilim planned in Earth terms hundreds or even thousands of Earth years ahead. Just look to the Mayan calendar to understand that truth.

The Nefilim in charge of Mars, Marduk, got his dad, Enki, to understand that the base on Mars called Lahmu was not stable. The folks had to be moved eventually. So, thought needed to be given to this move.

This meant Earth needed the ports and technology of Mars to be moved to Edin. It meant more bodies and the rise of a technological white-collar Igigi working class. Earth would need more workers to accommodate the lives and the needs of the Anunnaki and Igigi's workers too. So now the Nefilim needed more servants and workers of black and white slaves here on Earth. The white Earthlings got what we call the urban city domestic jobs. Why? Because the whites are more than just Primitive Workers. They are created as I now repeat not for mining but for domesticated service. Servants to the gods and their ruling space crew.

Today, according to our scientific analogies of what our rovers told us on the exploration runs, they uncovered on Mars irrefutable proof that Mars once had water. Today we see ice caps here and maybe there. Then there were lakes and rivers as well as oceans just like here on Earth. The atmosphere was destroyed and the chemicals that made up the living force escaped back into our common solar system's atmosphere. This is according to the tablets found and written 155,000 Earth years ago.

Act Three, Scene Five: A Visit to the Moon

The moon is another issue. Before Earth became both the mines and the spaceport for all activities, Enki and his son Marduk went to our Moon.

The moon plays many roles regulating Earth and our metaphysical realties of physical life here on Earth. One such role is casting the Sun rays back to us as a mirror during our evenings. What that means is we are getting energy for living and for creation day and night. It is the energy of creative wants and needs. That is why the wolves howl and are the noise once depicted at night. The wolf does not follow human rules or our rule makers the Catholic Church, or the illuminati, made-up stories of how witches came out with ghouls at night, and this made the wolves howl. Why do they do this? To keep their constituency indoors and away from the light that leads you to truth. The night is when imagination can carry you away with dreams of flying to the moon as well as Jupiter and maybe Mars. It is the evening time to dream, and then you may see that you were made to be more than just to listen to these bishops and cardinals with their chosen rulers telling you this is what you were born to do.

This time period of father and son on the moon without King Anu is very important. Enki on the moon gets very poetic. He talks of how enchanting the Sun and moon are for those alive and living on Earth. Enlil the brother did not see the world this romantic way.

Know Enlil was the general and one lifestyle politician. Enlil's motto was very simple. He was the controlling Earth command god. His motto was these Earthlings must never learn to dream and want and then learn how their dreams can become true.

Enki, we shall learn, so disagreed. Enki did what he could to make sure we Earthlings never ended up that way. But his son Marduk and Enki's half-brother Enlil would soon play chess with their pawns—mankind. With the coming battles of the Olden Upper World; "olden," like the Anunnaki spelled it. The Olden World is the world of the Eastern Mediterranean and Eastern North Africa—the original civilizations of Nefilim-Anunnaki creation.

On the moon, Enki cut the view of Earth from the moon into twelve parts. This is where our current astrological signs come from. Right here and now. This happens by connecting the stars shining as a weak spotlight into your eyes as dots connecting the bigger picture image that will help you remember what you are looking at. The house of our twelve Earth-based constellations viewed from the moon looking at Earth is where the concept of constellations, whose motions affect Earth, begins. This concept may have been first created by Enki and Marduk. That is why the names of those constellations back then are not the same as now. Why? We do not see and are not aware of what Enki himself saw when gazing at the stars surrounding Earth from Enki's view up on the moon.

The twelve constellations are different depending on your view from where you are on Earth. An example I learned while briefly living in Bolivia is that what was the Orion's Belt of the Northern Hemisphere, down below the Equator, was now a star light and star-bright poncho.

Earth-based philosophers over Earth time changed the original Enki name of the twelve imagined symbols he saw by connecting the star beams he saw of our galaxy looking down on Earth from the moon. These different symbols try to explain in Enki's sacred talisman images the energy concept of those twelve houses too.

Now is the time to share with you all what some elders knew as I was getting initiated into astrology. Look at our galaxy from outside our galaxy, where Earth appears. We are in the right-hand lower corner of that viewer's point of view if we stretch the map out. There is no circle, as I believe space is just a matrix. Just space. The empty space, called black holes, awaits the imagination of the invisible but living hand to fill it in. This consciousness uses empty space to take on physical power to light the black holes, which some called the Big Bang theory. The thought put into action begins testing new dimensions as well as galaxies. End the thoughts of the energy of life called consciousness of wants and needs, and instead of a Big Bang, we will have a collapse of everything, and everything will just go back and sleep in an absolute zero energy to the eternal matrix of the Supreme Being and its Nirvana. But the creation of our consciousness has no end. And as long as our consciousness has wants and needs, the energy exists to prevent absolute zero from ever happening.

If wants and dreams of consciousness should ever end, the whole galaxies and universes of space will lose their energy of life. And without energy and gravity, space then and there will collapse back to nothing. Imagination is the air of life. All of space with objects exists because of the gravitational force created by the rotation of these stars around each other. End the gravity, and you will end the universe and galaxies. They are all matrices.

It is so written that Earth is so important to the consciousness. We are standing near a new gateway. A gateway that can become a

Matrix of Love. Our Earth is so important to the growing consciousness for it is here where love shared in actual physical form has an opportunity to grow and prosper. Not just controlled to serve the few, but an area where consciousness can live and prosper learning love as a many splendid thing. We are the experiment. There are energies around Earth in physical form trying to wake up mankind the servant-slave and end the darkness that rules our existence and the dense planet Earth.

    Marduk, here on the Earth's moon with dad; Marduk, being Enki's living oldest son, gets his father to promise him, Marduk, a bigger role on Earth. And now the roles to become captains of Enki's world order are chosen between the grandchildren Utz (Uta), Ishtar, and Marduk the son for the coming world Nibiru colonies' disorder. Notice Enlil and the elders of Nibiru had no say. And it will not end well for the beings so created who live on Earth.

ACT THREE, SCENE SIX: THE COUNTY OF EDIN AND ITS CITY STATES

Now the tablets tell us about the time they called the Anunnaki Ninety-Second Shar, the new *sippar* (city) called Nibru, as opposed to Nibiru on Earth, was completed. This was the fifth city of Edin, which we spoke of earlier. King Anu came to visit Earth and gave the port his blessings. All the Anunnaki of Earth and the Igigi from Mars are assembled. This port is where the landings from and take-offs to Nibiru would now happen, as Mars was being phased out.

This was the new era of Earth. Ishtar, as opposed to Inanna, Anu's granddaughter, highlighted the celebration with her dancing and singing. She was the first one who we read about who can entertain the troops . . . so to say. She was also Marduk's direct descendant, as opposed to Enlil. Marduk was coming back to Earth, and he was setting up his team to rule Earth.

Ninurta went south to Abzu to bring slaves back up to the Upper World to his friends and to work the party. The first captured slaves of our Earth begin here. Enlil, the dad, is so upset because he threw the Earthlings out of the Upper World, and now they are back and brought back by his son Ninurta.

Ninurta convinced his dad that since they will be leaving Earth soon and going home to Nibiru, what's the harm? Let it be. The problem is they did not leave Earth soon and with a growing population of children expecting to control the world the way their parents did, the Earth was about to learn what the living can do when their sole purpose of getting and shipping gold back home changes.

Now with Homo sapiens living back in the Upper World, Enki, as I said earlier, realized there was something wrong. The first model human of category two was starting to become less advanced again. The model, when reproduced, comes out less than the parents.

Time to tinker again. Tinker tailor, soldier spy. Rich man, poor man, beggar man, or thief. What was the roulette wheel of gene manipulation going to produce this time for Enki?

Round four of the creation of Homo sapiens.

Our Earth-based DNA is different depending on where the twenty-three chromosomes began. It's that simple. These Nefilim manipulated our DNA program in physical form nonstop. We are all a form of consciousness living inside the prison of our bodies. And each body is different depending on its DNA. Our creators who called themselves gods, not a Supreme Being, made us for a purpose, as we have learned. We are their beasts of burden of life here on Earth.

So, the DNA is set up so we are run by fear, not by our high consciousness and its eternal powers. We still do not understand how to connect to the higher invisible, nonphysical object's powers.

To do this, and it's easier said than done, we must learn how others do this by communicating with those living in the eternal matrix of thoughts and new ideas. The Nefilim themselves communicated with some thought power by using their ME. It is interesting that I see this ME as an AI (artificial intelligence). It is programmed by some source to see and create new things from ideas with no boundaries as the brains of beings are limited to see only what they are programmed to see. This Nibiru civilization apparently understood and lived by their interpretation of their consciousness's connection to the galaxies of all creation. They did believe in the Supreme Being as the creator of everything.

    Enki decided his creation must become civilized. Civilized in a step-up manner. A little here and a little in the future, for life on Nibiru was so predictable. So boring, I assume. You had your caste at birth, and there you stayed. This is similar to the Hindu belief system. On Earth, this caste system is taught to Earthlings from the granddaughter of King Anu, Inanna, Enlil's daughter, as we shall soon see.

Act Three, Scene Seven: And Now Round Four of Mankind Models

Enki impregnated two young Earthlings with his Nefilim sperm. A boy and girl were born. Enki told no one, yet this new game he played. He actually told his spouse that he found the two floating down the river in a basket by the reeds on the banks of that river. Enki took them home to be raised as his children, which they were.

They are called the Gracious Ones. They were born 108,000 years ago on Earth. The names are Adapa (foundling) and Titi (one with life). This is the beginning of the D-gods that we will soon learn about.

These are the first and final model of the Homo sapiens that we learned about a few paragraphs back in our book time. Enki then secured their survival on Earth so they could multiply here on Earth. Almost Nefilim, they were. However, each subsequent generation would have less Nefilim blood than the one before. These two were created in Enki's image and after his likeness. Meet our long-lost creator.

So once again back in this Earth time we have Enlil, the supreme god of Earth, versus his serpent brother Enki, the doctor.

Enlil was the manipulative, angry, and controlling god of the Bible. Enlil did not want change. He liked order the way it was and did not want to change it up.

Enki was the misunderstood romantic of human creation. Enlil ruled his community with fear as his weapon. Enki wanted his creatures to live in and with consciousness of the Supreme Being as their guide. A life with abundance, not a life of servitude. Is it possible? I believe so.

Enki and his spouse Ninki brought up Adapa and Titi as Anunnaki children. Satisfied that these two were capable of being civilized and intelligent, Enki ordered from Nibiru foods with seeds so the food could be reproduced here on Earth. Four-legged animals start being produced here on Earth. Now Enki and his son Ning began making new creations as these domesticated animals that needed to be eaten existed. I am curious if these creations exist somewhere else. I am not sure, but I believe it is Nibiru. Why? They needed to raise domesticated animals for food as the mankind slaves' and servants' population was about to really multiply. The creatures and the Nefilim needed to feed their body machines.

This knowledge of feeding was, in addition to the Nefilim, only to be shared with the Earthlings, who were slaves, to feed their gods, the Nefilim-Anunnaki. This, back then, was not for general mass consumption. This was only done in the Anunnaki-Edin urban area as the other beings ate like other Earth beasts.

Adapa and Titi had their first children. The first offspring were twins. Anu, who was monitoring Earth from Nibiru, was so impressed with Adapa on Earth, he commanded that Adapa come from Earth's Heaven departure port to Nibiru immediately.

Orders were put in motion. Adapa was flown from Heaven on Earth to Nibiru. Adapa became the first mankind spaceman. Enki's two sons, Ning, the mad scientist, and Enki's youngest son, full-blooded Nefilim offspring Dumuzi, were chosen to join Adapa on the flight to Nibiru. This was Ning and Dumuzi's first visit to their home of their full-blooded cell and blood DNA Nefilim bodies.

On Nibiru, just like the story of Pocahontas in our 1600s, when the Native American is taken to England from New England, Adapa is the hit of society. On this circus tour, Adapa is treated as an equal. As an equal, he is offered all the delicacies of Nibiru to eat and drink. This apparently included the elixir of long and everlasting life.

Adapa, we are told, turns it down. Enki told Adapa not to drink this drink before Adapa left Earth. Adapa did as his father told him to do.

Before the three offspring departed from Earth, Enki made a video clip of himself telling the story of how Adapa came to be created. This was to be given to his father, King Anu. It was. Ning, who had the video, gave the footage to Grandpa Anu.

This footage carried a visual image of Enki, who explained to his father, Anu, the creation of Adapa. In the message, Enki asked Anu to please not give Adapa the everlasting life. Enki did this by private communication because he did not want public knowledge that this boy Adapa was in fact his child.

Enki, not being mean, wanted his child to fulfill his Earth destiny. Adapa was created to live on Earth as an Earthling, not become one from Nibiru. Not a Nefilim lifeline. Big move.

Grandpa honored Enki's wishes. However, the King spread the knowledge of the fact that Adapa is Enki's Earth offspring. The King told the people of Nibiru the following: "The welcome to the Earthling must not be overextended, on our planet he cannot eat nor drink. Let his offspring on Earth fields till and meadow sheep." Adapa was not to become one of us on this trip. No everlasting physical life in our Heaven in Nibiru.

Adapa was sent back to Earth. The Nibiru tour was over. Ning left with Adapa. Ning brought the seeds of civilization food. The seeds were fruits and vegetables that we still today eat. Dumuzi came on the next flight with the animals that still live and are bred by mankind. These animals included lambs and ewes. But it is noted that the food and drink of everlasting life did not come to Earth.

The story of this Homo sapiens creation called Adapa was now public Nefilim knowledge on Nibiru and Anunnaki knowledge on Earth. Enlil went crazy with what his mad man scientist brother had done. After the initial outburst, Enki became philosophical. Enlil said in public, "Destiny by fate is overtaken." We created a new Earthling. Let it be.

Let it be for the moment. As Enlil played chess, Enlil would make his move when he was ready to end these Earthling experiments. That moment would soon come when Earth was about to be hit by the winds created when Nibiru ran off its course on its travels to and from the Sun. We call this event The Flood. But it was more than a flood, and it was not made by the god. It was a solar system catastrophe.

Back on Earth, the game of Mankind's destiny continues.

Act Three, Scene Eight: Ka-in and Abel the Story

Adapa and Titi were an Earthling couple. They reproduced as all creatures are supposed to do. Let's look in on the twin sons who Titi gave birth too. Their names were Ka-in and Abel. This litter was taken over by Enki's Nibiru-blooded children. There was compassion from the father to raise his creation from the father's seed.

The twins were named, as I just said, Ka-in and Abel.

Ka-in was taken in by Enlil's Nibiru son Ninurta to learn the trade of farming. Everything regarding agriculture, we are told, he was taught. Ka-in learned to dig, to plow, to plant, and to harvest the crops.

Abel went with Marduk who was, I must repeat, a full-blooded Nefilim, who was royalty on Nibiru as well as Earth. Marduk was now full time on Earth. Marduk taught Abel how to take care of the domestic food animals.

The crops were to be grown to feed Earthlings, and the domesticated animals too, as these animals must be fed so we can eat them. Also, the domesticated animals were to be watched and fed in the area designated around Edin, or else they could be stolen or eaten by other Earthlings, as well as other animals, which the Anunnaki called beasts. These domesticated farms were established in Enlil's territory.

When these crops and animals were ready to be served as a meal, we witness the first time the Earthlings feed their gods. Interesting game.

Soon temples would be built by the Anunnaki using their slave laborers. They were built so the Earthlings could celebrate their royal Nefilim-gods at the anointed calendar date married to the moon's rotation in the stars. And these dates were the big celebrations where they fed their gods at these celebrations. And not only did Earthlings multiply, so did the children of the Nefilim gods. The male Earthlings were not circumcised so one would be able to distinguish who were the males of mankind. The daughters of the Earthlings were not physically marked, so the Nefilim did start reproducing with the daughters of Earthlings. Just as it says in the current bibles.

And it gets complicated and morally dirty. The first reality TV show called The Anu Family Dysfunctional Style, served as the prototype for dysfunctional families. Shakespeare published similar stories for plays in his day, or TV shows like the twentieth century *Dallas* and *Dynasty*.

So, the tension between cousins Ninurta and Marduk rubbed off on the Earthling twins. Now they fought to see who had the most important job, farming or animal husbandry? Drought came to these lands, and the agriculture—grass and wheat supplies—would get scarce. Making the drought worse was the domestic animals like the sheep were eating the grass of Ka-in.

Ka-in and Abel had words and fought. Not knowing sticks and stones can do more than just break your bones, Ka-in killed Abel with a stone. Remorse set in, and Ka-in fled. Then Ka-in was caught and confessed to his acts. Earthlings have a consciousness, as we see then and there—they were aware that premature death was a consequence of wrong behavior.

The Nefilim, we learn, deliberated on Ka-in's fate. A Nefilim ruling order legal system took control of the situation and showed us all that they also on Nibiru rule the Earthlings. They decided to banish him from Edin. Ka-in was taken by Enlil to the New World. We shall learn this soon. And so, this is Earth's first excommunication—when someone who did wrong is thrown out of society.

Another question: Have you ever asked yourself why the Bible as the storyteller talks about only royal families and their Earthlings? Obviously, there were more than just these few Earthlings. Why them and not others who did exist? It's an easy answer when you become aware of the need to create memories of the past as the rules of life. It is because the Book of Enki, now modified and edited and called the Bible, is tales reduced to writing that are oral stories we humans were, back in those days, required to hear. Required by the few who created this paradigm of a system run on fear and control. These families in these biblical stories are the chosen demigod families. They are the few who ruled the rest of the Earthlings in this Nefilim Earth-based society of social order and control. Disobey, and you will be killed if you are mortal. And as we just learned, if you are not mortal Earth beings but Nefilim royalty beings, then you will just be excommunicated by the Nefilim.

These stories become the imperial stories of those who controlled our past societies. Society today is based on those old societies. So to control your current thoughts, those old stories are based on a god who created mankind's wants and needs to look over us and protect us when we do good for that god and punish us when we do wrong.

These Nefilim stories were transcribed thousands of years ago, Earth years that is, into Earth-based language by Earthlings. The Samaritan texts are the purest and closest to the original Enki text. Why? They were the first Earthling writings as mankind was finally taught to write by the Nefilim, as the time was becoming shorter before the Nefilim would leave Earth, and they wanted mankind to become civilized, as if they were the minor league of civilized Nefilim life. "Live our ways, and one day you will be brought up to the major leagues of civilized life and enjoy our everlasting Nefilim life" is one thought. Or they created Earth to be civilized in their orderly fashion so when the need for gold on Nibiru occurs again, the Nefilim would be able to visit their minor league planet and get the gold the Earthlings were storing and hoarding for the Nefilim.

ACT FOUR
THE SEEDS OF MANKIND'S RELIGIONS AND WORSHIP TO A SKY GOD

ACT FOUR, SCENE ONE: THE GENESIS OF MANKIND RELIGION

It was the evening of a day during the ninety-fifth Shar of Anunnaki time on Earth, which is 342,000 Earth years, when the Nefilim-Anunnaki were here on Earth. This translates to about 100,000 Earth years ago. We are told that Adapa and Titi, Earthlings' first model couple, had a son whom they called Seti. This, I believe, must be the biblical Seth.

The first couple then had thirty more sons and thirty more daughters over the next 7,200 years. This is definitely different DNA from what we now know about, as the earned DNA of this first couple gave these first humans a longer life. Tinkers and tailors is the theme of what the Nefilim were doing with their living machines of burden at this time period of Earth.

These sixty children became farmers and the tillers of the lands and waterways. They were in charge of feeding their local Nefilim royalty called local gods as well as themselves.

Time passed, and now we go specifically to the ninety-seventh Shar. Seti has had all these children over the course of this time of two Shars, which is 7,200 Earth years.

Now in this ninety-seventh Shar, we learn that a son was born to Seti called Enshi. This name in their Nefilim language meant "master of humanity." All of a sudden it is important for the tablets to let us know that Enshi is important in this story of the Nefilim creating the imperial civilization. A civilization based on a royal family who ruled over the many to keep the system working. Then those royals had their priests who studied the skies and ccould forecast what metaphysical elements were coming their planet's way.

It is important we begin to understand this simple truth by seeing the tree and its branches of the creation of a sky god and mankind's religions.

The Nefilim knew astrology. They could forecast what was coming to Earth. The Nefilim, to Earthlings' understanding, were from the skies and called themselves gods. The Earthlings believed the Nefilim were the creators and keepers of Earthlings.

Earthlings had to obey the gods. And the Earthlings knew there was one boss, the big god called the king, who ruled them from the sky. And these gods had a staff who communicated with the king from instruments that talked to the king in the sky.

They also knew that there were instruments and machines run by people who would search the sky to see what was coming their way. Understand what I am drawing with these truths.

Now hear this story as I tie the knots of these branches and show you a picture story that tells you about the roots into our belief in a sky god and the priests who speak to a sky god with local rulers for us. Never do we learn that these beings, who are called Nefilim, meaning gods, are just beings like we are. They came before us and built their own societies so they could control life on their planet. They are now going to build societies on Earth so they can in their present and future times control us Earthlings.

The lad Enshi is taught how to write and how to count by his granddad Adapa. This implies that the other Earthlings did not yet know of these tricks. We were taught knowledge, which is only what your teacher and your teacher's system wants you to know. We do live and learn wisdom as it cannot be taught but can be shared. However, the system will teach you not to follow those who speak of things outside the A or B system of control. They are not in touch with god's mandate and are heretics to society's rules and order, which perpetuate ignorance and fears of anything outside the system of control.

Enshi was brought to Nibru-ki, the special city known as Heaven of Earth, by Ninurta, the son of Enlil, apparently disobeying his father Enlil's wishes. Enlil's wish was to keep the created Earthling's, regardless of parental creation, crew dumb and numb. Inside these city walls of Nibru-ki, the boy was taught how to anoint with oils those who were welcomed into the Nefilim Sacred Schools of Knowledge where the Earth-based space travelers called Anunnaki as well as the Igigi, now collectively Anunnaki as Mars was no longer a spaceport, were taught the arts and the sciences of Nefilim society. The graduates were called priests.

This is important to grasp as I am trying to make you aware of the roles of elders inside a society. A society can either open the gates of learning the rules of math and geometry as well as languages and the sciences with the ability to discover the wisdom one gains when an elder dedicated to sharing metaphysical truths can bring to a society as a whole unit. You will create the worlds with an order of knowledge blessed by wisdom, so soon society will not need laws and guns to keep society living under rules and regulations solely created to keep those in power in that power position. We learn how to share. We learn how to let dreams exist as people learn dreams in the here and now can come true.

Or you can keep this sacred knowledge secret and teach the masses to believe in fake gods who live by themselves and do the magic that unfolds each day our Earth turns around the Sun and the Sun turns around our solar system and our universe. You get the masses to pray to a sky god whose image they give their power of thought to and hope that everything will not change, and life will remain predictable and boring.

Knowledge is power. And it must not be owned by the few so they can stay in control of your living physical energies. Awareness is the goal. Living aware without fear is the touchdown of the game.

Our lad Enshi in Nibru-ki also learned how to extract the elixir from the special fruits the Nefilim brought to Earth from Nibiru. This fruit is translated to us Earthlings as *inbus*. Love to find it. Maybe instead of oil we should search the Middle East sands for this elixir. It is maybe the Fountain of Youth.

The ancients used to believe the juice to become aware and know the wisdom was frankincense. This juice came from the dew of various fruits found in certain sections of what we call the Near East, now called the Middle East or Levant, but what the Nefilim called Edin.

I too went on the hunt for these essences called frankincense as well as myrrh. I tried to anoint myself with these oils to: one, open my third (inside) eye; and two, especially with myrrh, to heal any open wounds. Myrrh did work to a degree. Frankincense did not work as I was not ready to flip my brain switch to off. I have since learned how to do just that as I did continue my quest and did open my inner eye to travel and see the beyond our locked matrix of existence.

These two oils were what the Earthlings used to anoint the Nefilim during their servant role. Look at old drawing in caves as well as copies of those drawings sold to you on Egyptian papyrus, and you can see the servants anointing their superior.

What did the legendary three Black Kings bring as gifts to baby Jesus? Gold to wear and frankincense and myrrh oils to anoint Jesus the new Christ in some future time as if this were in our timeline the new now reincarnated Dalai Lama to magically glow as he grows to become Christ in human form.

Where did these Black Kings come from? The outer regions, meaning the East and the West of the Olden Upper World that had gold, frankincense and myrrh, and black meaning darker than the Aryan whites.

So much knowledge over Earth time starting with Enshi, and as we will soon learn the chosen few Earthlings, was imparted to the chosen, anointed Earthlings. There are plenty of examples of who they were. The game still exists with the chosen Vatican-approved royal families of Europe and those royal families that England anointed in the Middle East after WWI in the 1920s.

Bored? Curious? Or both? Look up how the English anointed their new ruler, be it a king or queen, when the ceremony turns to making the royal title official. The scene is carried on by a head priest of that society's imperial religion, which in the UK is called the Church of England. You can see a reenactment of how the Egyptians used to anoint their priests and royal families and the head ruler called the king and sometimes a queen without a king, who in the UK is head of church and state. That is why the Vatican and the UK had their troubles as the Vatican is the head of the church, and the other kings and queens that the Vatican authenticates, their royal rule is only the head of that specific state.

Now we have black gold. Oil. Oil runs our society. But the truth is that using oil to move physical machines instead of air is just so primitive. Follow this truth. Air and Sun energies are not scarce. It is abundant. So, the controllers of our world need the necessities of life to become scarce. So, using oil, black gold, which we are told will run out, is a means of control. This needs to end, my friends. Now morph into a game where our currency is scarce and controlled by the few to own and control us as we are now nothing short of interest slaves. Keep reading and I will keep sharing.

So Enshi was anointed. Anointed to what? To share with the few the secrets of the wisdom of existence. He became the world's first Earth-created student of the sacred knowledge of existence here on Earth. His teachers were called lords, and it is here that religion of man began. The worship of the Nefilim second-tier royal families were called lords. The first tier were called gods, and number one was God.

Follow me as I continue the horrors of what these Nefilim did to us by capturing our energy and promising us a heaven on Earth, which they switch to a heaven on Nibiru in the next physical life we incarnate to when we reincarnate and choose to come back to their system of ownership and control. This is the bait and switch that they used when our collective not-yet-individual consciousness fell into their physical bodies of creation.

Yes, understand here and now that we are not our bodies. Our bodies are the physical car we get to live in and explore life in physical form living as a physical beast with the consciousness to be civilized and create an Earth playpen where we all can prosper and ascend as we discover the joys and pains of life in physical form. We came as their beasts of burden locked in by the DNA or jail cell Enki and the Nefilim family so created. Enki and his Nefilim crew of priests we call scientists knew how to capture our traveling consciousness into this Earth-based body.

When we learn the truth, we will set ourselves free. We will get out of the bondage we have here in our Earth bodies. We will become the planet of love in our UNIVERSE. Just what Jesus, who many do believe was sent to Earth to share as the messenger two thousand years or more ago at the start of the Age of Pisces, was sent to do. I go deep into this thought and share many truths I uncovered exploring these thoughts in book two of this series called *Taking Jesus off the Cross*.

Maybe the Age of Aquarius is really all about some conscious energy using us in body forms to help us put together the trail of our tears showing the whips used to control our consciousness and keep us in slave bondage of ignorance and fear. Think about that.

One more thought I must share. The universe and its galaxies are made up of many thought consciousness beings. We are not the only thought beings. We all left the source, which I call the Supreme Being, to live a thought fantasy in physical form. Our thoughts do create galaxies and new universes that become dense and become a new solar system as the thoughts' energies get intense and become the machine that generates the energies to make the gas of thoughts liquids and then make them solids and alive with the chemicals needed to create beings in physical form. And then create with the machines so thought beings now in a physical machine can live and experience thought life in physical form. And each universe so created as a matrix by its gravitational rules gives us a different shape and different machine organs as well to run our whole physical machines we called a body. Act Eighteen of this three-book series goes into depth to explain this metaphysical truth.

These Nefilim-anointed civilized human pets back then were also taught in this era how to make instruments. Instruments to play music and then to hum and sing along with the air the strumming and/or blowing created by using the physical machine instrument. There was no written language yet for Earthlings. But they did know the vibrations of energy that humming could give you, the vocalist, as well as the listener.

This is the era in which civilized humans also learned how to make fire, how to dig for water, and how to refine gold. This is what the

First and Second Temples of the Hebrews were all about. A big furnace to refine gold and worship their Nefilim God Anu and his Nefilim Head Prince of Nibiru called Enlil. And just as a coming preview, I share that Solomon was the mankind-anointed king who did this with his few who knew the secret metaphysical knowledge of making solid gold into a liquid gold. First it becomes a gas and then when taking liquid form the gas solidifies and falls to Earth where these particles became manna. Manna to eat and thought to now be enlightened by the bread from heaven.

Water became the gathering point for these civilized humans. Societies were built by the riverbanks or seas and the oceans. It is where the promiscuous sexual activity as a societal game began. This is why our DNA loves water activities. Sunbathing and socializing. Showing off our bodies and more.

Then the Nefilim gods, the Nefilim Earth-based Anunnaki lords, got into the act of making babies with the daughters of mankind. The world was populating. We are about to enter the biblical age of the beginning of the demigod race of mankind/Nefilim and their stargazing prophets. Enshi, whom we just read about, is the first of many who become myths of our ancient times. How else were the ignorant Earthlings to explain what they saw.

Now with Mars depopulating, the Igigi started to look for things to do on Earth as they did not all have chores. Choice became easy. What better than reproduce with their created animals? This is actually in our Bible. It is where the gods came to reproduce with man and create a new royal bloodline. It is the holy grail mankind has been looking for. The holy grail is the vagina that with Earth-based female DNA produced a child that also had first-generation Nefilim-based DNA from the sperm the Nefilim used to create a new physical life. And remember, this group was called the Aryans, which is what Hitler said was the German bloodline.

Think of the bathhouses of the Romans and Greeks that we learn about. Imperial societies are brainwashed into accepting as the ordained way of Earth physical life. The imperial order of ownership and control is taught as a way of life. Our schools actually stop awareness. The schools are nothing short of just brainwashing chalkboards. Remember we are taught that the Greeks were the creators of Earth's democracy. I ask you for whom was this democracy created? Not women nor society's slaves. Only the freemen. Just like the US Constitution, which specifically excluded, when written, slaves and women and those freemen who do not own property.

This is a very dark energy game using imperial religions and their imperial government that enforces the imperial religion's ordained rules and resulting order. How quickly do we populate? How do we control the many, no longer just the few? Teach them the imperial way of life. Governments of the few ruling over you. This is done by having the gods who you are made to believe in say this is OK and the only way for you to get to your heaven next time. Next life.

Follow me for this thought to conclusion. Take your life's beginning. Using mine, I was born in Earth year 1952 AD. Figure that every twenty-five years someone was born who helped make you. Going back to 1 AD on the Jesus timeline, that means there were seventy-eight versions of me before me.

Just think how our population on Earth exploded over those two thousand years. Billions now exist. Just think how many were born since 1952. See what we do when creation just goes without thought as to what happens with these newborns? What are they to do on Earth? Really, why are you here? You were made to serve the few, and then when those few are done with their game, what do you do, or for that matter, what do any of us do?

The answers we need to figure out as a society of mankind. We really do, for this game of my god has a bigger dick than you does not work. We need to build a community for all. A community that allows those who want to create and make a better world the opportunity to create art. Art is what makes up both the Earth and our hearts. And we the community need governments who serve the people. Rules that allow the many to have health, welfare, and safety to the best of our human capabilities.

The Nefilim, if they were aware, never dealt with love in any form. These tablets show me these truths until Inanna become involved in the game of living here on Earth.

ACT FOUR, SCENE TWO: THE BIRTH OF PRIESTHOOD

Where did this begin? Those anointed to control the many for the few.

The scriptures in this era tell you about a man named Enkine, which is a Nibru word that translates into "understanding the annuals." Marduk now appeared as one of the gods of the Nefilim in our Earth history. Marduk began his turn to try and rule Earth as promised to him by his dad Enki on their earlier trip to the moon. Remember Marduk was the full-blooded Nefilim created by the son Enki of the King of Nibiru, whose mother too had the full-blooded Nefilim bloodline. Marduk believed he was destined to rule over the lower creatures his father and mother created on Earth.

Marduk needed inspiration to train his first priest. The thought that he was the future god of Earth got him going. He wished to educate Enkine into understanding the blueprint of the Nefilim Earth-created life. So Marduk took Enkine to the moon to start the lad's education. Marduk taught Enkine about where the energies of the galaxies and our common solar system came from and how to see what is coming tomorrow by understanding the currents that enter our world order.

Back on Earth, Enkine was stationed at Sippar of Nibru-Ki, the place of the chariots, the fifth city of the Anunnaki colony's star here on Earth. Here we get the first Earthling priest—the supernatural functions of an initiated, anointed priest. Then this Earthling, we are told, was taken to Mars to serve as an inspiration to the few remaining Igigi who were still on Mars. An inspiration to do what? Show the few what they too could produce with Earthlings as they partnered in individual physical life creation.

In the texts, we learn that the final exodus from Mars for all Nefilim came in the 104th Shar calculated on Nibiru's circulation of the Sun, while the Nefilim were living in the colonies they made on Earth. This translates to about sixty-eight thousand Earth years ago. For some reason, we are not informed by the tablets what happened to the first Earthling priest again. Maybe this is none other than the missing prophet Elijah, who is thought to have gone to Heaven, or Nibiru. Maybe not.

But the inspiration speech of Marduk did work. The Igigi were going to become Marduk's army of officers to help the armies of the Earthlings take control of Earth from Enlil. Enkine was brought to the sky never to be written about again in any tablets I have found or are aware of to date.

You now can see here how the priests' caste system was created. Marduk misused these teachings so needed to know truths, but Marduk used his priestly order of humans to convince the other humans of Marduk's version of servitude.

Marduk ran Egypt with his priestly class. Marduk had his priestly class authenticate the living pharaoh successors he chose to rule, who had to have some Nefilim bloodline. They had to have the mother's blood of the previous pharaoh to be chosen as the successor, or Marduk would pick the next in line. The priest ran the Egyptian system for Marduk. The pharaoh was just the ceremonial head.

Now I share what the tablet I am reading shared with me about the lifeline of the first civilized man, Adapa. Adapa died in our Earth time 55,000 BC. He lived for fourteen Shar approximately. That equals about fifty thousand years. This is real. Can you imagine what you would do with time like that on your side?

This also leads me to conclude that the Nefilim definitely went back to the laboratories to shorten our Earthling life-spans. If not, the population on Earth would become a problem to control. We were reproducing here on Earth like rats, not just rabbits.

Okay. Ready for the twist in the story? Follow please.

Marduk fell in love with an Earthling. The Earthling was named Sarpanitas. Marduk wished to take Sarpanitas to be his spouse. This was not allowed in the Nefilim Charter authorizing the creation of mankind. No Nefilim could take the Earthling with a womb as a spouse, and this Nefilim was a prince on Nibiru who so wished to be the god of Earth. This is the beginning of the concept that you cannot marry out of your race of creation. So, after much deliberation between him, his dad Enki, his uncle Enlil, and Grandpa Anu, the King of Nibru, it was decided that if Marduk took this Earthling as his spouse for love, Marduk could not go home. Marduk was excommunicated from Nibiru. Marduk was forced to give up his title as prince. He did just that. Marduk wanted to be the only god/Nefilim by birth that would stay on Earth when the Nefilim got the Anunnaki and Igigi to pack up when their King of Nibiru said it was time to come home to Nibiru.

Marduk now realized that he was the only god from the Nibiru Heaven who was banished to Earth. So, when the others left Earth to go back to Nibiru, Marduk would be the only Nefilim, a.k.a. god, left on Earth. This was a big development.

The things we do for love. Or the things we use the words "I love you" to get us.

Act Four, Scene Three: Marduk and the Nefilim Igigi on Earth

Marduk and his spouse Sarpanitas, after the ceremonial wedding, were sent away out of Edin to a land of their own. Marduk was sent to the land we today call Lower Egypt. This was his new domain. Marduk would rule this land for thousands of years as the Ra. Ra, the Sun god. Sun god because this was now Marduk's universe, and in this land the Sun rose and set as Marduk decreed and therefore decided. Marduk would now rewrite Egyptian history and confuse Earthlings over the difference of Higher and Lower Egypt.

The Igigi used this wedding to totally leave Mars. On Earth they could take off their breathing suits and live there for good. The Igigi moved en masse with Marduk at first to Egypt. And as I wrote above, the Igigi became the tribe of Marduk when he made his move against Enlil to become the one and only Earth god. This is the coming story of the Hebrews and Egyptians as well as Assyrians. Marduk got control of the second and the third. The first group were Enlil's pawns.

With the Igigi now in Egypt, they wanted what Marduk was allowed. They wanted Earthling spouses. So, they got them. The term they used was Titi, or females in the scriptures.

Across the Red Sea in the lands called Sipper, Enlil pondered with resentment and growing hate. He knew Marduk's wants and needs. Enlil was very similar. In his mind, he had to own and control the Earthlings, as he was the chosen Nefilim god (I keep mentioning god as the Nefilim ruling class so we all see where this nonsense began), the Nefilim royal of command, as so decreed by his father King Anu here on Earth. Enlil wished to go back home to Nibiru too. He knew that his destiny was not to die on Earth. Enlil was the next King of Nibiru. He knew instinctively what Marduk intended to do.

Marduk's controlling ways turned off some of the Igigi. Those few then chose to settle elsewhere on Earth. Where? The lands east of Egypt as well as north and west. But not south as it was way too hot. In fact, even the white race of Earthlings did not travel to live inside Central Africa, as we will learn in Act Nine of this series. This started the Anunnaki and Igigi Nefilim exodus to the Indus Valley as well as northwest to the Balkans mountains and its valleys.

Remember, the Nefilim did not appreciate the Sun's heat the way some of us do, such as I. Enki loved the heat so he stayed in it. Enlil did too apparently, as he chose it. I love the energy of the Sun. But I am not the majority. So many of the Nefilim moderate climate seekers went to the mountains and lakes with their Earthling servants of our world. This is the beginning of the populating of these Earth regions with the white Aryan race.

Now Enlil got ready for a coming war with Marduk. Enlil needed his pawns and his Earthling checker pieces. So, he sent his son Ninurta to find the offspring clans of Ka-in. Remember, Ka-in and his families were excommunicated. They were sent to distant lands of Earth from Edin. They were sent to the Andes Mountains.

Now visualize the Andes Mountains and the region we call Lake Titicaca.

Act Four, Scene Four: Earthlings in the New World

The continent we know as South America and Central America is now discussed in the texts. It is referred to as the New World. It was an outpost and not ready for the Nefilim to civilize yet. Soon it would be.

North America was sheets of ice, as was Europe. The ice sheets stopped their creeping advances south about 20,000 Earth years ago. These regions were uninhabitable for the Nefilim, and this is why they were not written about in the Book of Enki yet.

These Northern regions of Earth would soon be capable of housing mankind. How this happened is being researched today. The newest findings I could find say that the southern Earth oceans began to release carbon dioxide. The release of these carbon dioxide gases warmed the globe and caused the melting of the continental ice sheets and ushered in our current worldwide climate of winter, spring, summer, and fall that we have today.

It is important that we humans understand that we did not initially cause this carbon dioxide problem. What started twenty thousand years ago never stopped. We are still living in that metaphysical reality.

The Great Flood, which we will soon learn took place here on Earth a little more than thirteen thousand Earth years ago, was the final piece of metaphysical elements from the beyond hitting Earth with winds causing floods from the South Seas that changed the lands we call Asia, Europe, and North America as well as the islands outside those continents.

The Nefilim were here for all these natural and universal generated disasters hitting Earth over the last 450,000 years. They saw our Earth change and what change means to living beings as the change brings new lands and seas and different air for us beings to live in this planet in physical form.

It is important to remember these Nefilim beings who call themselves gods lived one Nefilim year, and we here on Earth have to understand that means 3,600 Earth years. So 20,000 Earth years for us Earthlings was a little more than five and a half Nefilim years. It is nothing in their world awareness of time. In our world, we cannot begin to understand the passage of time. Just try to imagine a pet trying to understand our life-spans. Try to imagine the pets trying to figure out what we humans are to them. Would they not think we were gods as we believe that term god means?

What is the meaning of god to you? Imagine the Earthlings then watching Nefilim come down from the skies. Watching them make fire and build urban cities for the Earthlings to live in. Imagine the Nefilim bringing domestic animals so the Earthlings could eat them. Imagine the Nefilim tilling the lands of each region so the conditions become ripe to grow plants and grasses that we and our domestic animals can eat.

These Nefilim were gods in our eyes. The Nefilim manipulated our Earth bodies and created the magic substances that poured into our DNA that made us different from any other species on Earth. They lived forever in our minds and did not age to our eyes. They built our world. We did not. We are just their pets who can learn. We can adapt. And all we are doing now is catching up to our creators and their understanding of metaphysical truths that create the physical things for the land and the seas and the skies so they could travel here on Earth and travel to and from their Heaven, Nibiru, in the skies of our universal matrix they needed to colonize Earth and save their planet Nibiru.

Enki and his crew trapped our collective consciousness here in this matrix I call Earth. The gravitational metaphysical forces that run our planet Earth keep us here as a living consciousness without body when our bodies give out. We stay alive inside this dimension. This is fully explained to you in the third book of this series titled *We've Got to Get Out of This Place*. Now I will just, when I can, make you aware of the game we play while choosing to live inside a body. Alive inside a body, we then have to submit to a system that runs the place we incarnate into to learn physical life on all levels.

Earth is dense. We are dense physical thought beings made to live here on Earth as a servant or slave to the system. The Nefilim built this system. I am trying only to make you aware of the system, and how we fall in line and perpetuate a system in which you must kill beings to survive. Earth has energies that keeps our consciousness here as we play the game of thought of reincarnation to Earth's physical playing field, instead of ascending and continuing our existence in other dimensions, universes, and galaxies created by our thoughts and desires as we try to learn the games of all physical life.

So now looking back at time here on Earth in the Andes region before the Great Flood, let's see the birth of those New World cultures as taught to those Earth beings by the Nefilim gods and gangsters.

Enlil led as a teacher a group of Earthlings. Enlil taught this group how to make tools. He taught them about mining, manufacturing, smelting, sailing, shipbuilding, and how to fight a war. Our first Earthling spies and soldiers he created. Enlil was tinkering and tailoring the second mankind creation of the Nefilim, the descendants of Ka-in, who was moved to live his days outside the Upper World, a.k.a. the

Olden World of the original civilization of the Anunnaki-Nefilim space Earth travelers. There is still a difference maybe to this day of the humans from this region in our Western Hemisphere, the New World as the Nefilim called it, and the humans from the Mediterranean area called the Upper World.

These few Earthlings who were part of Ka-in's tribe back then were moved to the Andes with Ka-in and became our South and Central American ancestors. Study their culture and you can learn why they are different from the other mankind created by Enki and his little helpers at a later date. Ka-in is the godfather, as well as the patriarch of the first family bloodline of these first inhabitants of the Andes. This is the beginning of the Andean world.

I studied their past. I saw that it was filled with star worship. They had calendars that kept time all based on a system we do not fully understand. It is based on numbers of six, not ten like our society today. Marduk changed the game of six to a base of ten.

Why? Energies in space are easy to compute using six as the base. We all circle our energy force. A circle is 360 degrees. Six is the base number, but so is two and so is three. Two is how our brain works. Two is how our computers work. I will table the rest of this conversation for a later date. But know there is magic in numbers that induces thoughts and builds structures when you learn the game of math and all its implications. It all builds a matrix design by creating fixed space as opposed to the vastness and the emptiness of existence.

Act Four, Scene Five: Edin Before the Great Flood

Now let's flash in on our Edin region back then in time. A few years had gone by. Marduk was in Egypt, but his father Enki was still with Enlil in Edin. Enki had that sexual appetite, which Enlil did not. So when his nature summoned him, his personal obelisk rose and found its landing space in the womb of an Earth-created woman called Batanash.

Batanash was the spouse of an Earthling named Lu-mash. Lu-mash was Enlil's choice to be the priest of this region. Lu-mash was so anointed to be the workmaster for the Nefilim-Anunnaki at Edin.

See what sexual desires without thought can do? This caused a huge rift between the brothers as Enki produced with Lu-mash's spouse an Earthling. One out of wedlock. This Earthling was known as Ziusudra. In the Bible, Ziusudra is misnamed Noah.

The secret of Ziusudra's true bloodline being of a demigod, it is written in Enki's text, then shall remain with Enki and Batanash. But Lu-mash and Enlil knew what Enki was up to. Enlil did not close his eyes to truth. Lu-mash did.

As a coming attraction to the story of the flood, I leave you with this thought. Enlil went crazy and wished to destroy mankind in his recurring role as the angry god of our Hebrew-Christian Bible. Enki saved his son as Ziusudra/Noah, the boy, is his seed. The story is about to unfold. Our story gets mixed up in the Bible of today's world separating the three Earth-based Nefilim/gods who were known as Enlil, Enki, and his son Marduk were merged into one energy that our Bible calls god. The translators using the concept of Talisman make these three gods one. And the truth is that they all came from King Anu's seed, which made them royalty in Nibiru's world order.

Act Five
The Great Flood

Act Five, Scene One: The Great Flood, a.k.a., The Crossing

The Background

Enki adored his new demigod boy Ziusudra, just like he did his offspring Adapa. A demigod means half Nefilim, half mankind. This boy, Ziusudra, it is written, was pure white skinned with hair the color of wool, his eyes both big and the color blue. An Aryan for sure.

Enki and Ninmah, two of the three children of King Anu, the third being Enlil, raised Ziusudra. Ziusudra was taught priestly rites. He was made aware of sacred knowledge just like Adapa was before him. Ziusudra was taught how to read. The scholars who I read who know the tablets well are convinced that the Nefilim had a special language, which today we do not know. It was the grandfather of the Indus and the Balkan Danube scripts. This is what I believe the first languages on Earth were all about. However, there is no trace of how they began or what they mean. Why? The coming catastrophe that we call a flood wiped out the recorded tablets in this region and no one saved them. Enki did save his tablets.

It is interesting how we were able to transcribe the text of Enki. This translation became possible when Napoleon found the Rosetta

Stone in Egypt, on which three languages describe one event. Using the one language that the few who then translated the stone knew, mankind was able to unlock the secret languages of earlier Earthlings' creators and the pets called mankind. That is except the two I mentioned above and the Mayan dialect.

Physical times on Earth in this era are not good. The Earth is rumbling and being tossed about by the energies of unpredictability caused by the rotations of planets and comets and meteorites shooting around our Earth's gravitational forces. Not to mention the living few had nothing new to do, so culture was at a standstill. The Anunnaki were just waiting for their command to come home. To return to Nibiru. Many were now very bored with mankind and this experiment of what really amounted to the new pets of Nibiru society.

What do we do when we get bored? We cause chaos. We shake it up. So did our creators. Enlil was convinced that the mission on Earth was wrong. The one creator of all did not give the Nefilim-Anunnaki permission to create a new living creature with consciousness of any sort or means.

Enlil wished to end the experiment and just let mankind exist on its own. Enlil did not want to save them from Earth's invading metaphysical forces. Enlil had no living investment from Earth. Enlil's offspring were full-blooded Nefilim. His half-brother Enki and half-sister Ninmah had living skin in the Earthling game as they created the prototypes and successor bodies of mankind as if we were cars with our DNA engines using Earth for our factory parts, not Nibiru. This gives us a different Earth life warranty as we learn is less time than one formed from Nibiru's womb.

Also be aware that there was a physical problem with Earthlings. Unlike the Nefilim, who while living on Earth in their Anunnaki jobs did not get sick, the Earthlings made from Earth particles did get sick. They did not have all the bells and whistles of eternal life on an Earth-based timeline like the Nefilim did.

The Demi-Nefilim or demigods had a much shorter shelf life than their one Nefilim parent, but this did allow them to live longer and better health-wise than one-hundred percent of the humans the Nefilim created. Mankind in the days of Ziusudra as it is written was besieged with diseases of aches, chills, and fevers that led to early Earthling deaths.

Remember, we learned earlier that when Earth was created from Tiamat, the micro life was transferred to the new planet that once existed on the moon of Nibru, which collided with Tiamut. These microorganisms combined with the alien microorganisms of that new Earth world. A new combination must have mutated, and as a mutated force, it did not all work for the common good of our Nibiru-made Earth DNA. A different blueprint for fighting off bacteria that was new to our world on Earth was needed. The Nefilim withheld this sacred knowledge if they even knew the problem.

These thoughts regarding bacteria newly created for Earth cells that became organisms of life I leave to those who do this research. And now we understand the possibility that viruses can attack Earth by entering our atmosphere. We have learned that viruses do survive the takeoff as well as landing of ships sent into space to explore space and then return to Earth. I believe a virus is the building block of life from the air, and a fungus is the building block of life from the ground.

For me, I am happy just connecting the dots of existence and showing you the fossils of the past as the basement of our distance. Who are we? Why are we here? Think about it later. Back to the story of the flood.

Let's flash to Ninmah in Edin.

Ninmah, the doctor of life with magic potions that can save the Nefilim on Earth. To me, Ninmah is the nurse of love. Ninmah was a true healer. She had her potions, and they were more than a number nine, as the song "Love Potion Number Nine" of my youth shares with the listeners. Enlil and Ninmah had arguments with many small battles. The two were about to have an explosion. Enlil told Ninmah to let the Earthlings live or die on their own. It was not the duty of the Nefilim to save their existence. The three knew of the coming metaphysical unseen energy about to whack Earth. It was a coming catastrophe of winds and rains of resulting heat and cool weather caused by the energies unleashed by the crossing of Nibiru into Earth's and Mars's orbits around the Sun. Our universal energy track was going to bend and maybe break. The three knew that Earthlings needed to prepare for the event or just be allowed to die.

You cannot tell a mother to let you kill her kids. Ninmah plotted with Enki to save their version of mankind.

The Nefilim had a society based on stargazing to map the energies they saw happening over time in our universe. They did this to map out all issues Nibiru may have had on its 3,600-Earth-year lap around the Sun. They knew Earth was not the center nor in control of what the universe did. They knew the waves in our air surrounding Earth, like a hurricane, were about to get really bumpy, and rocks from the meteorites in space could come down to Earth caused by the crossing of Nibiru, Planet X. This coming crossing was a wave that was too big to just ride out. The universe itself was having too many retrogrades. And the Anunnaki were all made to get in their chariots and watch the passing storm from a place in space where these waves would not interfere with their ships.

Well now, the question is what did the Nefilim do with Earthlings?

Enlil revealed his master plan for the human race. Do not interfere. Just let fate take over. It is not our destiny to keep these beings alive on Earth.

Enki disagreed. Enki had Nefilim blood in his creations of mankind with his seed. Enki kept his dissent quiet, to himself. Now the stage was set to see what Enki could do to save his human seed.

Switch your vision to the command post of the Anunnaki. Enlil as the commander of Earth made everyone take an oath to swear that no one would tell the Earthlings of the coming space calamity. Enki did not take this oath. Enki stormed out of the meeting and figured out how to save mankind.

The stage is now about to be set. The actors are setting the stage for the play of mankind's and Earth's future. Mankind's fate was in the hands of two very different half-brothers called gods, who were acting just like we humans do today.

Enlil, getting ready for the evacuation, took the ME to Nibru-Ki to the Sinai Peninsula. There, the ME was buried in a protective chamber.

Enki, with Ninmah, went to Abzu and started collecting all the necessary specimens, as they saw it, so they could recombine all the life-forms that they had created on Earth. "Get all not the one specimen that they created," as stated in the tablets. Male and female essences and eggs are what the scientist and nurse collected.

Then Enki went to Ziusudra in person. Enki guided him with exact plans, which were very precise, to build a specific boat. He then told Ziusudra how to make sure that the boat was sealed with a special substance Enki gave to Ziusudra so water could not get in the boat.

Enki, then playing protector of all Enki's creations, told Ziusudra exactly what to put into the boat. Ziusudra then put in the boat all the seeds and eggs that Enki gave him to save.

Now the Bible, in the translations of the Book of Enki to the Samaritan's Text, confuses the Samaritan term *Nukhu*. Nukhu was used by the Hebrews and the Babylonians, and it meant "comes to a rest." It was used in the translated text of the Book of Enki to say the ship came to a rest on the mountain. The word Nukhu was lost in translation and became "Noah came to a rest," as if it was Noah the leader of this ark. This is a great example of a Talisman representing the boat that saves mankind, concept name in the Jewish Christian bible Noah replaces Ziusudra the leader/captain of the Nukhu, the vessel.

The tablets further make very clear Enki did try not to break the oath that Enlil, his brother and the commander, made all the others take. The oath about informing the Earthlings about the events about to happen to Earth. The tablets say in order to not break the oath, which Enki did not take, Enki stood behind a curtain to tell Ziusudra what to do. This way, Enki's face could not be seen. He did this to say he did not speak to his son. The goal, as Enki told his son, was to ensure the seed(s) and eggs needed for civilized man to physically survive actually survived.

Ziusudra, unlike Noah in the bible myth, took his extended family and friends onto this boat. We also learn by these exact translated words the following part of the flood story, not myth but truth.

"The life essence and life eggs of living creatures it contains," by the Nefilim, a.k.a. god, Enki and Ninmah collected, from the wrath of Enlil, "to be hidden, to life resurrected if Earth be willing."

In the Bible we read and follow blindly without question that the wrath of Enlil is translated to the wrath of God, combining both him and Enki as the one god of mankind, and mostly obedient from them, till today.

INTERMISSION

If I had a screen, I would show you motion pictures of planet Nibiru, which some researchers call Planet X, crossing its orbital path around the Sun, which then on this trip goes directly into the ring orbital path of Jupiter and Mars as Nibiru comes close to our mutual Sun.

There is no red light to get Nibiru or Jupiter or Mars to stop and let the other planet go. No, this is movement without any thoughts, let alone control. If the planets or moons collide and get bumped from their fixed orbits, so be it. The energies are doing their waltz. And a new world of order on each planet will begin.

This passage of Nibiru was off course. The energy that the planet Nibiru created in space was one thing. Now mixed with the wake energy of both Jupiter and Mars created as they travel their orbit, we have a mess. We have a triple passing, and the paths of Mars and Jupiter move in a circular sort of west-to-east rotation. Nibiru does not as it does have its own orbital gravitation force, which I call rules. The three planets' energy wakes, which I call winds, create a cone effect similar to a tornado that no one can predict where it will hit. This one got caught in Earth's atmosphere, and like a nuclear explosion the winds attacked the ground of land and sea called Earth. My friends, we have the Great Flood of Earth. This flood happened thirteen thousand or more Earth years ago.

Act Five, Scene Two: Earth After the Great Flood

The visuals I just put into your minds were to set the stage, I hope for all of us, to understand what the Great Flood was all about. Let your imaginations go so we can collectively see and feel this wind and lightning throwing fire, running water stronger than any bulls hitting Earth back then in Earth's time.

The tablets write that this flood happened in the 120th Shar. This was 432,000 Earth years after the arrival of the Nefilim-Anunnaki here on Earth. In our Earth time, this is 11,000 BC. Which is thirteen thousand or more Earth years ago.

We now know that an angry god did not cause this flood. The flood was the result of Earth's reaction to the energies of the universe from the wake caused by Nibiru, which wobbled a different rotation path than it was projected to travel.

Enlil used this cosmetic hurricane and tornadoes with its thunder and fires that became winds with rain created by the atmosphere of Earth try to undo what the Nefilim created from nothing at all. Enlil wished for the end of all their creations on Earth.

Enlil's goal was to leave Earth the way they found it, absent the metals the Nefilim, which included gold and silver, took to bring back to Nibiru. He wanted fate to take over and let nature continue its evolutionary path of creation. Little did he understand that maybe he and his royal Nibiru fate, as chosen by the energies of the Supreme, was to help Earth evolve quicker.

Never did anyone think to ask what Earth wanted. Earth has a consciousness. And Earth is a womb. Earth is female. Earth, just like any mother, wanted species with consciousness. Why? This species had hands that worked, and they could help Earth become more beautiful. Mankind could in theory help dress Earth up. Make Earth the number one planet destination that physical beings of all galaxies travel to in our universe.

Crazy?

Maybe not.

Again, Earth does have a consciousness. And every living subject looks at everything else as its object to use and get what they, the subjects, want and need done. We maybe are the objects created for Earth to serve Earth. Maybe the Nefilim were manipulated by the energy of Earth to create mankind.

Just thoughts to share. Think about it.

The father Enki and the mother Ninmah of these living creatures did not let that death happen. This is nature working its truth. Parents do not kill their children except on very rare occasions when something intervenes with thoughts and gets you to believe a god of dark, or what you feel is light, wants you to kill in its name. I was involved in making a movie using this concept called *Frailty*. It is definitely worth a look.

Enki and Ninmah stopped the destruction of the Earthlings' apparent destiny. Saying this, I ask myself, did the one Supreme Source make those planets wobble? Does our creator of all creation want us to exist? Does creation care? What would God say if God was one of us? Or isn't God in actuality one of us as we are one of God's drops from the sea of consciousness?

Or does the one and only source of all creation sit and watch and just wait for us all to stop all our wants and individual needs. To understand nothing is better than living in the loving womb of the source of everything and more. If it could make life, then I believe this source is feminine too. Mom wants us home. Father is what the source creates so energies could reproduce. Once home, we just are in the bliss of Nirvana.

Mankind is created from masculine energy and given life and form from feminine energy. And understand that something divided energy to make this matrix of thoughts and bodies into two energies. The Hindu religion teaches that the Supreme Source was bored and divided itself into two energies. Male and female.

In the Hindu thought pattern, it goes further. Brahmin is the creator who became two energies. Those two energies, Shiva and Vishnu, are run by the energies of wants and desires.

Maybe Enlil is the Shiva the Destroyer and Enki is Vishnu the Perpetrator. Let that sink in. Maybe Nibiru, another female energy, was angry and did want its creations on Earth to disappear.

I share this thought that the planets are the higher living creation. We are all part of our mother's physical design. The mother is our physical creator. Ours is the energy that leaves our mothers and gives our mother the force to create more of us. Our individual consciousness is nothing more than a drop of the collective. This drop is given life by the Holy Ghost who resides inside the neutron of all our living cells.

Now see Earth after the storm. The tablets give a great detailed description of what the Earth looked like when the energies of winds with fires and earthquakes and the resulting water waves attacked Earth back then. These were the energies that caused the Earth to flood.

Question for you the reader: Ever ride a boat and another boat crosses your path at a higher speed? That's what happened here with

Earth and Nibiru. We on Earth were tossed and turned. We had to find a new balance. The water is contained by the land that is really nothing more than land with a huge pool on the land's property. Well, these winds stirred up the water and made the water revolt. This revolt caused the water to come over the contained top and go as far as the water in the stream of air could go. That is until the winds moving the water calmed down. And the mountains were slammed with energies of wind and rain as well as a flood from the water being pushed along.

This big water explosion began when the ice broke up in our Antarctic. This ice became a force heading north and overran everything on the Earth in its path.

The Nefilim wrote what they saw while watching Earth from their spaceships outside Earth's and Mars's as well as Jupiter's and Nibiru's orbits and their atmospheres. And we have learned that Earth and Nibiru do have a collision in their past. The energy waves, really waves of confession, first hit our southern bottom, breaking the ice cap into many loose pieces. This ice, now extra pieces, melted into loose water that overflowed the full glass of our oceans. The extra water poured over and then some, running on nonstop airwaves on the worldwide floor of our land-based world. Think of your bathtub. An overflowing flood as we could not stop the faucet that made the ice melt and create an overflow on Earth.

It takes a while for the water to find its calming point when someone somehow stops the faucet from running. In this case the ice was now partially melted down south. At this point the water became calm and began to be absorbed by the land, now soaked. Water was absorbed by land. All one big circle.

Hear this as you read, water has a consciousness. Water is alive. Water was created so consciousness could balance its wants and needs in a physical form. Water serves creation in this universe's matrix. No water, no physical life.

The Earthling boat heaving and rolling in the storm of the Nibiru crossing comes to rest on top of a mountain now surrounded by water. The Nefilim called this the Mount of Salvation. We know this top as Arata.

On my recent trip to China, I saw and studied the rooftops of the buildings inside their Forbidden City. As I took a look at their structure, I saw that these tops were the reverse structures of the boat that I saw drawn out from the written instructions so given by Enki to his son Ziusudra. Enki told Ziusudra again what to use to build the boat that would withstand the water force so created by the crossings.

I believe all of mankind's current cultures are connected. The Chinese came out of the Indus Valley and may themselves be an extra creation made by the Nefilim tinkering and tailoring their human pets of their creation. I explain this in Act Eight of this Book of Earth series. We create new species; do we not do it? We do it with dogs and other pets just as the Nefilim did it with us.

Are these sacred roofs of Chinese creation on their sacred temples really just taken from the design of the boat that saved mankind back then in the year of the flood? Ponder that thought.

Act Five, Scene Three: Back to Earth Thirteen Thousand Years Ago

The first thing Ziusudra did when our hero came out of the boat alive was fall to the land and give praise to his father Enki. Not to the one Nefilim who tried to destroy all called Enlil. Know the difference, and you will learn the role both played in controlling our fate here on Earth. Our Bible combines the two Nefilim as one bi-polar energy.

Now from the skies the Nefilim returned. They returned to survey the land. Enlil and Enki embraced and smiled, we read, as the Earth would survive. Then we learn that Enlil saw the Earthling Edin survivors and went berserk. How could anything alive not drown in the uncontrolled waves of the seas?

Enlil attacks Enki vocally. "How did this happen?" Enlil yelled. Enki told the truth. Enki saved his son and his son's bloodlines. Enki then persuaded Enlil that the Supreme Being of all made the final call. The creating energy of everything and more let the Earthlings survive. The mind and more called the Supreme Being of all could have ended the experiment of physical life here on Earth. The Being chose to let the play of mankind life on Earth continue.

Now we hear from Ninmah who says she is happy and elated that her children still breathe: "The annihilation of mankind shall never be repeated." Then Enlil, angry but accepting his defeat, told Ziusudra to "be fruitful and multiply."

I smile as I end this section, for the pieces of the puzzle in my mind are now connected. I see how we began. I see how we continued our existence in life living form here on Earth. And I understand the whole concept of those Nefilim-gods who fell to Earth from ships leaving Nibiru-Heaven to make mankind

Now looking back in time, we learn everything built by the Anunnaki-Nefilim space team in the Edin region was destroyed. That is, except the landing platform for the Nefilim spaceships to land on Earth in the Cedar Mountains of today's Lebanon. This platform was higher than the rest of the Anunnaki structures. This structure today, according to my hero who studied these texts most of his life, Zecharia Sitchin, who said it is none other than the stone platform we find in Baalbek, Lebanon.

This Baalbek structure was taken over by the Roman Empire thousands and thousands of Earth years later. This structure became the so-called Roman Temple to Jupiter. Jupiter was the Roman's version of Zeus, the Greek top god. Everything else in the Anunnaki horizontal view as the water subsided was now under the new soil moved by the gushing waters.

I mention Sitchin here because without him and his students, as well as fellow soldiers, looking and exploring the artifacts that Earth has held secrets from our wandering minds, none of my learned wisdom would exist regarding the Nefilim and their space traveler team called the Anunnaki and their homeland Nibiru. This dedication of their lives to learn the truths of Earth's creation is why I can connect these dots. To actually spend the time to digest and uncover the secrets of the Earth is so priceless. Their research was the key to unlock my total being to put the pieces of this puzzle in place so I could share the truths of our creation and civilization. And I know I am not the only one.

Back to our Earth space traveling crew, the Anunnaki:

The Anunnaki studied the flood's path of destruction and put the pieces of the new Earth puzzle together so civilization could start all over again. This living experience taught them how to build structures that could withstand the test of all unnatural catastrophes of time. The test of unforeseen events that we blame on the creator of all. Really maybe all the creator did was rebalance the unforeseen energy forces that shook the balance of not just us but the balance of our universe and our galaxy.

Saying that, I must now let you all know that it was written that finally physical beings living on Mars came to an end. From this Nibiru crossing across the universe, Nibiru waves knocked out the atmosphere that allowed physical life to exist on Mars. The last few remaining settlers on Mars came to stay for good on Earth. Even though this is written, I believe that there are still living energies, be they bacteria or viruses, alive on Mars.

Now imagine the spaceship passengers back on water-soaked land. What do they do? Enlil went to get the ME out of the Creation Chamber, which was near the Celestial Chariot sacred spot on Earth. We are told about this chamber now. I guess Enlil's team was shocked that the chamber actually survived, so they said that the chamber was diorite. Diorite is apparently one of the hardest stones known to mankind. Much stronger than steel.

Who put that rock there in Edin? It is not found in this region of Earth. Just a thought. If you look it up, you may be led to the volcanoes that existed in the Andes Mountain regions.

Inside this locked chamber as if it were a big closet with boxes, we are told Enlil's team took out the seeds they brought from Nibiru. The seeds of creation that would allow them to re-create their gardens in their new Eden. Ziusudra was not the only one with the seeds. There were other copies here on Earth.

The world on Nibiru was not good as Nibiru's atmosphere was also shaken. The Anunnaki crew needed to get more gold as the atmosphere on Nibiru had holes reappear as well as new holes. These new holes were caused by the energy that came back from Earth and Mars and Jupiter as the floating boats called planets, on their orbital tracks, swam too close to each other in the ocean of space. This means that they had work to do on Earth as they needed more gold. No one was going home yet. And more Nefilim were about to come, and the need for those pets called humans would increase.

Lessons learned from the Great Flood, the Nefilim, using their ME, would now build new structures to land the spaceships here on Earth. These new structures are the big Egyptian pyramids we see appear all of a sudden in lower Egypt, which we call Memphis. Understand and stop believing the imperial religions of mankind's lies that a prehistoric Earthling could have put this together. There were no Erector or LEGO sets for us children to build. The pieces were not yet created for one to then assemble. There was no Play-Doh mold to copy.

It is important for me to write here and now that Enki did not save all life here on Earth. It is written that most Earthlings in the south, the land of Abzu, were killed. Life as a numbers game had to start over again. The first mold of mankind was thought to be dead, except for the Aborigines we discovered underneath the equator in our Southern Hemisphere in the land we call Australia.

However, I do not believe this about the black slaves. I believe they ran off into Central Africa, the lands between the North Tropic of Cancer and the Southern Tropic of Capricorn. I believe there was a super race of beings in these jungles where whites did not go. And this race stayed alive by not interfering with the Nefilim until they thought the time would be right. Marvel comics created their mythical Black Panther, and during my life working with Stan Lee at the turn of the last century, we discussed at length Nibiru and the Nefilim as well as the Anunnaki and the creation of mankind in all its prototypes.

Act Five, Scene Four: A New Physical Order on Edin: Abzu, South Africa, and the Andes Mountains

Mining ore as before on or near Edin was impossible for the Anunnaki and Earthlings. The wild uncontrolled waters carried away what nuggets of gold existed in those river basins and creeks. The mines in South Africa were destroyed by the Great Flood.

Ninurta took to the skies and surveyed Earth. The sky pilot returned with new news. The winds from the crossing had eroded the mountains of the distant land beyond their homeport ocean, the Atlantic. This erosion exposed the rich sediments of gold that were hidden inside the Earth. This mountain range is today known as the Andes. The gold was now falling out from the exposed mountains as nuggets.

When you visualize the flood, you must remember that winds caused by the crossing of Nibiru did damage to the land. These winds tore apart our hills, mountains, and valleys worldwide. It was the biggest hurricane to hit Earth. We talk of only the flood because the second set of writers of the Enki story called the Samaritan tribes understood only what they could see, and all they saw was the world horizontally from their land where they stood. And their image was their homeland called the Upper World lands. The Samaritans knew nothing of the Andes Mountains and the civilization of Ka-in's ancestors. The Ka-in crew did survive too.

This hurricane of major winds and tornadoes hit the region called the Andes and, as I wrote, made the gold fall to Earth from these mountains as gold nuggets. These nuggets were loosened by the winds of the hurricane. This is where the ancient El Dorado civilization of Bolivia and Peru begins to really take its place in the annals of Nefilim-Anunnaki Earth time. Someone or thing created the Lake Titicaca. This lake has a shape similar to the animal we call a Jaguar. Who did that? Nature or the Nefilim?

This is the Inca Empire's true beginning. Enki and Enlil, two of the three competing gods of Earth, were shocked. These gold nuggets meant that for right now, no mining or smelting was required. All they needed to do was collect the gold.

So, a new port to fly in and out of needed to be created by the Nefilim. This port today is found in a region known as the Nazca plain. I have been there as well as all over Lake Titicaca. When I arrived in 1996–1997, this land and lake and mountains mesmerized me. I knew I had been there before. I knew then and there I would be back again.

I returned in October of our Earth year 2018. That visit inspired me to go and write this history of our creation. I returned to the books I read before and the new books that those earlier books led me to today. I could not stop. I traveled and saw what I needed to know and appreciate to tie the dots of life together for me to give you this Earth-based consciousness lotus astrological sign of our past here on Earth.

Who are we? How did we get here physically? And why do we follow the rules of order that the few make us do so a community living together in a social unit can survive? These are the topics my mind examines as I write to you the story of our collective past here on Earth.

Act Five, Part Two
The Andes Mountains

Act Five, Part Two, Scene One: The Incas

Ninurta now returned in a big role in the creation of mankind. If you remember, Ninurta had been to the Andes Mountains before. He went with his father Enlil to get this region under their control if Marduk tried to grab control of what they were calling the New World. Ninurta stayed there. The locals, who had been living there before the Great Flood, knew Ninurta. He was revered by the living Earthlings as their god.

The height of these mountains protected many of the then living from destruction by the winds or flood caused by the crossings. The time had come to put the descendants of Ka-in to work for the benefit of the Nefilim and Nibiru.

The Anunnaki called these people the Incas. It is funny how the Spanish referred to these folks as Incas too. How did they get this name? The answer is that the Vatican has the books.

The people living there called themselves Quechua. That tale we will learn over and over again, but let's say the Vatican, who gave the maps of the new world to the Spanish and Portuguese sailors, knew what the Nefilim knew about the land on Earth and left it in map form. These map tables were and maybe still are in the possession of the Vatican. That simple. Why? Because the Vatican wants you to believe in their

Christ as the only god. Never do they want anyone to put together the true story of creation.

The Incas were happy to work as directed by their god, Ninurta. Why? It gave the living something to live for and do—to live and serve their Nefilim (god) after they are fed and rested. To begin their new Earth chores for this god. Their god wanted gold. They never learned why, so they thought it was for show-and-tell.

We know now from reading this book the Nefilim wanted these new villages in the mountains to be built in gold and instructed the space crews of Anunnaki to build the land accordingly. It was to build their Earth cities in gold. And now the living Earthlings would worship gold. Because their god wanted it this way.

Gold became the attraction the Earthlings knew they needed to find and needed to hoard to bring their god back to the Incan regions. So the thought of the Earthlings who knew only what they were told by their god was that urban gold cities would get their creators back. God knew magic, and magic would save the people from nature and the wild animals of the mountains and the jungle that surrounded their mountains.

They got the gold and god appeared and helped the Incas survive. Even Enlil was happy these Inca creatures survived the Great Flood. He now had slaves who would listen and do, not compete for being top dog. Remember, these few came from mankind creation number two. They were not as bright as, say, Ziusudra and his kin.

There was societal order in these lands created back then after the Great Flood. This order was shared with me back in October 2018 by an energy I know and love but one that I feel is from another universe. He came into my path in Cuba, and we went back to his Bolivian homeland together to explore the region and for him to share with me the sacred knowledge he had by being from these parts. The man is special, and I will for now leave his name out. This was my second visit to the energy of the Lake Titicaca, and I was now ready to understand.

Act Five, Part Two, Scene Two: The Story of the Rules and the Societal Controls of This Incan Community Who Call Themselves Quechua

The Quechua is the name given by the Incas (king-lord) race of mankind to call their peasants' tribe. They are the descendants not the ancestors of the model two humans who were selected to go with Ka-in when he was sent away for killing Abel. They live in the Lake Titicaca valley, and they know the mountains and all the gifts and secrets the mountains hide in plain view. They believe they are the descendants of Atlantis. Atlantis in their minds was none other than the urban area of the five first Nefilim cities on Earth.

They had no written language to record knowledge that we know of. When it was time to teach mankind how to write in Edin, for whatever reason, apparently the Nefilim did not teach these Earth beings they created to write their thoughts or spoken words down. They did have a system to count, and it dealt with knots made on rope, which functioned as this culture's math counting system.

The Vatican had this knowledge of the Incan past and El Dorado. How? It was the keeper of the stolen manuscripts of Enki and the later translations of his book by human civilizations, so they thought when they destroyed the Library of Alexandria. These books are the Vatican's and coconspirators' secret knowledge. The Vatican came to South America with their conquistadors back at the end and the beginning of their timeline called 1,500 AD. The Vatican came with their conquistadors using their swords shaped as crosses to steal all the gold that the Anunnaki had the Incas build their cities of gold with and on.

The Quechua, as they called themselves, who were the descendants of Ka-in model line, created a living order. They had a language that predates the languages of our so-called history of living mankind. This language became the Linga Franca of the Vatican's conquistadors. The Vatican's own private language that foreigners could not understand.

The Quechua had a living social order divided into four cycles. Each cycle had different stages that were that were seven years long. I will now break down those cycles as I was taught what they were by my friend the visitor.

Cycle One is Childhood.

Stage One starts the first moment you are outside the womb. That start is the first year to continue to the end of your sixth year of Earth. When we begin life in Earthling form from birth to seven, we get our teeth. We begin to live physical life.

Stage Two of this cycle of Childhood is when you start your seventh year on Earth. This stage and the cycle start on the year you are now living, not at the end of that year. Also, they end when the next Earth year of life is to begin. So now this fourteenth year will begin on the thirteenth birthday. We go through puberty. We become animals of Earth that can reproduce and learn the basic rules to survive and become part of the reproduction machine.

Cycle Two: Youth

Stage One is from thirteen to twenty. It is where you learn to use your creative energies. And those creative energies include sex.

Stage two is from twenty to twenty-seven. This is where we learn how to negotiate our wants and needs. It is where we can make life mistakes.

This stage is when you become aware. Many cannot live with this awareness. It's hard to live and accept the peaks and valleys of life. The inability to roll with that new flow can take you out of your physical body by causing death. This age bracket is so dangerous. One that we elders must help the youth pass through. Awareness is no friend to those who are raised dumb and numb. Youth One and Two are where our leaders get the young to go and kill others. This group believes what they are told. They learn in the schools that are still run by the imperial olden Upper World not to question imperial authority.

Stage Three is twenty-eight to thirty-four. Here you prepare to be an adult. You start to see the mistakes of youth, but you still are capable of making and living your mistakes. The rules in these societies had different leniency for mistakes made as a youth and before adulthood.

Cycle Three: is Adulthood. Adulthood is four seven-year stages of being an adult. This is where you discover your life mission. It is where you put it in motion. Where you get to get it going. We all are not here with the same mission. The four cycles are thirty-four to forty-one, forty-one to forty-seven, forty-seven to fifty-five, and fifty-five to sixty-two. Look at your life and now judge yourself within these time frames. You will see different versions of yourself.

Cycle Four: is the Elder.

With luck and good health, the cycles of being the community elder now begin. Five divisions. Sixty-two to sixty nine as the first one. Second is sixty-nine to seventy-six, the third is seventy-six to eighty-three, the fourth is eighty-three to eighty-nine, and the final is eighty-nine until your end.

As I reflect on what I just wrote, I see the community had some interesting lifestyles. They lived totally by the moon. The calendar had thirteen months. Those months matched the menstruation cycle of the women of their community. The man with the life-bearing womb. The pathway matrix to getting and living life.

This was then fifty-two weeks with one extra day. That day was celebrated as the day everyone should be forgiven so all can start anew again. This included all debts. Debts had a one-year shelf life. Down under, this day was December 21. Their summer, and on our calendar it is winter. It is the south's longest day of daylight and the shortest light day of the northern world year.

The leap year make-up day, as our days are less than an exact twenty-four hours each day, was not discussed, so it probably did not exist. Time is just a thought to give us reason to be and believe in our social order of community control. The day began at sunrise. There were no clocks. Time is used to control us to do certain things at certain hours so that we do as we are told.

The people living back then lived by an order of natural Earth existence. The community as a whole addressed wants and needs. So often by examining and explaining the natural order contained in yourself, that causes disorder of your natural flow. People had property, but it was not their property exclusively. It was their property to protect for the whole community of mankind. There was no concept of accumulating. Capitalism is a game of theft. Entrepreneurs and creators are what society needs. Capitalism is not creation. It is perpetuation with the goal to make it for the few, not the many. We do not need another banker in a society based on scarcity like ours is today.

Then, everyone had a job. A job was a function to serve the community, not just themselves. If you were not able to work, your function was you served the community because your inability to work meant someone needed to take care of you. This was work to be taken care of. I now believe this concept came from the Nefilim, as you should remember both Enki and Enlil had to get permission to create the chores as well as permission of whom to give the chores to. Everyone has a reason to live and be a member in good standing in their community.

There was no stealing, no lazy behavior, I was told. No lying, as there was no need to be better than the rest. You were what you were. If you did not live these truths, then you were evil, and the community would deal with you accordingly.

We will learn about the Aztec and Mayan civilizations later. And in my other book *Highways of Man*, we will learn about the other two tribes of Mesoamerica Nefilim eras known as the Olmec and Zapotec as well as the Toltec. But understand these societies were based on what the Nefilim were doing in these lands at the time of their society's creation. There are no written records that we have found, and I believe they may not exist. There are many structures with paintings and graphs that do explain what the locals believed.

Studying the records left over Earth and the movements of the Nefilim, we can trace a better understanding of what is left on Earth from their past. The Mayan calendar is definitely related to the space travel of the Nefilim and what they saw as the coming events of energy coming to Earth in the future, which they could predict.

Act Five, Part Three
The Age of Leo

Act Five, Part Three
Scene One: The Giza Pyramids of Egypt

The Great Flood changed the way the Nefilim would get the gold to Nibiru. Mars was no longer available as a place where small quantities of gold could be sent from Earth to be repackaged and then assembled into larger quantities and placed on a bigger spaceship to return to Nibiru. Mars was needed to do this because there was less density in that atmosphere, and it was easier to move the ships with heavier weight than just space travel and get the goods to Nibiru.

The Nefilim had to adapt to the new conditions of Earth and Mars as well as the moon, as they still needed the gold.

The Anunnaki, the Nefilim on Earth, and their pets called mankind were now gathering gold in Earth's Andes Mountains. This gold was their focus, but their home on Earth's range, their sacred space, was still the Upper World where Edin and other urban societies were being rebuilt.

King Anu had come to Earth and was now with Enlil trying to figure out what to do to solve the transportation problem of getting the gold back to Nibiru. They were in the air and vertically surveying Earth. The issue was where the new command post was to be located. Logic would place the spot in the Andes Mountain region. But nostalgia of their home on their Earth range would place the spot back in the Upper World as they called the Edin communities. Again, these terms were describing the point of the Nefilim entry into Earth from the beginning. I write this so our minds can see the meaning of the words I use.

Also know this is when we start reading about the age of the astrological signs. Each era is about 2,200 years old. The Nefilim really believed that different energies can and will reach Earth to start a new metaphysical era of us beings on Earth as the Sun turns in our galaxy. And this turn is left, what we call counterclockwise. So now we have the Age of Leo.

The original air command and control post in the Edin regions was wiped out by the Great Flood. The gold merchandise they now sought due to the flood was in the mountains of the New World.

There were thoughts by the elders to move everything to the New World. To build their new urban society in the Andes regions. Nostalgia set in. The king and prince decided from their view in the air to maintain the original home and build civilizations for the few to have their plantations of home life and keep the landing settlements of ships from Nibiru near Edin.

Questions are being asked trying to figure out how to create the new spaceport. And if it is to be built near Edin, where do we locate the towers needed to let the sky pilots know they are near the landing strips? How do we on Earth communicate with the pilots so that we can have them land their crafts on the exact spot we now choose? All questions we will now learn the answers to.

The Nefilim, as we are aware, were sky watchers. They needed to build their Earth towers in line with the stars in our Earth's sky. The astrological dots of stars that we call Orion's Belt was how King Anu and his son Prince Enlil, the next birthright ruler of Nefilim, decided to build their new towers to communicate with the Nefilim pilots.

The new tower control spot the two selected was to be the Nile river region that today we call the lower Nile. It worked as it was a delta. A perfect land to build the everlasting beacons of pulsating lights sent out into the atmosphere from Earth that captains of floating spaceships could see and use to navigate their way to Edin.

The exact spot chosen is what we call Memphis-Giza Egypt today. Like Orion's Belt with its three stars in that constellation, this Earth spot would have three Earth-built bases with lights on the top of the big structure to shine brightly into the sky; these Earth monuments would communicate with the heavens above. They would be called the Great Pyramids.

Mars had pyramids to do this for the Nefilim too. They are still on Mars. As a sidebar, please look up pyramids on Mars. Just think what we have not been shown let alone told in our schools of brain control.

The builder and architect of these Giza pyramids we discover was Ningishzidda. a.k.a. Ning. The son of our first Earth scientist, Enki. Enki, again, is the first son born to King Anu, but he could not become the ruler because he had the wrong bloodline, meaning the wrong mother.

The later civilizations of this region we today call Egypt call their builder Thort or Tehurj. These two words mean the "divine measurer" and/or the "god of science and knowledge." Ning is that real Nefilim. Thort built the pyramids using his mathematical awareness of how to keep structures standing throughout the wear and tear of time. Its sacred knowledge is in the angles the structures are placed in so they can withstand the movements of Earth caused by Earth and the winds that come into Earth's atmosphere.

These big three pyramids were not built to be tombs as our history wishes us to believe. Others, as we will discover, were built to hold the dead human pharaohs wrapped in cloth so the Nefilim, if they so choose, could get the bodies and give the dead the everlasting kiss of life in Nibiru. This will happen in the coming astrological ages of Cancer and Gemini. The Nefilim needed to have societies run by Earthlings who reported to the chosen Nefilim local ruler (god). These Egyptian civilizations mummified their human dead leaders and built their sand pyramids to place their dead pharaohs in their living mausoleums dedicated to the now-departed king/pharaoh.

These three Great Pyramids were designed, I must repeat, with the intent to become the landmarks that are indestructible to flood and the natural decay that occurs just with passing time. These pyramids were to be the shining beacons so the space travelers could spot the landing grids and air control towers for the Nefilim pilots to land the Celestial Chariots.

In the ruins of what was once the Royal Library of Nineveh, the maps the Nefilim and their Earth-based employees called Anunnaki used to dissect the atmosphere and mentally begin the building of the pyramids and land the ships here on Earth was found. Yes, we have the blueprint of this creation.

The Nefilim learned so much from the Great Flood. They witnessed from a space flight vertical view the survival of the landing platform at Baalbek. They used the principles of building that earlier site to create the new structures slightly southwest in Giza of that original area.

It was important in the builder's mind to build these pyramids not by natural landmarks but on a land that had no mountains, only water-clogged valley. The pyramids, according to Ning, were artificial peaks. The pyramids needed the delta region to create everlasting peaks.

The Pyramid of Menkaure, the smallest of the three, was built first. The structure is really four smooth sides of rising angles. That simple. The slaves called mankind did not create any of this design, nor cut the rock nor move it to the location to be put together. Machinery unknown to us did the building of cutting the stone and placing it on their LEGO design designated spot and then lifting it into its place. This advanced machine created by using their ME also was used in locating the stone and moving it to the building spot. This stone may have come from China. Maybe the Longyou Caves.

The next pyramid built was the Pyramid of Khafre. This pyramid, like Menkaure, does not have a major network of chambers or passages. This is exactly how the Samaritan text describes the building of the first two pyramids.

With the Nefilim group's approval of the first two pyramids, the Great Pyramid was built. This pyramid, as translated in the Samaritan text from Enki's Book of Earth, does have chambers and passages that were not in plain view. Meaning secret passages. Each chamber had a purpose, and it was not to be buried to reincarnate and be back again.

Also, the temples, as opposed to the three pyramids, of these Egyptian regions that were built were built for the pets to worship their gods. Again, these temples, as we will learn, is where the gods required their pets called mankind to celebrate and have the feast celebrating their Nefilim-god—one of the many gods living and ruling the family land called Earth.

Originally the gods who ruled the lands were run by full-blooded DNA Nefilim who lived forever on Earth's time as understood by us Earth beings. Then, as we shall learn, the Anunnaki had a population problem of Earthlings to feed and take care of, so the Anunnaki created civilization and had Earthlings; they chose to be the kings and priests of the gods' land. They were given knowledge of how to do what the Anunnaki wanted them to do so society with Nefilim rules could be created and served here on Earth.

We shall learn that the Anunnaki men liked (fancied) Earthling females, so what is called the demigod, half mankind and half Nefilim, came into existence. Then you had the wild female Nefilim come and mate with mankind, and this too created a new breed of mankind. We shall soon meet one of this DNA creation.

To connect the dots of the manmade pyramids we see in Egypt, listen as you hear or read my words—I need to repeat this concept. The living mankind Egyptians built the Upper Egypt pyramids so the dead mankind rulers, as opposed to the Nefilim royal rulers, could be seen by the spaceships in hopes that the flying crew would pick up the mummified rulers and take them to Heaven so they could have the eternal gift of life given to them by their Nefilim (gods) whom they served so well. These three Great Pyramids were not built to take home to Nibiru the dead. No, they were built to get the gold to Nibiru.

In the tablets we can decipher that the chambers of this Great Pyramid had pulsating crystals. Purpose? Pulsating crystals were used to transmit signals and light to guide incoming astronauts down to Earth.

The Pyramids of Giza are different from the tombs of the Valley of the Kings. And these tombs are different from the copy pyramids that appeared, as I said, in the Age of Gemini. These tombs in the Valley of the Kings were built with Nefilim machinery, as were the Great Pyramids. Those tombs do have inscriptions as they tell a story to be found later in Earth's timeline to explain life back then when they were built. This is deliberate.

Those tombs were built for burial of the kings who were the offspring of the right bloodline of the Nefilim and were part human and part Nefilim. That simple. But these demigods did not have the Nefilim everlasting life. Only the full-blooded Nefilim did.

These three Great Pyramids did withstand nature and its changing moods of love and hate. The building was not, however, people proof, and it is we, the people, who destroyed the original structures for our own personal greed and to create false legends to control our minds and imaginations.

In the Great Pyramid one can find an inscription to King Khufix above the king's chambers in a small space. This is believed to be a later addition put there to throw us off the path of truth. Some so-called experts try to convince others that this king built the Great Pyramids around 2500 BC. This was done so we stop asking questions and do not learn when and why the Great Pyramids were constructed as well as how they were constructed. If you question the artifacts without having a stake in the answer, you would understand that we are a part-alien race to Earth. Also learning that truth then you can learn the how our history of god and religions were created and why. We are a consciousness that is not from Earth as its beginning.

I confess that it took me many years of studying with readings and visits to put this timeline together I just gave you of Egypt. It is confusing and must be really analyzed with current awareness—not lies to perpetuate the story others want you and need you to believe to continue their ruse so you believe in their system of control.

To honor the Nefilim builder of the Great Pyramids in poem back then, it is written in the text a monument was to be created nearby. The monument must have been the Great Sphinx of Giza. The Sphinx has the face of the builder, Ning, and the body of a lion. Why a lion? Apparently, the star sign of that age was none other than our Leo the Lion. The scriptures say the face of Ningishzidda, the peaks' designer, let it be.

The lion, which some call King David's symbol, is used to this day on the family crest of those members of the European royal families who claim they get to rule and be worshiped by divine decree. This is the priestly order from Egypt that morphed into the Sadducees of priestly Hebrew rule in Jesus's time that used the lion to prove continuity to their creators. David was a chosen king by merit as he killed the demigod half-man and half-Anunnaki called Goliath who ruled the land of the Philistines.

Have you ever noticed that the crests of the Vatican's chosen European rulers all have the lion in their family crest? This is where it came from. Know that the Vatican did bless all the kings and queens of Western and Central Europe on behalf of their god, who is not Nefilim created but is based on the tales of the Nefilim here on Earth. Their version of Christ was created by a vote by the bishops of the Mediterranean region at the Council of Nicaea in 325 AD. The reason this was done is Constantine needed to create a sky god religion to authenticate the ruling order of the Roman Empire being in line with the Nefilim (gods) from Heaven. Anything that disputes this claim of authenticity of the Vatican's rule over you will immediately in today's world be met with propaganda created to say that the information is wrong and only we the Vatican know the truth.

This Sphinx, not being smooth stone and placed on an angle, did erode. Scholars have concluded this erosion was done by water being able to seep into the structure's molding of the stones. Measuring different water lines causing excess water into this region, we are told, places the building of the sphinx around twelve thousand years ago. Which is the Age of Leo if today is now the Age of Aquarius. Remember, each new age is about 2,000–2200-year run, so go backward in the lines of the ages, meaning counterclockwise, as these signs are married to the movements of our Sun in the galaxy's sky.

Act Five, Part Three, Scene One (B): Dividing the Lands of the Nefilim Colonies on Earth The Age of Cancer

First, I must share with you that the division of lands is what was habitable back in those times. Remember, the Ice Age was ending. But *was* is the key word. The lands of the northern half of Earth were not fully habitable yet. These lands in which the Nefilim lived were different from what we can live on now. So now it was time to divide the Earth colonies of Nibiru up in that era of life on Earth.

Now it is time for royal family jealousy to take its dark energy hold. Poor Marduk, the now-forgotten son, takes center stage. Marduk is very jealous of his half-brother, the head Nefilim on Earth of Science and Math knowledge Ningishzidda. All the accolades are being given to the scientist of their time. The architect of the sky he has become.

Marduk once again feels passed by for promotion to what he believes is his turn to shine from the sky as he was promised to rule Earth. This jealous and self-absorbed boy will soon be the seed of our current society's unbalanced lives. This Nefilim was one evil Nefilim being. His coming rule of Earth as we shall discover is the straw that stirs the pot of Earth's mankind fears and ignorance that leads to division and division's dissension.

Remember, Marduk was the first son of the first son of the king of Nibiru. These two first sons of the next generation of royalty, Enki and Enki's first son Marduk, are from illegitimate mother bloodline succession rules. Neither of them would be able to be king of Nibiru following the line of Anu. They were given different routes to be the leaders of their generation. That is unless there were a power grab revolt.

Marduk was promised by his father Enki that he would be in command of Earth. The command post was given to Enlil, as we learned, by King Anu. Enki did tell his son Marduk that the time just had to be right. Marduk's sign was the sign of Aries. Marduk was told, "just wait your turn." Yes, the Nefilim's team of Anunnaki lived here on Earth time for hundreds of thousands of years as their physical body of creation had one Nefilim year of life for each 3,600 Earth years. You do the math. Crazy, but true.

Marduk was not the only Nefilim-Anunnaki child who wanted his own fiefdom. But he was the leader of this uprising questioning the control of the big three. Those three were King Anu and his boys Prince Enlil and Prince Enki.

Act Five, Part Three, Scene Two: What Do We Do With the Children's Children of the Nefilim Royal Retinue Who Colonized Earth?

Now across the universe, the Nefilim, using their version of FaceTime, began a heated debate. It's all about the children's children. The debate is who gets what. Really, what do we do with our extended life on Earth? What is our purpose? We want to rule not just be relief players. We want our own kingdoms, so let's divide the Earth into sections where each one of us creates our own version of civilization. Let's experiment to see which way is better.

The peacemaker of that time period was none other than Ninmah. Feminine energy stopped the warring male gods. Ninmah's name was changed for her role in keeping the peace between her brothers Enki and Enlil and their sons and sons' children. Ninmah would now be known on Earth as Ninharsag. The name means Mistress of the Mountain Head.

This was during the Age of Cancer as the lion was now over. Maybe ten thousand Earth years ago.

The Elders Council of Nibiru divided the lands between the siblings and their followers as follows:

1. Ninharsag was given the Land of the Missiles, a.k.a., Tilmun. This land today is the Sinai Peninsula of our world. Then it was out of bounds to Earthlings. It was declared a neutral territory under Ninharsag control.

2. Enlil was given for him and his family the habitable lands of the East. The East is also known as the Olden World or Edin. The lands East of Sinai. Get it? This was the region we today know in our history books as Mesopotamia, Akkad, Babylonia, Assyria, and Sumer.

3. Enki was given the dark coastal hued lands of today's North and Central Africa. The Nubians were the people then living on this east coast of Africa. He was also given Abzu, a.k.a., the Lower World. This land division included his son Ziusudra's habitat. Ziusudra is the Noah hero of our Bible story of the Great Flood in case you forgot. Notice how no one got, let alone discussed, the noncoastal regions of Central Africa.

Please remember there is a difference in the creation of the Earthlings. We were created at different times and with different intents. The intent to control us is inside the DNA mix that our creators used to make living slave or pet bodies. What they could not control was our inquiring consciousness that will try to free itself of the mental roadblocks I call chains inside our body form. We as a consciousness will learn how to manipulate our own DNA to make us the equal of our creator. This they called the Age of Aquarius. The age when civilized beings' society on Earth would once again become enlightened, and this dark energy of using beings to be a slave race would end.

The New Testament talks of Armageddon. It is the battle that was forecast to come in the Age of Pisces, which is Jesus energy versus Christ energy. The energy of love versus the energy of control is the battle. And the Age of Aquarius, it is forecasted, will bring an end to that world of control and create here on Earth a world of love with peace for all beings.

It is important to know that our space galaxies of existence have different consciousnesses exploring the possibilities of living life in physical forms associated with the material matrix of a universe. Each consciousness as a whole, not individual parts, travels the galaxies and stops in the universes to live life in that matrix form. Our consciousness got trapped as we were tricked into stopping here on Earth believing it was the land of good and plenty for the whole, not knowing it was for the few who promised us once we got here, next time we could have what we have living here in physical form.

Knowledge with wisdom is the answer. And now I get to my very important question for society to answer. Who owns knowledge, and who controls the teaching to make beings wise, as I wrote about in my book *Sacred Knowledge: A Rock 'n' Rollers Guide to Higher Consciousness*?

Enki now decided to please his rebel son Marduk, and to Marduk, Enki gave the dark-hued lands of today's Egypt. This was the battle to this day of Sudan and the Egyptians as well as north and South Sudan.

Now the slave worker mode is broken. For these gods with their own lands to watch over wanted servants to do what they were told to do. The Nefilim, as it was not just Enki and his son Ning, (gods) tinker with our mankind's DNA again. The goal was to give Earthlings a little more so we could do more than just menial work and physical tasks. We needed to be able to serve the civilization the Nefilim-gods were about to create and allow to be populated by their beasts of burden slaves, mankind. We were again initially created in body form to be physical white and black slaves. In the minds of our creating physical gods, we were not their equal but domesticated pets, their pawns on their checker or chessboard of Earth-based lands.

Although we are focused on Egypt after the Great Flood, Upper Egypt combined with Sudan and the land we call Ethiopia became the experimental land of black beings of Enki and his children who were scientists. They experimented with creation. Both animals and material. The Nubians were the black primitive workers who were the slaves and servants of the Enki clan. They worked and created items in this region that we have found that in our world are more than fifty thousand years old.

I have seen some of these relics, and in my possession I have, so I am told, an artifact of the god Thoth, but which Thoth god, the Nefilim's or the Atlantean as we will learn about in the next two books of this series? This artifact is molded in a stone that was unique to find here on Earth. An Egyptian artifact that Aly, my Egyptian guide back in 2010, gave me and told me that it is maybe over fifty thousand years old.

A little side story to share with you. I went with my son Barron in September of 2010 to Egypt. I was the guest of a man I knew as Aly, who was a Coptic Christian who worked for the KGB and the CIA, he told us. He was employed to take the people sent by their respective spy agencies of the USSR and the US to learn the sacred and now-secret metaphysical knowledge of the pyramids and temples of Egypt—the buildings of these pyramids and the temples of antiquity both before the Great Flood and after the Great Flood. The before and after buildings were two different mindsets of creation. One was to open portals to energies, and one by Nefilim and their pet's mankind was to duplicate the previous buildings again, searching for something as those who made it did not have the wisdom, let alone the ability, to make the temples or the big three pyramids the way the Atlanteans did, as we shall soon discover.

This game is a game of traveling the path that I am living in today's existence, searching for wisdom and the sacred knowledge of mankind's physical matrix beginning and what came before us here on Earth. To play the game, I have learned I must be prepared to constantly look for light and not get caught in any shadows that hide the truth in plain view if I open my third eye to truth. It is like unwrapping a gift that comes to us in an energy box. Many layers before you get to the truth, which is buried in our Earth's sands of time or can be heard in the passing airs of ripples spreading across the universe. "Keep exploring," is all I hear in my mediations and out-of-body experiences. I have come across many guides, and I must say both the Atlantean Thoth and Paramhansa Yogananda as well as Enlil, who did come to me as I wrote Act 13, were my three special Book of Earth Series guides.

Aly is dead now. He was involved in overthrowing the then president of Egypt who was rumored to be leaving the IMF to hitch up with China. Aly was one of the secret leaders of the Arab Spring revolution. He was a trip to know.

Aly took my son Barron and I to the temple known as Abydos. Here one can see what the living on Earth knew fifty thousand or more years ago. I could not believe what I saw. The lies that one can read on the internet say it's a forgery. It's not. This temple was originally a cave built by Thoth to hide the Atlantean secrets of metaphysics from the dark energy that took over Upper Egypt when the Atlanteans left this Earth when Earth became the dense physical planet we now have and the Nefilim took it over for their own personal use to mine for gold.

As I read and rewrite this section of this book, I am now able to share that this temple was created to hide in plain view, a stage where the key to the Halls of Amenti resides as discussed in Act Sixteen of book three of this series called *We've Got to Get out of This Place!* The Nefilim knew something was there, but it was hidden from them. The

Atlanteans who we learn all about in that act considered the Nefilim to be dense energy and not living with light.

I will say right here again that I do believe Earth has been a portal for consciousnesses from many galaxies' beings to explore life in Earth's physical forms to understand the games one can play in love with light, as well as in shades of darkness. I am here only discussing the species that created mankind's DNA. The how they did it as well as why they did it and what happened after that species called the Nefilim left Earth to us, their physical heirs of Earth.

Barron and I, back in 2010, saw drawings in the temple that looked so much like a helicopter and submarine plus a battle tank. This was built before Earthlings were being civilized. These were drawn by the Nefilim masters using slaves' hands, not their minds, to draw as they were told. These drawings were not done by Thoth and his Atlantean race.

On the side of this temple, one can see a mural drawing of objects that look like cells. They call the wall the Tree of Life. Living cells that combined using our DNA to make our bodies, and the machines called organs inside our bodies, work. Work so we can have a physical trip learning how to live with the quality of life and physical death. A true wild toad ride from Disneyland.

This era is also where the concept of Earth-based male sex domination began, which copied the Nefilim rules of civilization. This game of life requires a king to rule the community of the living, not a woman. A woman can actually rule only if her king lets her do so. But a male then can only royally rule if they have the mother's blood for the blue-blooded line of pharaohs and kings.

It is important we all understand so we can continue this exposé of where the terms New World and Olden World come from. It is here and now. The three land categories of Edin, Egypt, and Abzu we just went over were referred to as the Olden World. The New World as a term was applied to those in the Andes regions and the rest of the Western Hemisphere that would soon escape the Ice Age.

Act Five, Part Three, Scene Three: The Need For a Smarter Mankind Model

This division of the Olden World and the growing population of Nefilim-Anunnaki Earth children created the need for the civilized slave worker. The new model being was needed to perform the task of keeping the few satisfied with something to do during their spare time. So what they did was continue to build their urban centers for the rich and royal families and friends to create a society of arts and create a culture. But building a new society, we have learned studying our history, is based on physical and domestic slave labor.

Now the Nefilim-Anunnaki with extra time on their side started soliciting the female race of mankind. Male Anunnaki started producing babies with female Earthlings. It was no longer just a King Anu family thing. The offspring became a different race from the existing ones of mankind. They were part Anunnaki and mankind DNA with a consciousness that somehow got trapped inside these bodies by something Enki and his son and sister knew how to do. This new race wanted the privilege of the Anunnaki. They knew they were more than just a creation to serve. They were the demi-Nefilim-gods whose physical bodies were made from Earth.

Even though they had female servant or slave blood, they still had Nefilim-Anunnaki genes. They were soon to be those who would try and rule the Earthlings.

Now remember the civilization of Mars and those who lived there as Igigi? Well as we read, they came to Earth when Mars's spaceport was closed, and on Earth they multiplied—right outside the Palace of the Chariots in Egypt, Marduk's exclusive territory. The Igigi did not follow the rules and resulting order from Nibiru and their civilization's guidelines. They wanted control of the missiles in Sinai. So war for land ensued. Marduk, it is written, lost two sons in the battles of the half-human, half-Nefilim/Igigi half-breeds.

Remember as we continue these stories are culminations of many Earth years. Not years we can understand as we are used to mankind years.

While these family squabbles continued, Enlil was worried about the safety of the spaceport. So Enlil, without permission from Nibiru, created a second spaceport. This new spaceport was built to the lands beyond the sea that were Ninurta's lands. The port was built in the Lake of the Mountains, a.k.a., Lake Titicaca. This is when the Nazca plain we spoke of earlier with its landing strip marks was first used by the Nefilim for Nibiru (Heaven) to Earth-Eridu flights.

Now getting very philosophical, I must share that by having offspring, a.k.a., children, we create a need to have them serve us and look for something to give them to do. Woman and man share energies of their unique body parts and create that energy that uses the female body and creates life and gives us more children. The more we get the more we must divide what we have to take care of our children. This division of papa and mama's possessions do create the dark energies of greed with envy and the ability to create the desire to murder to protect our domain.

Children are not always a good thing to have in unlimited numbers. And we have learned this truth constantly by watching what mankind does when the population grows and living space for that expanding community of people must be found. Everyone needs their own space in physical form.

This review of the Nefilim on Earth shows this truth. Makes me wonder what the Nefilim did to stop population explosions on Nibiru.

The Catholic Church (Church) has a system with understanding that there must be a limit of children so inheritance does not divide the Church's physical properties by family today. The Church is a male paradise. One cannot marry nor can one acknowledge children. The property the Vatican owns is communal. The Church owns it, not the individuals of the Church. There is no inheritance.

The Church had the books of Earth's history as written by Enki, and the way the Church is run is to make sure it withstands the dark side of human wants and property needs. The Church knew the history of the Nefilim on Earth as the Nefilim wrote their history and left those records here on Earth for future beings to discover. The Church share not as equals but in a caste system of caste equals, and no family can claim this is all theirs. The Church is really the first communist commune. The 1 percent of Cardinals who vote in an electoral college control all the others and that 1 percent lives and abides by its gold taught rules. It is also why the woman are not given a position of any real control.

Please ask yourselves, why are we alive? For whom and for what purpose? What is the end game of physical life?

Enki's Book of Earth also finally shared stories about love and romance. The good, the bad, and the ugly. Here is the story of one royal romance gone wrong on Earth.

We are now about to enter the territory of families and their stories of ruling order.

Act Five, Part Four
The Age of Cancer

Act Five, Part Four, Scene One: The First Royal Family Civil War

A little background on these lovers and their royal families for you as I recount the feelings we call love and what it can do to the families of the lovers.

Dumuzi was Enki's youngest and, it is written, cherished son. Dumuzi, so the story goes, was sensitive, caring, and very artistic.

Inanna was Enlil's Nefilim blood daughter. She was beautiful beyond description, as well as extremely competitive and artistic. Inanna was also known as Isis in some of the coming ancient societies that existed with mankind at the helm. Inanna is not Ishtar, Enki's granddaughter, and do know they get mixed up in our moving myths of Earth.

In our myths soon to be created, both are referred to as the Goddess of Love. Venus was her name, as well as many others. Inanna was a peacemaker between warring properties too. Whatever Inanna wanted, Inanna got. This is not yet her age. She is the Age of Gemini.

Inanna and Dumuzi were strangers in their night. Exchanging glances, they fell in the energies of love, now the desires for physical sex with love before their night was through. They were totally in love. There was nothing one would not do for the other.

And here is what love can do when you are competing for your exclusive by family birthright position in a very cruel world. Maybe here is where we have some social orders saying first cousins cannot marry, although first cousins did marry in Queen Victoria's time. These first cousins became king of the UK and Germany called the kaiser and the King of Russia called the czar. These three caused World War I. Look how many people died fighting for their king.

Dumuzi was given his own lands to rule by Enki located above the Abzu. The land had buffalo and cattle, Enki's domestic animal creations, to feed the people not just meat but cheeses and other mammal delights. The domesticated animals we still eat today, I believe, for the most parts are all scientist lab or cloned creations of Enki and team.

This land of Dumuzi was very close to Marduk's Egypt. And the older brother Marduk was naturally jealous of his younger brother Dumuzi. Marduk was jealous of not just the land grants, but Dumuzi was being pushed by his spouse Inanna to compete for different chores that Enki was just giving to his brother Marduk without considering that maybe Dumuzi could do it better.

So Marduk's current reality of being top dog of his generation was now put into a contest by a younger brother motivated by wanting a bigger role in the Anunnaki Earth world order by his spouse Princess Inanna. And that motivation was strong. So, what does big brother Marduk do? Let's set the younger brother up in a sex act with another lover and show this unfaithful act to Inanna. The act of disruption to Dumuzi's happy wife and therefore his happy life. A very sick play to be played out.

The director of this play is Marduk. The male actor unknowingly is Dumuzi, and the female lead of part one is Marduk's half-sister

Geshtinanna. The evil brother Marduk gets his half-sister to commit the act of having sex with a committed spouse, with the promise that the offspring of this sexual act would inherit the throne because of their line of seed. This would make Geshtinanna the queen's mother if this was England.

Geshtinanna was the sex object Marduk used to help him end the relationship of his brother Dumuzi and his relative Inanna.

The sister was a simple sister in her ways of seduction, and she got dreamer boy in bed. It is written that Dumuzi, while committing the breach of sexual exclusivity, flipped out and ran away. While running, he slipped and fell on a rock in the river and died in this unforeseen accident.

Enki learned of his son's death. It is written that he said in grief, "Why am I punished, why has fate turned against me?" Although the Nefilim had everlasting life here on Earth, we do learn that they do die from unforeseen accidents. My son Barron died the same unforeseen way in this life of mine. You flip out inside, and then if you have wisdom and know the truths of life, then and with remorse and forever-silent tributes, you just move on. But straight up moving on is hard. I tried in my own way to help the others survive this tragedy. It is hard. So, I can only imagine what Enki had to learn to deal with then and there.

His son was full Nefilim-blooded as his mother was Ninki who was full-blooded Nefilim too. Meaning subject to eternal Nefilim life. But we read that he was not brought back to life. Dumuzi was not brought back to life by any ME machine as Horus of Egyptian folklore would be written about. This boy was dead. The father freaked out. Ripped his clothes in grief, and this ripping in grief became a Hebrew tradition. Enki also put ashes on his forehead, a Catholic tradition of mourning. Get it?

Now Inanna had a sister named Ereshkigal. Ereshkigal was very jealous of her sister Inanna and her given position in the Nefilim-

Anunnaki celebrityhood world of fame and eternal fortune. Ereshkigal now offered to help Inanna find Dumuzi. In written prose, we learn that this is one evil sister as Ereshkigal poisoned her sister Inanna with the first Earth witchcraft potion.

Ereshkigal lived in the lower world Abzu territory and was known as the Mistress of the Lower World. That lower world is near today's Central Africa. It is where the African religions of potions and magic comes from in our world today. She announced to Marduk's team that her half-sister Inanna was plotting to destroy Marduk and therefore she must go. Ereshkigal trying to side with Marduk now proceeded to try and kill her half-sister Inanna.

It's time for witchcraft. So, this potion had sixty diseases. Again, the first Earth witchcraft came out of what today we call Central Africa. The potion was released, and Inanna disappeared.

As I write this, I see the slave creations called African man watching the exploits of this superman Nefilim race. They do not know what is going on. They are freaking out and they create their stories to explain the behavior that they witness. The tablets are helping me connect the myths of mankind with the truths of where these myths began and how because this knowledge was withheld that I am sharing now, we were allowed to believe untruths so those who now control us do so with fear and perpetuated ignorance. Hopefully this book will allow all of you to end the superstitions of religions. This book explains the gods of their old and their new world.

Enlil freaked out. "Where is Inanna," he yelled to himself and everyone else that was in hearing range. No answer. So, what does this loving, creative Lord of Command do? He got his half-brother Enki to create a machine without physical limitations to find Inanna through DNA scent. Drones were created like we have in our world today. Drones with the power of scent!

The drones that, according to others, resembled the mythical creations of Greek and Roman mythology called Erinyes of Furies, found the lifeless body of Inanna. What does Enki do?

Well, our world's best scientist, it is written, administered the cure. Boy, I wish we as a race looked for the cures instead of digging for oil, which Earth buried for a reason.

The cure was the Water of Life, which was sprinkled on the nude body of Inanna. The skin absorbed the essence and got the body moving again after the Plant of Life was placed into the throat so the plant could work its magic and bring the body to life before the consciousness returned to the eternal matrix of collective consciousness that everything comes from and goes back too. If you go back to that eternal consciousness of all, you cannot return as what you once were in this matrix.

Now this game played by Marduk morphed into a civil war of the royals on Earth. The war of the Earthlings Enlilites versus the Earthling Enkites! You see the birth of Israelites or the superrace called the Nubians. You see they have different skin colors? The original Nubians created for Enki on his ranch of Eastern Africa lands that once had a superrace of mankind until the DNA got diluted and watered down by birth were dark skinned.

The side of Enlil wanted Marduk dead. Enki's side had a problem. Marduk caused the play to begin, but he was not the one who caused the death. In our legal system today, Marduk might be liable for making the play begin, but he might be set free as he was not responsible for the unintended death, which was caused by the departed running away and falling to his death as an unintended act of the crime.

We can argue both sides. The departed never would flee if he was not set up. Yes, he may have been set up, but where is the crime? The departed was the one who took his dick out when he should not have strayed. So, is it okay to stray? Thoughts that one must figure out to enact a code of law and order for all or just for the few. Questions do we make different laws for the masses, not the elite. The endless questions of society rules and resulting order are the laws so created for whom and why?

Questions that will never get an answer! Life is complicated but everyone has a personal view as the game is played. Safe or out? Replay? Not with life.

Enki's side had a problem in our tale, which can now be read as a Romeo and Juliet tale. Juliet (Inanna) blamed Romeo's (Dumuzi's) death on her lover's family, not Enlil's. Inanna was going to get revenge, and so the world turned and turned to a new equilibrium.

Inanna challenged Marduk to a duel. Just like Alexander Hamilton versus Aaron Burr, only these two had more than old fashioned pistols to kill one another with a lot of collateral casualties at the same time. *Star Wars* begins! And since Earthlings could not yet write and could create only oral tales, imagine the oral stories so created by the witnesses living then watching the Nefilim gods fight it out.

The tablets give us their version of this story written by those who knew and who we now know. Marduk headed north! To Giza is where he ran. Now he changed direction and went to hide out in the Great Pyramids. Which one? Well, the one with the chambers of course. The Great Pyramid, which was then called Ekur.

The pyramid proved it was indestructible to everything except human theft. The weapons of Inanna did not pierce the stone. Now we have the James Bond chase scene inside the halls of wonder and with its secret passages and dropping doors to close off invasion.

The pearl inside was the great pulsating stone. The crystals were hidden in a chamber where the pulsating stones activated the lights necessary that once shining in space would lead a traveler of the skies to Earth. This chamber was where Marduk hid out. Locked in.

Locked away, Marduk could die from not getting the water or food, as living physical life, including the Nefilim we now surmise, needs food and water. Sides are drawn. Let him out or let him die.

To the rescue was the Solomon of that time. Ninharsag ended the deadlock with his judicial decision. The solution was to divide the land-world even more. To this day the issue created here and then reverberates. These Nefilim made a mess, and we are too ignorant and fearful to learn the truth. We are worshiping our slave owners, not the Source of All Creation, what I call the Supreme Being. The Pulsating Energy of All Life.

Marduk was to be placed into exile as Ka-in was before in these Nefilim rules of order. But first Marduk had to be taken out of the hideout, which he could not do. So to the rescue comes Ningishzidda. The architect himself cut a doorway in the stone so Ninurta, Inanna's brother, could get Enki's wayward son.

Once Marduk was out of the chamber, the crystals were examined. There were twenty-seven crystals of Nibiru, we are told. Apparently, upon examination, it is said that a few were damaged and pulverized. The good ones were kept but the bad ones replaced. They were not put back into the chamber. This chamber was left empty. And the myths about the chamber with our wild imagination are left in space. Stories after stories about what was there and what happened to it.

The answer is in the book/tablets themselves. The crystals were moved to the mountaintop near the Celestial Chariots, Mount Sinai in our world, the domain of Enlil.

ACT FIVE, PART FOUR, SCENE TWO: THE PEACE TREATY

Now back to Earth and the resolution. Enlil and Enki had to create new titles and new areas of lordship or princedom as the British called the sons and daughters of their royal king or queen as the UK has today in their Queen Elizabeth children and grandchildren world order. Look what the British do when they need a title for a grandchild.

The big change was Marduk lost Egypt. Ningishzidda got what we call Egypt. Inanna demanded her place under the Sun. She got it. Inanna got the Indus Valley as the population of these Aryans, half Nefilim and half mankind, version two or maybe three, were growing and needed to be put in order.

As for my curious students of history, this is the region of the Kama Sutra sexcapades. Inanna was the Anunnaki sex goddess. This is how the Kama Sutra began. The sixty-four arts of love with pleasure and passion! Sounds like a song.

The history of this Indus region and their Hindu practices, which I call a religion, are in prose. The Vedic praises to the gods, that is. Inanna was the queen of poetry, as we learned before. I believe it was she who created or at least produced this art with her staff of worshippers and fans.

Things on Earth were getting strange now. Anunnaki were not the majority anymore. There was the intermix children as well as plenty of new Earthlings of different time creations running around.

The growing population was getting hungry and restless. Obedience was needed so the gods themselves could regain control of their pets and half-breeds. I am talking like this because this is the mindset of our creators. We were never anything more. Just a pet that one could love or abuse. One to serve but not one to serve. The scripture says the gods wanted to remain lofty over the humans. How do we keep them observant?

Act Six
The Creation of the Earthling Civilizations in Edin, Egypt, and Elsewhere

Act Six, Scene One: The Visit of the Nefilim Royals King Anu and Queen Antu

This takes place in the Age of Gemini.

King Anu and his Queen Antu came to Earth to create and then orchestrate the new fate of mankind. It is important that we understand the Nefilim now believed that the Nefilim were the creator beings whose job was to create a new species of physical animal to administrate Earth. Really, using other words, the emissary acting out the roles the Supreme Being wanted them to do. This issue has two sides to the thought as Geminis supposedly do.

Choice one: their Earth actions were predetermined and called their fate.

Or choice two: their actions were determined by their decisions done in line with their concept of the Supreme Being's intention. This I call destiny.

These questions really to figure out in a very high plateau what to do are decisions of fate versus destiny. The final decision of what the planet Nibiru should do was made by a Nefilim parliament of fellow lords of their sky. A unanimous vote was given for the Nefilim to give mankind their own civilization modeled on Nibiru.

Anu the king and Antu his queen had not seen their children in a bit of time. The kids were looking older than the parents. So it is said. While coming down in this era of Earth time, mama and papa said to their sons and daughters, "Do not worry that your Earth years have you looking older than us. For when you get back to Nibiru, we have the cures to get you back to your Nibiru state of aging."

Why the trip to Earth? To make a decision about how to proceed with their Earthling creation called mankind. It was obvious to the ruling crew that mankind would survive. It is said in the book that the will of the Supreme Being Creator is clear to see. Earth belongs to the Earthlings. But what are the Earthlings? Slaves to work for us? Yes, a lesser race that needs to be shown how to build a society. Why? Because they were now too many to exclusively rule so the parents needed helpers. Hence the creation of urban civilization.

How do they survive? It is now the job of the Nefilim gods to help mankind survive before the Nefilim gods leave Earth.

The first Earthling cities of networks as a federation began with rules and order for different cities. The country area outside the cities was left on its own. The division of rural life on Earth as outsiders began. Those on the inside lived now in urban cities with suburbs. Soon these urban networks would be centralized as empires. In time the urban cities and the rural areas would then be absorbed into nations as mankind led its own destiny. That is ahead of our current story. For now, the urban cities are the thing. In the cities is where mankind is trained to obey its local Nefilim rules and resulting order.

Back to the visit.

Enlil and Enki took care of their dad. They built Anu a new palace in the middle of Edin. This new home was called Unug-ki. The name means "the delightful place."

Enlil built a new home in his region where the old Nibru-ki stood before the flood. It is written that this was a seven-step ziggurat pyramid. This was Enlil's stairway to Heaven. Also, seven is their magic number for Earth as the gateway to Earth required going past six planets before they reached Earth. Remember Nibiru circling the Sun from the outside planets and then crosses our airspace as it goes inside the inner planets of our common solar system.

The Led Zeppelin "Stairway to Heaven" song now plays as a tune in my head. This book I pray makes those lyrics a prophecy. All that glitters is gold. But it's whispered that soon, if we all hear the metaphysical tune, then the piper will lead us to reason. And a new day will dawn for those who stand long. And the forest will echo with laugher. This book must help us as a collective consciousness end our inbred fears called beliefs in the gods of our creation who we learned are not the Supreme Source of existence and everything else. We all come from the same Supreme Source. Our first parent is not male or female but the Creator of thought and action, the Supreme Being.

Enki built his new home where the first Nibiru home once stood. The area was known to them as Abyssinia, which in our recent translations of these scripts in the Bible is called Ethiopia. It was administered by primitive workers called Nubians. I am repeating myself so we all get the truth. The Africans came from our so called common first mother, Lucy, the mother of mankind whom the Nefilim called Lulu. Lulu, we must remember, was a male species, as we have learned, that could not reproduce.

I feel right now is the appropriate moment to share evolution or creation of mankind. Darwin was right in his hypothesis of the evolution of life. However, regarding all life Darwin was not aware of this story of mankind. The Bible was right. We were created in the image of our gods called the Nefilim, not the Supreme Being. We all come from one source. Our consciousness comes from the one source whom the Nefilim called the Creator and I call the Supreme Pulsating Being. Our consciousness as a group left the Supreme loving womb to experience our own creation called physical life. We are from a collective consciousness, which we then break away from to have our own individual living experience in physical form.

Getting right into the heart of this debate, evolution or creation, I must give you the following known data. All life on Earth—again, all life on Earth—comes from one source of DNA. Our human genes have been scientifically proven to be identical with the function of producing amino acids and proteins to the genes of not just vertebrates but also the invertebrates and plants as well as fungi and even yeast. This is the naked truth, as I say.

These findings have allowed scientists to trace the evolution process from the simple to the complex organisms living here on Earth. We who are the most complex organisms here on Earth that we know about to date. I dare not bring up the dolphins as they are from somewhere else. But we humans can do more physical things than any other. And what we cannot do, we know we can figure out a substitute that can do it for us. Like live under the seas or fly in our air.

Now as we the humans raced to discover the codes of human DNA in the 1990s, it was discovered that we humans have 223 genes that do not have any predecessors on the Earth genomic evolution tree. These genes were found to be missing in the entire known and charted evolution of vertebrates.

These genes, the scientists admit, involve the important physiological and cerebral functions exclusive to man. The difference between us and the chimpanzees is almost three hundred genes. Those extra genes are all of the 223 previously mentioned.

So now the question goes, without evolution, were those genes placed inside our DNA? This book answers that question with a yes.

This creation is too much for the scientists to admit because they cannot physically prove it. Well, can you prove you love your significant other? No. Your actions do, but a physical defined product does not exist. We cannot see and touch everything. Some things we can only see or mentally feel, and that is our metaphysical truth.

Someone gave us non-Earth-based created genes. And this gift explains the sudden appearance of mankind. And we were tinkered and tailored more than once. Which explains Neanderthal and Cro Magnon as well as the difference between our DNA acting in different specimens of mankind with different diseases around our globe even today. We are all from the same model but different engines. This book is how we became what we are today. This book is dedicated to opening our minds so we can collectively leave the world of servitude and build our Heaven here on Earth for Earthlings. Not gods from their land called Nibiru who created us so they can be served by us in their campground called Earth. That simple. That true.

But before I go back to the story, I must share with you what the scientists with their alleged high IQs said to explain this new collection of Earth-grown genes. The scientists say these genes got into our bodies by a horizontal-linear transfer of genes. We were infected by a bacterium, which also cannot be found. The bacterium gave us these genes.

Maybe the bacterium was the same as the Nefilim I write about here, who said, "Let's create an Earthling in our image that has the capability to do what we need them to do, but not become us." However, in time we can become them. How? Let's evolve together and understand the who and the what as well as why of mankind. Let's take back our living game of life.

Now that lesson is inside our heads, and I will continue the tale of mankind for all of us to learn and grow as one family of mankind, without religion but with the Supreme Pulsating Being who wants us to become all we can become with love as our beacon of light.

Act Six, Scene Two: The Coming Age of Taurus. Maybe 7,200 Earth Years Ago The Creation of Imperial Religions The Creation of Imperial Governments

So now the worship of the gods of our creation begins. The worship is needed to keep the Earthlings in line and do as they are told. Fear of those in power is one way to keep a society in line with the resulting law and order.

Enki, in the tablet scriptures, volunteers to educate the Earthlings and lift them up to be civilized. Enki also was the one who started the Schools of Sacred, now Secret Knowledge. Enlil and Marduk were the opposite. Enlil wanted peace so he could finish his chores and leave Earth with peace. This was his coming age. Enlil was the Taurus, and he was now in charge of Earth besides being the Lord of Command as Anu granted him hundreds of thousands of Earth years ago.

This is so hard to understand because we understand life in body form only by what we see and know others have experienced. We cannot begin to understand beings who can live forever in our understanding of life.

As we learned, with the temples came the priestly order of humans who were selected to know the secrets of the Nefilim on an as-needed basis. With the priests came the Earth kings who would rule as directed by their god. Their god who owned their lands, which the humans were to toil under and serve, not be served.

The above is really the beginning of the Old Testament. And this actually took place around 7,200 years ago. The Bible does not yet begin, but soon it will. Why? Because now the Nefilim decided to really civilize man, and that would take some time to play with mankind's DNA to make it happen.

Why the beginning? Because Earthlings now were taught how to use their brains in menial tasks. They would write what they were told or remember what they heard. They were not taught yet to dream and be idealistic. That development would come.

Enki taught Earthlings how to write, how to farm, and what to farm for their own profit. And here I feel is where the food was changed, which changed our life expectancy as the years in the Old Testament get shorter and shorter. The first genetically modified foods.

The elders of our Bible did live many more Earth years than we do now. They had different genes. Different planet-based mother DNA too.

The plants we eat and use on our bodies are where we can change our lives. The plants are the elixir of life. If the plant can extend, it can shorten life too. The Nefilim brought their Nibiru domesticated feeding plants to Earth, as we said before. But not all of them; only what was needed to run a society of humans with a shorter life-span than the Nefilim.

Please do remember the animals we eat need to eat the plants that we choose to feed them, which are the same plants we eat. Disease runs rampant here, and I believe this is where we lose the longer life-spans. And this is the beginning of Earth-based diseases.

The kingship of Earthlings, it is written, must have a crown and scepter as we do in Nibiru. So here begins the tradition of the first and second estate of governments and their religions and their armies to protect their way of life.

Now in this Earth era, King Anu wanted to see his grandson Marduk in his latest exile from the Olden World. So first the crew went to learn what El Dorado was all about. They were off to Peru/Bolivia.

A palace for King Anu is built near Lake Titicaca, which may not have been created by the Nefilim. The palace was covered with gold. Even, it is said, the statues and flowers were gold painted if not made up of gold.

At this new palace, King Anu was taught the new metal of Earth—a metal called bronze. Bronze is made of tin and copper, which was found all over the Earth. This knowledge was shared with Earthlings, and this is the rise and fall of the world-traveling Minoan civilization during the age our history of Earth calls the Bronze Age. This age is represented by a bull. So is the Age of Taurus, during which Enlil was the ruler of Earth. I am connecting dots.

Ever wonder why we find bull statues around the world in our archeological discoveries? Wonder no more. The humans traveling the world for the bronze creation and distribution network, which traveled by sea, brought with them their Nefilim god and that god's astrological sign, which was the bull. We will learn this Nefilim god is my spiritual friend Enlil. In Act Thirteen, I share our bonding.

Marduk, who was up in our land we call Central America, came to meet his grandpa Anu in today's Peru and the lake they called Anak, not Lake Titicaca. This name means something in the societies of the Andes region. The Bolivians call Anak the father of the giants.

Marduk, during this time period, was busy building societies in what today we call Central America. Marduk populated this area with Earthlings who were moved north from the region of La Paz and Lake Titicaca. Under Marduk's supervision, I believe they built their society based on gold. I believe the flying serpent god whom these people of this region worshiped was in fact his dad Enki who came to check in on his exiled son.

The Aztec Empire and Mayans had their bird gods. Enki, I believe, is the god that the natives called Huitzilopochtli. This is their god of Sun and war. These societies of the New World were also civilized to build and survive by the Nefilim family feuds of this era.

The written picture stories of their own creation were deliberately destroyed with intent by the Vatican and their conquistadors in the 1500s. Why? So we Earthlings would not know nor ever understand the creation and growth of this Andean and Aztec-Mayan civilization's past. We do not even know about the sites one can find in Oaxaca where I did go to learn about the Zapotec civilization.

King Anu, on this visit, felt pity for Marduk and pardoned the lad. This was all Marduk needed to begin to plot his return. The phoenix that would rise from the ashes to rule our Olden World urban orders world with his laws and his disorder. Marduk was the ram, and the Age of the Ram was the next sign to control Earth in about 2,000 years, which was the time of Abraham and Moses.

This last interaction with King Anu here on Earth time was, as I said, about 7,000 Earth years ago. Our 5000 BC. In the timeline of Nibiru, that is two Shar. Again, a hard concept for us to understand. Everything is relative and, in my mind, my vision all comes together as one big story of living creation here on Earth and back in Nibiru.

King Anu instructed his princely crew to give mankind limited knowledge of the stars and the sky, which you could see if you really looked with open eyes inside the Mayan calendar. Give them laws of justice, which is what they needed inside the cities of Edin. "Righteousness teach them," were his words.

And the result of this edict was the coming religious gods wars fought over righteousness. But for whom?

King Anu, it is written, then departed.

Well, those words said by Anu were 7,000 Earth years ago. Again, in Nefilim time, two Shars. Where are the Nefilim and their space traveling Anunnaki? Gone are they, or are they still here?

The stories I will now share are now told in these tablets on Earth times.

Act Six, Scene Three: The Bible Era
Mankind From Above is Given the Nefilim Rules to Govern Themselves and Have a Predictable Resulting Order That Will Run Earth for the Nefilim

We have entered the era of the confusing Bible. The Bible, which is a mix of the stories, forms the point of view of the two gods Enlil and Marduk. Really the Era of the Taurus Bull Enlil and the Aries Ram Marduk. So do know the Bible was not a true running account of Earth time as it was written at different times with different agendas.

Everyone has an agenda. I do too. I just never understood why we can't all be friends. Now I do. And I write to show you why that sentence is true. Because when you understand the game of our story and see that what you have learned is written to control your emotions so you believe in the writer's system that separates and divides, you will understand why we can't be friends.

I write to forgive and unite. Time for the promised Jubilee.

I write to unite, and I write to give a solution so we can all build a paradise here on Earth and make this the love planet. Not sex, but love. Giving and taking so we live in our hearts, not fear so we want more than we need. And with fear we team up to take it instead. With real love we are building a team to create it. Love-based community of mankind. Our magical twenty-fourth chromosome, the Supreme Being of Everything and more!

THE BIBLE ERA begins.

Now back to Earth.

Mankind is about to start writing its own history using the tales of Enki's past as if these events happened yesterday in mankind's sense of time. This may be true in the Nefilim sense of time, but as we just saw, the preceding tales are four hundred thousand Earth years old. In Nefilim time, that is only 111.1 years around the Sun. We need to understand that truth. Humans cannot begin to conceive that other beings can live as long as the Nefilim-Anunnaki gods did here on Earth. They believed these gods fell to Earth, and when they left Earth, went to Heaven in the sky to have their eternal lives. That truth is so important to understand as you unravel the Bible and try to figure out the times these events happened. For here on our timeline these events are written by man on Earth's time of Earthlings.

The Nefilim, living on Earth and following King Anu's advice, wanted to each be the kingpin of Earth man. This desire is why we have different gods and different beliefs. We call those gods the big "G" God. It needs to stop, my friends. We need to learn the truth of how what we do know all comes from the misunderstanding that the Anunnaki were combined into one and that one gets misunderstood in translations to one god. THE ONE GOD. They were not the one God. They were the Nefilim, which means gods. And these gods all came from the same Supreme Energy Source. And yes, they created our physical bodies.

The Bible is nothing more than a collection of stories of royal Nefilim family feuds. Where brothers and sisters are fighting with each other over control of how we build a society for mankind and the desire of a certain being we call Nefilim or half human, half Nefilim demigods who want to be worshiped for teaching mankind how to live. That is as long as the species stayed as slaves to the Nefilim god's rhythm.

The best way to understand the creation of society is to envision what the Romans did when they went about building their roads of commerce and trade. The Romans created outposts with local leaders chosen to rule in conformance with the Roman-appointed governor for that region. Then when the big boys came in, everyone made sure the big boss was satisfied and kept happy. Festivals were held in the boss's honor, and whole communities would appear to sit and be happy that the boss came to town and that the little old "me" got to say to the boss I love you and thank you.

So, building the Olden World to have a society, the big two, Enlil and Enki, gave powers to field generals of sorts to build the community. Every community had their temples where the local folks could come worship their gods and their god of the territory.

Each city and the resulting towns and villages were to build a temple to serve the gods. Churches were not around then and grew from the communities. Communities where the community folks living in rural areas without the gods of the urban Nefilim/Anunnaki-built cities in attendance. The church in these rural areas being the center is where people would gather and share the gospel (news) from the east and the west, from the north and the south. The crossing of life. The church was the center.

The Catholic Church calls itself Catholic because it means "true church." Catholic in Latin translated to English means "true." Get it! Absolute power play and resulting power control over all of us. And hear this in your minds: if one of us believes and we interact with you, those wrong beliefs do affect you. How? Because you respond to the fear and ignorance that the followers of that belief impose on you.

The Vatican's church was brilliant in a very wrong way to create the villains of the church. For if you want power to control as opposed to share, you must then divide. So, you make your side *us* and you make the other side *them*. You lose the *we*. You lose Team Earth.

The religious holidays of the Nefilim on Earth were built around the Earth's seasons of life. These holiday seasons number eight. The winter and spring and summer and fall with the halfway point being a lesser but still a holiday. A day for the pets of the Nefilim Animal Farm to serve their masters and thank their Nefilim gods and lords for giving them life and substance. A festival would also occur. Each festival had a manager. Those managers were called priests. The priests reported to their producer, the local Nefilim ruling god. The local god set the play. The managers called priests were the actors as well as the directors.

Before this local god took the stage and spoke to the attending flock, a green room was prepared to see and greet the local man authorities. Offerings were brought. Backstage, food and drink were given. The stage was the temple where an audience could gather and make their scarifies to their Nefilim god. In truth, it was just one big rock 'n' roll show. A show I know very well how to stage and move on down the road.

The priests would keep their jobs as long as the god was looked after. The priest was the go-between for the gods and the people. This is all religion is today. The priests are also today known as rabbis and imams and cardinals and bishops. These selected few try to keep favor with the now-imaginary God's rules of antiquity and keep the crowds of the living in line with this ancient game of ownership and control.

The rulers now started teaching the people called mankind how to build and keep society moving and growing with the basic needs of survival. The people were taught how to make bricks to make buildings (masonry). They were taught how to write and speak one local common language. They were taught math to a limited degree. They were taught agriculture. Basically, this was the beginning of an arts and science curriculum.

Then the vocations side was taught too. The vocations of that time were to feed and clothe the people. How to farm and how to feed the people were the first two. Then came clothes as a uniform before styles. Then how to make wheels and chariots to transport goods and people. If you notice, this was not done in the local areas of the Incas and their mountain ranges.

With a mankind population growing, the Nefilim needed rules and regulations for the pets called mankind. So, with this need the legal system came into being. This legal system of justice, it is written, began in the city of Sippar, in a place called Ebabbar. Translated, the name means "the shining house."

Here is how the Nefilim created our civilized societies' rules and order based on their Nibiru rules and resulting order.

The Beginning of Mankind's Kingship

A king was chosen at first to rule the lands under the control of the Nefilim royal family, who called themselves gods, and the priest. It was said, "Let's bestow kingship of crown and scepter on humankind." This crown was given in the city of Kishi.

Ninurta called the first king of mankind mighty man. Kishi was called the Scepter City. The city that housed mankind king was just one of the five. The king was moved around to these five cities by the Nefilim stuck on Earth till they were authorized to leave. Only Marduk could not go home. Each city got to house the new king of mankind who reported to the then Earth-ruling Nefilim.

Soon the Nefilim gods would have their family feud and new kings would be chosen representing different gods. But right now, we had one king for the god's Olden World order. When we talk of god, it is a sky god who comes down in a chariot from the Heaven above. This is the Nefilim and planet Nibiru whom they call god and Heaven.

The ME was used to make each society workable in their own Earth environment. We must learn this truth. Each society needs rules for its habitat. Living as I do in London, New York, Miami, and LA, I know very well that one rule of order does not fit all. The Nefilim knew this and tried to live it.

Ninurta was in charge of the Sinai region. It was he who built this region, and he used the ME to help him create those local communities.

Inanna got her hands on the ME too. She used her sexual allure and seduced Enki to get these powers, we learn. Enki, according to the texts, had to admit he gave her the powers to his brother Enlil. Inanna used these powers, it is written, to build her Indus river region. Enlil gave in and then chose that the kingship would be moved from Kishi to Unugki, Inanna's given Indus region of control. As I said before, some energy made those seven mountains from the Middle East to India.

Now comes the Nefilim family dispute. The division of mankind. Marduk went berserk. Once again, he felt he was denied his rightful place of having all of mankind living on Earth ruled from his given territory by the division of responsibilities by the elders of Nibiru. Remember, Marduk could not leave to go home to Nibiru.

Act Six, Scene Four: The Tower of Babylon and Marduk's Run to Egypt

Marduk decided to take fate into his own hands and took control of the region where the region was reserved for his grandfather's visits, King Anu, on Earth. This region is Babylon. And this is how the Babylonian mystical and mythical folklore began.

This city needed bodies, so like the Catholic Church does to control regions when they wish to control the people, Marduk called for a pilgrimage of his Igigi Nefilim followers and their pet humans to Babylon.

Remember, Marduk lived on Mars and was the leader of the Igigi. They were his tribe not his by birth family. Marduk was at war with his birth family. So Marduk made this location the special place to know and serve the new Earth Nefilim god, and he now called himself the Nefilim of the Nefilim (god of the gods). This was to be The Sacred City and the city for the sky ships to travel to and from Nibiru.

The city under Marduk's usurpation or power was now being built to reach the sky. The tablets say they made clay brick and burned them by fire to serve as the stone. Babylon had no stone. A tower was being built to become the place where visitors to and from Nibiru would disembark on Earth.

The tablets go on to say Enlil the controlling balancer of Earth global order Nefilim (god) was not impressed. No, he was upset, and he pulled rank. What he did was take the tower to and from Nibiru down. There was only one to Nibiru. And that way was through Heaven, called Nibru.

Then Enlil set upon to create different regional languages so no one could get the populations stirred up as not everyone would speak with the same thoughts when voices came out of our tongues. He was not going to allow Marduk to wreck Earth and the Earthlings for his sick sport of killing the animals called Earthlings.

Marduk was the architect of the new Babylon. It was he who created the Hanging Gardens. The hanging gardens meant they were not being grown on Earth.

The total creation of the Ancient Seven (there is that number seven again) wonders of the world we must not wonder about anymore. They were created with the ingenuity of the Earth-based Nefilim known as Anunnaki. In fact, maybe the Nefilim also created the rainforests of our world. Some energy planted the seeds that enabled carbon to be used and create the beauty and joys of the various rainforests around our globe. The Nefilim-Anunnaki planted this Earth we live in with intention to create the beauties we still see as we live here on Earth.

I hear some of you saying this can't be. Why is this knowledge hidden from us? It's not hidden, it's like a song that has yet to be heard. It's like the tree that fell in the forest, but no one sees it down yet. These truths are all around us. Just look up the Baghdad battery, which our US troops took from the Baghdad museum during our second invasion of Iraq in 2003. Experts say this battery was at least 2,000 years old. An electric battery!

Act Six, Scene Five: Egypt and Central America in the Age of Taurus.

Now with the forced exile from Babylon, Marduk decided to go make his mess in another region of which he could claim authentic permission. The region is Egypt, and now the story of the civilization and its priestly order of control and ensuing battles for top dog begins. We the people were the pawns in the Nefilim chessboard of their time building societies here on Earth.

Marduk went back to Egypt and discovered that his younger half brother Ningishzidda had grabbed control. This had to be changed, and change is what Marduk brought to the community at this time.

Ningishzidda (Ning) was in control of Northern Egypt and the Nile regions as well as Red Sea had banished Marduk, a.k.a., Horus, here in the area we call Upper Egypt and its white sands Egyptian desert. This region is southern Egypt. This move explains the two Egypts. The brothers fought for about 350 Earth years over controlling the region; Marduk won when Egypt was united. This union took place under the Scorpion King, also known as Marduk, who united Upper and Lower Egypt. In Earth time, this would be about 3100 BC, which fits perfectly with the rise of the Egyptian Empire.

Enki got involved and tried to stop the family civil war. Enki convinced Ningishzidda to leave Lower Egypt and move to the new world, the land they call beyond the seas.

Please note how the sea is called the Atlantic. We are then told about Atlantis, a mythical city. We learn about the myth of Atlas. The As in our world come from the Anunnaki, who wished to take control of Earth's history, and these names with the As are all from the Nefilim-Anunnaki world.

Atlantis is real and not a myth—sure makes sense now, at least to me. The Nefilim made up oral stories of Earth's history of previous living beings and needed to erase the light of the Atlanteans using names and oral stories, such as creating the second Thoth as if it was then the Nefilim who did everything, not the energies living on Earth of that time period of Atlantis who left when the darkness of the Nefilim became too dense. In Act Eight we will learn of the Atlanteans and how they left Earth for the Venus energies of space. This connection with Atlantis and the Anunnaki is something for others to explore while reading these tablets.

Now remember that Ningishzidda is the architect of the big three pyramids as well as human DNA. Now he is called Thoth too. The son of Enki is consistently, like his dad Enki, referred to as the serpent. His logo is also the winged serpent. This is relevant for when we study the history of Central American indigenous peoples.

The Aztec god was called Quetzalcoatl. Quetzalcoatl was their god of wind, air, and learning. When the Vatican's killers came to the land we call Mexico in their silver suits of armor, the conquistadors were mistaken for being the army and soldiers of their god Quetzalcoatl. This is how Hernán Cortés was able to get close and then kill off the civilization that at this time of 1500 AD period probably had the best living lifestyle in our world.

The Aztecs thought their god had come back as he promised when he left. So they let their guard down and Cortés, in the name of Christ, the Vatican's version, killed all those beings who would not submit to the rule of the Red Cross.

The inhabitants of today's Central America back in pre-Vatican times, which we call pre-Columbian, were also known as the Olmecs. They did have African features. How did that happen? They were brought by Ningishzidda to help him build his pyramids in Mexico the same way the tribe helped him build the pyramids in Egypt. Even though he had ME to build the pyramids then, he still needed the help and service of animals like the humans the Nefilim so created.

How could the pyramids built on the same geometric proportions be in Mexico and Memphis, Egypt?

Simple. They were built by the same Nefilim species. But not at the same time. Mexico's version was built during the Age of the Bull.

The knowledge I am sharing is sacred knowledge. Sacred knowledge is basically the tales of where you come from. The people who control our current system of law and their resulting order know what I am writing, and they keep this knowledge secret from the masses. I am here to open our world to truths.

Let's go back to the Scorpion King myth. But the tablets let you know in no uncertain terms that the Scorpion King Narmer is real. This king worked and did what Marduk told him to do.

The pharaohs who came after the reign of the Scorpion King were all part of Marduk's required bloodline from the previous pharaoh's mother. A contender for the title of pharaoh had to have the same blood as the last pharaoh. This is demigod stuff. Mom was always to be the blood of the Nefilim.

This is where the Hebrew first then Jewish blood of a mother comes in. The Hebrews were Egyptian slaves of Marduk. To prove you were a Hebrew, the Hebrews copied the rules of how you are able to be a pharaoh. You had to have your mother's blood.

Here is a partial list of what Marduk did to transform Egypt into his land. And in doing so set us on a course of hate and destruction that still goes on today. All in the name of serving a god.

1. Marduk called himself the great god Ra. Ra in their language means "the bright one."

2. Apparently Ra changed the face on the lion sphinx to his son Asat's face. This was done to erase the memory of his brother Ningishzidda. However, the book of records stopped that game from happening eternally.

3. Ra decided he would have his own mathematical system. The Nefilim used to count with six being their magic base number. Marduk or Ra made the number ten the magic digit. We count in tens to this day, and here is where it all began.

4. The moon was how the Earth time was counted. But Egypt would now count time with the Sun. And so does our Western world of today. The moon worked because it had four viewing divisions. Those divisions are new moon, waxing moon, full moon, and waning moon. Each lasts for seven sunsets. So that is where the concept of the week comes from. The Sun had two. Daylight and darkness. So, every day is the same. No new Sun.

5. The Egyptian creator of religion went to Marduk. He created his order and required everyone that would rule to have the mother's bloodline.

6. Marduk also created the first concept of spies, which is similar to the KGB or Mossad. The group he chose was called the Neteru. They were Nefilim-Anunnaki gods themselves. And the name translates to the Watchers who watched the skies and the lands as well as any seas. What society calls scholars believe the Watchers to be the angels that the Bible

talks about. The Watchers lived and reported the events of the community to make sure Marduk stayed in control.

Some thoughts to share while I give all a break on the Anunnaki/Nefilim story. Rulers by birth are not the answer and never have been. That is what we see here. And history, which this series of books will show you, does not change. We need to have leaders by merit, not birth. However, there is the problem of ruling fathers as they think, "What do I do with my kids?" Got to give them property.

Charlemagne had three sons. When he died, his kingdom was divided into three separate Vatican-run territories. Charlemagne was the first German tribe First Reich regime. Remember, Hitler was the Third Reich. These three areas became, as we will discover, in Opus II where Marduk played his game in the name of Christ. The wars that went on in this kingdom are insane. It's insane how sons and grandchildren just kill each other to have the absolute control that their parent had. Something is wrong with our DNA that we still act like gorillas in the mist. They never stopped fighting in Europe. And I do believe Marduk was the dark energy that created the Christ who says you may kill for me and made the Jesus energy of love the missing figure of Christ the energy of control and death if you so disagree with the cross of the Vatican.

Now back to the Nefilim and our story.

The Egyptian pharaoh kings of this Nefilim-Anunnaki era were thought to be half gods—in the scriptures they are marked with a *d* before their name. This created a class system of priests and royalty ruling classes. One that we have not gotten over yet. Count the lands called nations that are ruled in form by a king and now sometimes a queen of birthright. This is where it begins. Now is where maybe it should end.

The problem with these rulers was they were not immortal, nor could they leave Earth and go to Nibru and then Nibiru, what mankind was taught by the Nefilim to call Heaven. Heaven is the place where you live with the Nefilim (gods) forever and ever more.

Enki never gave his son Marduk the formula for reviving the dead. And he never gave his son any visas for human space travel. Marduk's kings returned their bodies to Earth. The essence is something else. We do leave our bodies. If we cremate ourselves, I do believe you will end your DNA strings to Earth. Meaning you do not have to return to Earth in your newest reincarnation.

Enki did give his son certain information stored in the ME so the society of Egypt would be the top dog of its day. The ME helped Marduk. This info allowed Marduk, because he was then able, to control the flow of the Nile. This control allowed Marduk to be able to control farming and raising domestic animals. The ME shows you how using energies we do not yet know moves things around. Lapis lazuli and crystals were two materials that moved energies from the beyond around.

Feeding the people became a community project. The knowledge on how to do so became the community asset. But never did we learn that this type of project for the community, not just the individual, was really a community asset that must be owned by the community, not a class of citizenry.

Thank you, Enki, for keeping a record of what your Nefilim did here on Earth. Maybe we can learn naked truths.

Act Six, Scene Six: The Epic of Gilgamesh A Demi-God

One must understand the roots of the story of this king and why this story survived in the Middle East's sands of time. It is deliberately left out of the Judeo-Christian Bible.

Let's set the scene.

We are in the Middle East, north of today's Saudi Arabia and in today's Iraq. Northern Edin of the Nefilim time here on Earth.

Gilgamesh was from a 75-percent-pure Nefilim bloodline. The man was born to the female Nefilim goddess we know as Inanna. The father was Banda, who was half Nefilim (god) and half human. Banda's dad was Nefilim, and his mother was just an Earthling. Meaning Gilgamesh was born to be able to royally rule on Earth this time period but was not able to travel to Nibiru.

Inanna was the Venus of her day. Inanna is also the energy that the Egyptians would call Isis, and here is where the energy of Isis starts over again. This feline energy of Isis is the obsession of the Masons Order. The cities of Paris and Washington DC were created around the theme of Isis.

Inanna is also who Ninharsag named a constellation after, which we call Gemini. This era of Inanna rule would become known as the Age of Gemini—the twins. This age, we have learned, was about 6000–4000 BC. Inanna was both creative and very driven. The goddess had that energy of sexual desire. But we learned all this, so forgive me for repeating. But repeat I must as she is the most famous of all the Nefilim goddesses.

A quick review of Inanna. Inanna, at this time period, was in charge of the third region of the Olden World. This was the rise of the Indus region. The tablets describe the land as the land beyond the seven mountain ranges, which begin count at the base of Mount Sinai. The Indus Valley region is what we call it today.

Inanna's love of art and the need for physical sex rubbed off on the humans then living in her world of control. This is where the worship of stones began.

Her land, it is written in the tablets, is the land of the Sixty Precious Stones. Inanna loved stones and loved poetry. It must have been she who used the ME to create the language we call the Indus script, the language that the tablets say she created for her people to read and communicate so that others would not understand. This was done so a Marduk in the future could not unite and mobilize Earthlings to attack the Nefilim (gods) like he did again.

Not speaking the same language makes you different from the others who do speak the same language. Language separates us. So here the problem becomes speaking different languages makes you believe you are different from those who because of language cannot understand you. Throughout my life I have learned how to communicate with others when we speak and think in different languages. You learn to communicate with energy. I did this through song and dance.

When we study today this region and its Earth history, we come across the Indus script. We have yet to be able to translate it. The script is not yet deciphered. It was only used in this region. It does not appear anywhere else. There is no dual use of languages on any monuments in this region like we learned with Egypt and the Rosetta Stone.

The Rosetta Stone was found with three languages written on it. Those languages were Greek and Egyptian. The Egyptian had two forms. One form is hieroglyphic, and the second is demotic. This is how we deciphered the language of the Sumerians culture and their Samaritan tablets.

By the way, there are two forms of Samaritan dialect. One is Aramaic, which was used in the sacred and priestly educated classes who were trained by the Nefilim to speak the human languages and not the Nefilim dialects. This Aramaic dialect died out around one thousand Earth years ago.

The other dialect is a Hebrew dialect used in the next generation's interpretations of the stories of Enki's Book of Earth. These Hebrew bibles of chosen stories to share showing the creation of mankind were put together from 1200–100 BC and given its final form around 250 AD.

The Arabic language began during the time period we know as 100–400 AD. It is a derivative of the Hebrew language. So all these books in circulation about god and how Earthlings were created are really new mixes from an original source that wrote the stories as they were happening.

Enki's tablets were deciphered by those who studied the Samaritan written texts. I spent my life reading everything I could about those who studied these tablets and the discovered tablets found written in the Nefilim languages.

"Why the different languages?" I ask again. We learned Enlil demanded that new languages be created, and so Inanna did this for Enlil in her region. All done to prevent Marduk or a future Marduk from making Earthlings unite under one culture. And when this happens, they can put together the truth of existence under the Nefilim or their latter-day chosen representative control. The Indus and the Mayan languages discovered on regional artifacts are two of the languages whose codes we have yet to break.

Understanding Inanna's love of stones and her control of the region, we can now see how stones play such a role in the Indian culture. This culture from clothes and jewelry needs the stone as an artifact of their creative goddess of love and sex. Love and sex as sex is not always love but a need to satisfy one not always the other. Love is a shared concept. Your sacred place that you and your love partner will always know.

Gilgamesh is very important epic mankind should be aware of, and for that reason alone, it is not in the Jewish or Christian Bible. The Jewish and Christian controllers of knowledge do not want others to learn this story. This story shows in no uncertain terms that mankind was created by aliens from another planet, and those aliens made mankind and then started coupling with the creatures they so created to make demigods. This is the story of one of those demigods.

Gilgamesh knew his anointed position in society of his more-than-half-DNA Nefilim (god) like birth. Gilgamesh wanted the immortality of his Nibiru family. Gilgamesh wanted to go to the Earth port to Heaven, Nibru, and be brought to Nibiru to be made immortal. This epic is all about Gilgamesh's search to become immortal. In essence to obtain what he considered his birthright.

The tale tells you how he went into the land of the Tilmun. Tilmun, as we read, is the land of the spaceport that goes from the land known as Earth's Heaven to then be taken by the Nefilim (gods) to Nibiru for their DNA's everlasting life. This spaceport is also the place where the secrets of Nibiru were kept from humankind's awareness and knowledge.

In the mankind rewritten tale that we mortals have read as a myth after many translations, Inanna is not mentioned. Gilgamesh's mother, Inanna, is now called NinSun. Remember the gods had different names for different territories. Different languages, remember?

NinSun has an uncle in these tales, Ut, who NinSun begs to take her son to Tilmun. The text we read is not easy to understand until you put together the whole story and understand who the real characters were as opposed to what oral tradition changed over time. Gilgamesh was Inanna's child, and he wanted his birthright to be immortal as he was 75 percent DNA Nefilim. The tablets help us do just this. But you must know the characters and Earth's history with these characters.

Now back to the story.

To get to the sacred/secret place, Gilgamesh must go through a few roadblocks. Roadblocks installed to stop trespassers. Now we discover the devices used to stop trespassing in this area were machine control voices which deactivated certain blocks. Those blocks prevented entry unless you knew that certain specific version of open sez me. The magic password.

To the humans, these voice-activated posts were thought to be Oracles. Oracles were voices that were inside talking stones, it is written. Stones really being either sensor devices or a computer camera designed with watchers who watch, and when someone was trying to trespass, the stone was able to let them in or keep them out.

Oracles, so we all understand, were actual living bodies who had command posts that when alerted could talk through the stones and give answers to the questions being asked. Bodies that were Nefilim. Bodies that could use machines to fly and then hide in ways humans could not do. In the coming scenes of Abraham, Moses, and Alexander, you will discover these tricks.

A priest had to talk to the Oracle of those days. Remember, the priest worked for the Nefilim (god), and god had his representatives called Oracles. The Oracles knew what the god wanted the others to know to serve this local god.

The tale tells us how on his journey to obtain immortality, Gilgamesh encountered different roadblocks. Roadblocks to stop trespassers. We learn of the fire-belching monster, which prevented access to the secret tunnel entrance. A code got him through this fire-throwing sort of dinosaur machine entry point.

Gilgamesh got inside the spaceport and was met by our Great Flood hero, Ziusudra. Remember, he was a demigod made from Enki's sperm.

Ziusudra knew he was related by birth to Gilgamesh and showed him the secret plant. Ziusudra told Gilgamesh this plant gives the energy to keep a man young. The plant was from Nibiru and only grows in this sacred region of Earth. It was private for the Nefilim (gods) and the looked-after demigods of Earth's creation.

Gilgamesh was made by Ziusudra to understand that he could not go to Nibiru. He was forbidden. However, Ziusudra told him the story of the sacred life-extending plant.

Gilgamesh, upset that his goal would not be reached and that he must settle for door two as if it were a game, ripped the plant by its root and left to journey back to his kingdom on his Earth home. Not a friendly way of being. A bit aggressive. We then read in the myth that he fell asleep on this journey. While asleep, a snake, attracted by the fragrance of the plant, came to take the plant away. Gilgamesh returned home empty-handed. He died as a mere mortal.

Who was the snake of this story? We know the answer. It was Enki. Enki was taking back what was in his mind rightfully his property. This was not available to humans or mixed breeds of his genetic makeup except Enki's son, Ziusudra. To get the plant, you need permission from the big three. The big three are Anu, Enki, and/or Enlil. It was not Ziusudra's place to give anyone this secret plant's power.

The moral of this story is only these three gods of the creation of mankind could give one immortality. Not even the goddess Inanna, who was a child of Enlil, could give or obtain the powers to his offspring.

Gilgamesh was a great king, we learn, of a major city. The city of Uruk, a.k.a., the biblical city of Erech. Marduk got intellectual hold of this event and saw how one could sell to the Earthlings, if done right, the everlasting life in Heaven (Nibiru) concept, even if they could never get it. By lying, Marduk got control of the fear of death that we all have. He created the concept of if you behave, I will give you everlasting life in your next life in your next creation of being a physical-but-not-as-dense body being. You will be with me in Heaven.

Gilgamesh never got eternal life. In fact, Zechariah Sitchin, my favorite scholar of the Enki tablets, believes this king's bones are buried in what today we call the Royal Tombs of Ur. Ur being very close to Anu and Antu's royal visit to Earth, which we discussed after the Romeo and Juliet tale of that earlier era.

Act Six, Scene Seven: Marduk and His Games of Playing Tug-of-War with His Dominions in Egypt and Babylon

Marduk used this tale of Gilgamesh for his own purposes. He twisted the tales and lied and made the pharaohs and elite of his Egypt believe they too could become immortal. Marduk would give them the plant on their way to Heaven. This would be administered as part of their last rites by the accepted priests of the god (Nefilim) we now know as Marduk. It became the Book of the Dead for Egyptians.

Marduk told the ruling few under his rule that he could offer them a passage to Heaven to everlasting life. Marduk wrote his Book of the Dead. This book in reality tells the story of how to get to the Nefilim home planet of their creation called Nibiru. It tells how to get to the portal of an Earth spiritual dimension as opposed to physical dimension for the passage to Nibiru where one could live forever. But evermore? No. Heaven is not the one we believe in; Heaven then was the departure point to go and visit the Nefilim, King Anu, and get everlasting Nibiru life.

This is how Marduk, playing the role of Ra, the Egyptian Sun god, kept the control of his region we call Egypt. He promised them immortality if they followed his rules. Just made up for mankind by an individual Nibiru (god's) rules. Rules our manmade religion spits out as if they are eternal truths. Religions are just based on lies from these Nibiru tales that get us to kill and be killed as the soldiers for our current cast of fools still lying as if they actually report to the gods of Nefilim creation. Maybe they do. Maybe they don't. But I told you all life returns to the Supreme Being Creator in what is the eternal matrix of our creator's mind. We are all thoughts coming from this eternal thought matrix acting out our individual dreams in Mother Earth's physical form.

Marduk is the devil that dad, Enki, could not control. Nor could Marduk's grandparents, his brothers and sisters, or aunts as well as uncles. This is the black seed of the Anu family tree.

Marduk, who was now out of control, ordered his flock to build the stairway to Heaven again. The tombs, he said, must face the east so the daylight would reach them first. And then what? That is why some religions to this day face east when they say their prayers to their small Sun god.

Marduk also instructed his Egyptian soldiers to invade the lands of Africa, which he called Abzu, and get their gold to bring back to Egypt. This is the gold rush for pleasure and beauty, not for survival of a planet. This was the beginning of the fake temples being built in upper and lower Egypt. It is also when human's insatiable appetite for gold that serves no purpose other than glory became the games of war that mankind would play. Ask yourself, why do we worship gold? Well, we were taught to believe the Nefilim (god) favored those who got the gold.

Marduk told his dad, Enki, the Earth was his to rule. This is where the seeds are planted that today still get us to kill over gold and oil. Gold for vanity, and now black gold, which we call oil. Why? For the concept that it is necessary to keep society in the style oil gives mankind with gold being what is needed to hoard if the Nefilim (gods) and their new apocalyptic war of metaphysical unforeseen events will soon happen again. The return of the Nefilim (gods) and their need for gold. They will take gold to keep you alive.

Religion (from Latin to English means "to bind") as the worship of your private god is how we were controlled as a community of non-equals back then. Religion is how we are controlled by a community of non-equals today. Withholding knowledge of who we are and how we got here and why we are here and where we go next is how we are controlled. My goal in life is to give you these answers and then pray you wake up and get it.

Donovan sang it best when he sang, "He's a Catholic, a Hindu, an atheist a Jan, a Buddhist, and a Baptist, and a Jew. And he knows he shouldn't kill. And he knows he always will." This is where our idiot game of war in the name of our local Nefilim (god) begins. These wars were instigated by the Nefilim (god) Marduk, whose bipolar personality was mistaken for love. A Nefilim devil called many names in many societies. His energy was known as Ra, Zeus, and Baalbek, just to share a few, which societies he ruled on Earth when the Nefilim went home so no human could stop him. Remember, he, Marduk, was not allowed back to Nibiru. And stuck on Earth, as we will learn, he would die before his time was due if he had made it back to Nibiru.

When you get it, you will look to become a community of mankind. You will get the game of life. You will understand how to be the team of collective consciousness known as mankind that came to this world, this dimension, to make our dreams come true. Earth can then become the heaven of health and happiness for us all.

Act Six, Scene Eight: Mankind Checkers Versus Nefilim Chess An Overview

The game of living checkers with the humans being the fighting pieces and chess with the humans as the pawns.

The wars of mankind started right here near the land region we call Edin as well as the Sinai Peninsula. This was, as we learned, the Nefilim sacred space, and we are not taught this in our schools. Why? But here and now we know why it is a sacred space.

People in this stitch of time were expanding and leaving the sacred space region. They were the outsiders whom the Nefilim called pagans, meaning living outside the Olden Urban Nefilim settlements. The outsiders started to move into regions around Europe and China. The Ice Age was ending, and land appeared beneath these sheets of ice. It was very fertile, too, and could definitely support the living beings.

These cultures had elders who knew the game and created their own stories of creation and made rules to be controlled. The stories all have the same beginning, and the stories created new religions of controlling people in faraway communities of mankind.

However, the communities of the first two Earthling sections, Egypt and Edin, were very important to the big three. Those three again were King Anu and his two sons Enki and Enlil.

This region of the Olden World order had the spaceports for travel back to Nibiru and had the ME machine of weapons and more that ran the physical lives of the Nefilim. This knowledge and the weapons were important to protect. Apparently, the gold rush was over and all the Nefilim headquarters were doing was cleaning up the mess they made on Earth while creating a new being. They were getting ready to depart and go back to Nibiru.

Enki did not write about the other lands at this time. All Enki's tales were about the original Nefilim regions where they could settle and not be living in lands covered by ice like Europe and North America and China.

Marduk was playing cat and mouse. Marduk wanted absolute control, and every time his team got near the spaceport, Enlil awoke and would stop Marduk. As I said, cat and mouse games.

The first Nefilim divided region, Enlil's, had Nannar and Ningal as the royal Nefilim couple, Ningal being Nannar's wife in control. This region is Mesopotamia and again was called the Olden World, or Edin. Inanna was everywhere else. Just look to the tales of Isis.

The couple Nannar and Ningal liked to party. These two created the religious festival concept we still have in our world today. Those festivals were to be celebrated twelve times an Earth year. Each new moon had its festival. We lived on moon years in that region. Remember, Marduk made his regions live using the Sun as the guide. He was, again, the Egyptian Sun King. He was the beginning of our current concept called Christ. Christ is the Sun God. Christ's anointed birthday is December 25, which is the day the Sun starts its journey back north from the Southern Hemisphere. Really, it is when the Sun's wobbling changes and starts to wobble its rotational turns with the north facing the Sun as opposed to the South Pole facing the Sun. It's simple, and do understand that the rules and regulations governing our current Earth are made with the north as the dominant source.

The moon as our ruling light gives the Christian religion the Easter holidays, whose days rotate depending on the equinox we call spring in the Northern Hemisphere. The holidays of Islam and the Jews as well as pagan religions change each year. They are computed on the astrological sky and the energies of the other planets in our solar system. The Christian religion is just computed using the Sun, except Easter as that requires a Good Friday and that needs a Passover holiday, which changes every year.

Twelve was the number of the astrological signs that dictated the lives of our Christian order copying Marduk and his rules. When the Sun is the now-controlling timeline, our year sometimes has thirteen moons a calendar must deal with. To end this game, the Church of Christ would pick a day that was the same every year, so we are taught to celebrate the birth of their Sun God called Christ.

Ever ask yourself why September is the ninth month when it means the seventh? Ask no more as the Catholic Church changed our calendar to start the year on January 1 so it began seven days after their anointed day, December 25, for the return of the Sun on its passage north.

The British, in 1751, changed New Year's Day from March 15 to January 1, beginning in 1752. Why? Think about it. The Hindus, Hebrews, and the Chinese too have a different New Year's Days. Why? Pick up the pieces. See what you believe from a different perspective. Who is running your game of life? Not you.

We need to understand that our concept of every day being twenty-four hours is not true. Each day is a little more in actual time. We fix that discrepancy by adding a full day on the fourth year from our current calendar's beginning. Each day is a little bit more than twenty-four hours by a little less than a minute per day. Each year is off by six hours, which is 360 minutes. Divide that 360 by 365 and you get the missing seconds.

These games are made to control your living thoughts. Control you to believe each day of each year is the same. That way you do not question the rules that you are born into. Remember, life is a game. Yes, life is a game. Team sport? Individual sport, and we are the spectators. Why do our leaders play god? Where is the team sport?

The Nefilim, as our current worldwide Wikipedia spells the word, claims they are the people we call stargazers. They were ruled by the stars and the energy those stars released on our living world. They are mixing this up with the human Edin tribe called the Chaldeans. Let's go to truth. The living place of the Chaldean's community rise was Ur. They were Nefilim-created beings. They had their priests chosen by Enlil, the soon-to-be Hebrew god. The first big priest and spy of this growing order was our Abraham of Ur. The Sumerians call him Ibruum, and the Arabs call him Ibrahim.

This Abraham figure is the grandfather of all three Olden World religions. The wanderer from Ur.

In the Sumer region of the Olden World, the cities rotated who would have the king. It was peaceful at first, but war for control of this region was about to become a reality. As Marduk in his Egypt, the neighbor to the Sumer areas had one ruler.

Egypt, under the control of Marduk, did not follow this rotating king rule. Marduk was the god, and he had his priestly order that were also called the Watchers. A Watcher was really a spy for their local Nefilim god. This Watcher was to report what the people were doing.

Marduk started to believe his lies that he was spreading. Edicts were produced to control this effect. He claimed he was the one without equal, the one Ra above all the other gods.

Enki reappeared and spoke to his son. Told him to slow down. But Marduk told dad that his sign was the sign of the Ram, and it would be the Ram's time in a few Earth years to rule the Earth. Remember, these signs lasted about 2,200 years. This coming age of Ra was also the age of our time when the Ram suddenly appeared everywhere in this Olden World. It is the sign of dominance tying the just-ended era of the Bull, who was Enlil, to the new era of Marduk and the Ram. It was absolute mind control that Ra, Anun, or whatever he called himself to his pets, tried to place on the civilization here on Earth.

Enlil had an era of shared rule as a benevolent leader as long as Enlil had final say, was the sign of the Bull from Nibiru (Heaven). The Bull sign is associated with the moons of Taurus. As the signs are associated with the movements of the astrological sign, which goes counterclockwise, the next moon after the Bull is the Ram and what we call Aries in our astrological world order. So, I write this so one can see the confusion caused when Marduk took the helm from his uncle the Bull-Enlil.

Enki putting family before truth allowed his son and his narcissistic ways to stay in play. His son was telling the truth that with the coming of the Age of Aries, it was Marduk's Earth controlled game of Earth life to play. Our timeline for this would be 2220 BC until 1 AD. Remember, the Nefilim constantly had the mental battle of fate or destiny play out when they made decisions of what should be. Enki thought this was what was supposed to be, and he who could have stopped this son did nothing but let it go on.

Crazy way our fates are decided. By those who know and who are known. We always end up in the hands of fools.

Act Six, Scene Nine: Civil War—Marduk (Ram) Versus Enlil (Bull)

We are inside a time machine visiting Earth. The announcer says the time has come to learn how mankind's tug-of-war began. The Nefilim (gods), a.k.a., Anunnaki, used their pets called humans to wage the war as battle checker pieces and the pawns used in the game of chess being played by the Nefilim gods. The humans were dispensable and really disposable pets.

Only a few were needed to lead the team to victory. So those few became the third estate of mankind, the military. The first estate was the royals. The second estate was the priests. Now the third estate was the military. Soon comes the fourth estate, the lawyers and snitches of society as well as the accountants who make sure you obey all the rulers and pay the government taxes. And then we have the merchants and the rest of all of society's undesirable, or the deplorable.

A great Earthing leader was needed for Inanna and Enlil's team. Inanna found the perfect guy. The new warlord of the region we call zone one of the Edin Olden World time of human blood was Abrakad.

The Arab *abracadabra* comes from this legend in the world's past time. We need something; we wish for it, and when we believe, our wish can come true. They wished for a leader, and here he was, Abrakad.

Enlil gave the man Abrakad the crown and scepter. Our history books call him Sargon I; the Nefilim-Anunnaki knew him as Sharru-kin, the righteous regent.

Sargon had his duty, and his duty was simple. His orders were to make sure everyone in their god's Mesopotamia Edin behaved and followed Enlil's desired behavior. Sargon had an advantage that others in his region did not have to win the battles our history tells us about. The quote from the tablets I found is, "By Enlil was Sharru-kin empowered, Inanna with her weapons of brilliance his warriors accompanied." Meaning he had the weapons inside the ME.

Marduk was watching and waiting, learning the moves that Sargon and his army were doing to control the area. Marduk wanted to control the Olden World, and he was about to set out and try to do just that.

Marduk wanted Babylon back. It was his city, so he believed. Babylon was, according to Marduk, the gateway to the gods. Marduk got his chess pawns to attack. His army won the first battle. He took over the city in the heart of Enlil's Edin. Inanna flipped out and got Enlil to awaken and deal with this cancer of a being called Marduk.

The rivers of Babylon were filled with blood just like the song says. Inanna got Enlil's permission to make the next move. Inanna attacked. She had no army but used weapons of mass destruction and killed most of Marduk's pets called humans and destroyed the city.

Marduk, defeated in Babylon, decided to leave Edin and did not go back to Egypt. People were wondering where their god was. Marduk was waiting for time to pass till his star sign, the Ram, was the age of their Earth playground land. This disappearing act gave Marduk the new name of Amun, the unseen one. Yet he put in play his disciples. They set the stage for the return of this monster.

Natam-sin, the grandson of Sargon I, was appointed king of both Akhad and Sumer. The first king of more than one Anunnaki-controlled city. This is the beginning of empires, not just nations, that start to rule bigger territories as populations start to spread out and then connect.

The Nefilim-Anunnaki were waiting to get permission to leave Earth. Close up shop and return home were their wants and needs. They were prematurely aging and wanted this to stop. On Nibiru the aging would come to a halt. This is why Earth years were being used in the tablets so we the people would have a reference of our time according to our lifetime line. The Nefilim-Anunnaki, as I have said, in our world lived forever and ever more.

The Nefilim-Anunnaki crew was told from their command posts to clean up all the loose gold in the New World and when done get ready to leave Earth. They were also instructed by King Anu to continue to teach Earthlings to be civilized to survive without the Nefilim's (gods') supervision. The game now became whose rules and whose order should Earthlings follow. Which Nefilim (god) would be supreme in this Olden World?

The New World, our Western Hemisphere, neither Enki nor Enlil really cared about. Life was not urban in this region. It was primitive and based on living in and with nature as created by Earth. The gold would very soon not be needed anymore. The new world did not even have a need for a wheel. No alchemy of materials and water with fire to make a new world possible of city from stones and bricks and paved roads, with water running in manmade streams we call aqueducts. There was no Nefilim loved poured into this region. The region was left with no guidance and would soon become a land run by superstitions and sacrifices in ceremonies all to encourage the Nefilim gods to return.

Enlil and Ninurta, during a temporary peace with Marduk, went to check in on the New World. Their trips around the region are where the flying gods myths come from in our world today. The Nefilim (gods) took flight to see what was happening with the mining and the gathering of the gold and other minerals needed for life on Nibiru and Earth. Why not? They thought Marduk's threat was over as he was missing. Little did they suspect the warrior princess of the next twelve gods waiting in line, Inanna, who wanted to be queen herself, would make this next move of ownership and control. Inanna struck to take control by filling the Nefilim gods of ruling order absence.

Inanna used her warrior King Naram-sin to move to take control of the first region and destroy everything that was in the way of his (and really her) chessboard in the lands of Sumer and Akkad on the way to Egypt. His goal on behalf of Inanna's true goal was Egypt. Inanna wanted Marduk dead and gone. The family feud from the War of the Roses in Egypt was not over.

Naram-sin made a mistake, and Inanna did not advise properly on his move to get to Egypt.

The mistake is Naram-Sin went to Egypt through the Sinai Peninsula. The land Enlil called the Tilmun. The forbidden land to humans at all costs. Even forbidden to those whom Enlil apparently adored.

Enlil came back from the New World travels and unleashed his revenge. Without armies of mankind, he went straight to the ME weapons and wiped out all Naram-Sin's army and leaders.

Gods causing war among mankind for sport! Which god do you believe? The god causing the war or the god giving you salvation and protection from the sinful behavior of the other side's Nefilim-Anunnaki god.

This behavior is what we still do today. We kill for sport as we do not even eat our roadkill. This time period was around 2300 BC. A few years before the time of the Ram. And the Ram Marduk was getting ready.

Food for thought: is this violence part of our essence and placed inside our DNA given to us by our creator? Or is the violence streak learned behavior?

Parts of Edin were wiped out; confusion was the order of the first region. In Marduk's second region, Egypt, with his disappearance act, order was not the rule of the land. It was a ball of confusion too.

Enlil got a hold of dad, King Anu, on Nibiru to get the advice of what he should do to restore order. The move was to place a new king in the city of Ur. This king was to be the people's peacemaker. The command was to bring peace to the lands so the lands would once again be prosperous, and the people would live with the abundance of their necessities for their way of life. But what was their purpose to live? Really, what is our purpose to live in physical form? To serve whom? To do what?

Act Six, Scene Ten: Abraham

The new chosen Nefilim king of these lands was named Ur-Nammu, the Righteous Shepard. It is written that Enlil was so worried about the coming Age of the Ram, Marduk's time to rule Earth, that Enlil started consulting the stars to help guide him so he could carry forward the destiny of man. Or was it fate that Marduk was to rule?

Marduk, in his absence, as I stated earlier, from Egypt, was really traveling and setting up his taking control of the Earthlings on Earth as their one God. Marduk was gaining massive support by inducing fear among the then-living population of mankind in these Olden World collective regions. Marduk's son Nabu was helping dad enslave humans by creating fear to gain obedience.

Mankind was about to play tug-of-war again. The tug-of-war of the Nefilim-Anunnaki gods, not God, was about to begin.

Ur-Nammu died in a chariot accident. Shulgi replaced him. It is written that Shulgi was full of bile and eager for battle. The new king, it is written, had the power of the battlefield, and he apparently had the power of persuasion because he seduced Inanna. With Inanna's support came her weapons of destruction.

This King Shulgi overran the land of the first region called Edin. Once again, the peace and safety of the mission control center was placed in jeopardy.

Enlil wished to stop Marduk's ascension, and he needed to gain control of his region himself. He needed his priest and his priest spies to take control and end the dissension. Enlil needed to become the Father God of Mankind, the only king of Nibiru's colony on Earth as soon he would succeed his dad and become the King of Nibiru and henceforth in charge of Nibiru's colonies and stop playing the game of king for an astrological Earth sign.

In the present, the Nefilim would leave Earth soon and there was no reason to share the leadership of Earth with another of the royal family retinue. Enlil's thoughts were that he would be the only Nefilim (god) in control of Earth. Now Enlil realized the changing game board of Earthlings. The Nefilim would leave Earth, and he, as the one who would be in charge of Earth the colony, Enlil, needed his human spokesperson to champion his cause with the people using the temples to worship the absent Nefilim who would communicate with Earthlings on an as-needed basis.

This is the point in time with the anointment of Abraham to become Enlil's chosen priest and the leader of the Nibiru-Hibiru, a.k.a., Hebrew flock.

Abraham was a Chaldean—Watcher of the stars. He was already a wealthy man and was about to become the wealthiest man of his region and the father of all the remaining Olden World, Nefilim-Anunnaki-inspired gods' religions.

Enlil was now going to copy the moves of the other Nefilim-Anunnaki (gods) and use humans to carry out his desires to oversee at a distance and rule over mankind. The main objective for Enlil here and now was to protect the spaceport. This is where our legends make Sinai the peninsula so important. It is why the prophets seem to meet and talk with a god in this peninsula.

Marduk now appeared in the city of Harran, just after Abraham left to perform his duties for his god Enlil. Havoc begins with the people. They had more than one Nefilim god to fear, and something had to give.

Enlil used Abraham and Lot to become his spies. He needed them to report what it was that Marduk was doing and which people were following this other Nefilim (god's) rule.

Marduk became the god of most of this region. He played politics well, and has now united areas today called Egypt, Israel, Canaan, Assyria, Akkad, and Sumer. Only a few regions were not loyal to Marduk, the god of obedience, as he told his followers.

Enlil called for a council of the Nibiru elders of his rule. Marduk, to counter this move, called a meeting of all the Nefilim-Anunnaki to his temple in the rebuilt Babylon. Enlil did not go. Marduk wanted their blessings for him to take control of this Olden World region.

The Elders of Nibiru met with Enlil, and all but one agreed that Marduk must be stopped in his tracks. The dissenting voice of reason was Enki, the father of Marduk. Enki said that this was fate that brought Marduk to this point of leadership of Earth and fate that he should now rule. Let's let fate be the ruler of destiny. Again, we hear, what is fate, and what is destiny?

We see the confusion that lives inside all the One Supreme Being's creations. Even those who play god need reassurances they are doing what the one Supreme Being God wants. From reading stars to speaking with Oracles and machines, the hand of fate is in the hands of us living fools. Fate is a lie if we believe for some reason that a God or the God has determined what we should do, so god's outcome is the ruling light.

The truth is that even the One Supreme God is a secondary energy force, as even that Supreme Being got its individual identity from a source. So I, Steven Machat, believe in the Supreme First Energy Source of all beings in existence that exist or existed or shall exist in the future here, there, and everywhere as well as nowhere.

No third-party identifiable God gave us or owns our free will. We are the makers of our destiny, not a predetermined fate other than the fate we need to make up our own minds guided by our inner knower that tells us all what we want to hear before we choose to do it.

Notwithstanding Enki's pleas, the elders decided to destroy the local regional cities of Marduk. The reason was to end his game for control of the central region of the Olden World.

Abraham was Enlil's able servant. He had the chariots of that era and the finest horses protecting the spaceports from human trespassers. Kings and priests, it is written, came to Abraham from far and wide to gain Abraham's support to help those seekers with pleas to their Supreme Nefilim (god), Enlil, the Nefilim (god) of peace and order. Enlil was a pacifist. He wished for peace and would use his fists or elements in his control to get it, and if required, to get revenge.

We read about the angels visiting Abraham to gain knowledge of the doings in the towns by those not loyal to Enlil, but they were loyal, it turns out, to Marduk, the Nefilim (god) of requiring obedience to him, which he called love. The god whose uncle is Enlil. This is a family civil war.

It written in the Bible that two of these urban cities, from which angels, a.k.a., spies, sought information for Enlil, were Sodom and Gomorrah. From these cities Marduk's plot was to use the people pawns to get control of the spaceport itself.

The Elders of Nibiru decided to stop Marduk, and this stopping would require the Weapons of Terror. The weapons would be used in a preemptive attack. Just like we the "civilized world" of 2003 did against the Iraqi manmade living god Saddam Hussein.

Sodom and Gomorrah were just north of the spaceport. Egypt was to the west. There was good military reason for Marduk to start his war of control from these two cities of that time period.

The angels (spies) appeared, before the strikes of terror began again, to Abraham. They needed final information, and here is where we meet the soft side of Abraham the man as he pleads with these angels, really again Watchers of Enlil, to spare the righteous ones who are not vile or evil.

The tablets let us know that the angels who visited with Abraham were none other than Ninurta, the son of Enlil and Nergal, the son of Enki and half-brother of Marduk. It is they who warned Abraham of what was about to happen, so he must leave at once.

The angels went to visit Lot, as Abraham asked them to do, and were discovered by the local citizens who realized they were spies for Enlil. They escaped but warned Lot of the coming doom. As we read in the Bible, Lot was told to leave with his family and not look back. Lot's wife did not listen and did look back. The woman was turned to salt, we are told in the Bible. In reality, she was vaporized by the weapon attack, which was, according to the description in the tablets, the "one without rival the blazing flame" and "one who with terror crumbles; Mountains melt" and the "vaporizer of living things."

In Earth time this goes on in 2064 BC. It is the end of Enlil's regime as the head regent (appointed to be the head of the governing state by the absent royalty), who is not at this time period the king of the Anunnaki-Nefilim. It is the time of the season for the beginning of Marduk's (Ram) reign.

Enlil won that nuclear civil war battle of Sodom and Gomorrah, but he did not win the battle of time, and his moves or fate gave Marduk another chance to rule with a bipolar fist the Olden World. The description in the tablets lets you know this destruction of Sodom and

Gomorrah was a nuclear storm that was also using biological as well as chemical nuclear not just atomic weapons to kill the people. Nabu, Marduk's son, was killed in this battle.

The Nefilim-Anunnaki of Sumer also had to evacuate as the bombing released gases that got into the wind and now were coming to their town too. It was a mess everywhere in this olden section of Earth except Babylon. Babylon survived as for some reason the gas with the wind did not hit Babylon.

The Nefilim, who studied metaphysical things when eyes could not see let alone foresee and still get no answer, turned to the questions of fate or destiny. So now they had no answer to how Babylon survived the attack. So they turned to thoughts of fate versus destiny. The fact that Babylon survived led the Nefilim on Earth as well as living on Nibiru to believe that it was destiny for Marduk to be the new regent of Nibiru and to rule Earth.

The Anunnaki did leave Earth, we are led to believe, except Marduk. Marduk was the new regent of Earth for the Nefilim. Do remember he was excommunicated from Nibiru and sentenced to Earth for making or taking an Earth spouse. Marduk the Nefilim (god) of obedience, he says, became the one Nefilim (god) of vengeance. He stayed put to watch and rule the Earthlings so created. But apparently the work was not finished at the spaceport in Sinai. Meaning Enlil did not yet leave, and till his work was finished, he was staying put and would take back his Hibiru people and give them their land that today we call Israel.

The story coming is the following: This dark reign of Marduk went to Egypt, and Enlil's chosen people were taken into slavery. The god of the Bible who lived and when needed punished, known as Enlil, would have to get even again. But apparently his Sinai control post, his exclusive domain, would stay free from Marduk and his controlled followers.

Act Six, Scene Eleven: Moses

Earthlings were living a very dark Nefilim-made disaster. It was a mess. Mankind was fighting mankind over different conflicting deliberate orders from Marduk and his priestly order. This game of ruling Earth was a wrestling sport for this dark Nefilim named Marduk. Marduk fed off conflict. Marduk fed on the blood he caused by his actions making mankind hate each other and then kill each other in his game of dividing people. And this meant having each side of the conflict believe him to be their creating God, and as such, the one they owe their life force to and whose wishes must be honored.

Marduk was ruling the Olden World in total. Again, not the New World nor the lands of Europe or Asia and South America. Except the region we know as Sinai. He was waiting for Enlil to leave, as ordered by Anu. Marduk had different needs and desires. He was anointing Earthling kings to fight wars against each other's new empires for sport.

The people of Abraham, who were chosen by Abraham to be loyal to the rule of Nefilim Enlil and all their male and female heirs called Hibirus, were captured by Marduk's Egyptian division. They were brought to Egypt to be the slaves of his Watchers and the Watchers' human offspring called Egyptians, who were the upper society's higher class of Egyptian culture.

Yes, class structures were built into our learned behavior of how to run a society. As we will learn in our books, we have different classes, which are built into the societies of our time.

The keeper of the currency that makes mankind do one thing or another is the first class. Then these keepers bring in their leaders with their priests—religious representatives—who tell you what the unseen Nefilim (god) wants you to do and believe you are doing this to win that imaginary creator of everything and more favor.

Let's turn to Moses.

Screen opens in your mind. Man on a mountaintop with tablets in his hands. Lifting his two arms and now coming down as the tablets are crushed into pieces. Why? Let's learn the truth.

Who was Moses? We don't know. There are many oral stories from that time that we have had reduced to writing, and none share the same origins of this man.

Now let's ask when the Sumerians disappeared.

According to our historical records, the Sumerians were the people of southern Mesopotamia whose civilization flourished between 4100–1750 BC. This is signified by the animal image associated with this society, which is the Bull. The Bull was the symbol of Enlil's regency of control of Earthlings as mandated by the Elders of Nibiru.

We are told the Sumerian civilization disappeared around 1750 BC. Really, this means it was when their language as the official language of the region disappeared.

Sumer is the big city where the name Sumerian comes from as if this region was all Sumer. Sumer is a region of city-states under the regency of Enlil in his Edin. Each urban city-state shall have its own kings appointed and so anointed by the ruling Nefilim regent of Earthlings we now know as Enlil. When Marduk tried to divide this region with his premature claims to be the regent with his symbol the

Ram, which is the symbol of Aires, Enlil the Bull, the astrological sign of Taurus, created the Hibiru tribe of mankind using Abraham as a shepherd. A shepherd who was supposed to identify to Enlil who was part of his loyal flock. Enlil needed to know who was loyal to him as opposed to who was siding with Marduk. Enlil's real game was to protect the sacred weapons and ME from falling into the wrong hands of Marduk and his animal crew of mankind.

I must interrupt my tale here and explain the misuse of the word "Semitic." A Semite is one who speaks one of the various vocal languages that trace back in our time to the Samaritan language created by the Nefilim when they were teaching the Earthlings how to communicate with languages. This Samaritan language has morphed into Hebrew, Aramaic, Phoenician, and Akkadian. Those names are known as the various Semitic tribes of this region in this era, and their military ventures caused the end of their world order. They were absorbed by the winning tribes of battle. Each tribe had a common set of values, which they believe as a unit in theory are right and everybody else is wrong.

These Semite tribes' order was an order that included Sumer, and we learn that Sargon took control of this region after the destruction of Sodom and Gomorrah.

Now I ask the eye in our sky to please tell me what happened when they died out. The place was like the visual images of the movie *Thunder Dome*. I saw a dark age occur in this region. This fits in with the story of Abraham that we just read. It is not until Babylon rose and their King Hammurabi in 1792 BC got power did this region awake again.

This ruler Hammurabi created the written laws and order for his society's ruling class. These rules told those few what they could and could not do to the others. These rules described commerce and trade. They told you how much to pay for a slave. It goes on to say how much a wrongful death cost as you had to pay a fine for society to forgive you. Pretty outrageous stuff; look it up and read it. It is described as the Code of Hammurabi.

The Code of Hammurabi is mankind's first written code of law, which was given to us by Regent Marduk.

The Sumerian dialog language started to get replaced by the Akkadian language around 2000 BC. But it did stay alive in written form until the age of Jesus.

Now the stories will soon change in our Bible even more. No god is authoring the texts. It is humans reporting to humans. The ruling Nefilim, the regent of the time period, created the hateful energies that result in war. The stories no longer are written by Enki first in that Book of Earth.

We, now in the Old Testament, can really discover the bipolar god. We now learn that this bipolar god is Marduk during his regency of Earth in this age of the Ram. So now we can understand the god of vengeance when things do not go his way is also the god of love, when we obey the rules and order to perpetuate the last living Nefilim-god's control of Earth.

It is important for us to really, I mean really, understand this so-called being who plays god and is in control of our living lives on Earth by being superior energy to ours is from Nibiru, and this born Nefilim is NOT our Supreme Being. No, he is just another creature living inside this universe that came from the same source we all do. That source is the Supreme Being of energy without any physical body that only gets created when your consciousness takes a physical life. And know we are not the only forms created by thoughts that exist in this universe or any other universes in the galaxies of physical existence.

The Nefilim, when landing here on Earth, were able to take a form that suited their needs on Earth. That is why they were called reptilians or serpents. They could change form and were really cold-blooded. They created us as a warm-blooded Earth mammals. Mammals do not live longer than reptilians. They walked and talked as we do, but they made us as mammals. And when they reproduced with their creations as they did, that creation was warm-blooded, and as such, has a different timeline.

Enlil and Marduk were sort of similar in style. They were the same family DNA blood tribe. Both apparently had no remorse about killing. God, a true father GOD, if there was one, would not kill. In physical form you take on a different concept of being. You can kill, and that must not exist in a society of beings. However, you will kill other beings including animals and plants and eat fungi to survive.

But Marduk had a need to be seen and worshiped, whereas Enlil just wanted peace. And Enlil wanted to make sure that those who live did not get the sacred knowledge of eternal and forever life. If they did, they might travel space and kill other living beings in time. We, by being created in body form, gave life to a being who would try to control their environment as the top dog. We were they, the Nefilim eons ago unless we were stopped, who would evolve the same way they did. Enlil knew this.

Enki, the creator of our mankind, wanted his species to survive and probably thrive, but he could not control his son, Marduk. Enki does not appear in our Bible again, let alone any tablets found on Earth to date.

Enlil did not yet disappear when the cities of Sodom and Gomorrah were destroyed. I believe he sat and waited with his team who was stationed with him there in his spaceport in the Sinai Peninsula to wrap things up on Earth. They all would depart soon, but not before he left his mark on Earth with his creation, the Hebrews. I know by various communications I have had with his energy that Enlil is the "god" of

Moses as well as Abraham, and I will now present the story as we can decipher from the scattered Samaritan text of this time period.

According to the internet, our eye in the sky, Moses was born around 1590 BC. He was born in what we call Lower Egypt. Lower Egypt is near Cairo. But to whom was he born? It does not really matter, for he was the agreed chosen one to lead those Hibirus who swore loyalty to the one god (Enlil), who wished to depart Egypt and the enforced slavery of Marduk's troops. The game or goal was to leave and go back to their promised land by Enlil to Abraham.

Enlil reconfirmed this promise to Abraham's son Isaac and then to Isaac's son Jacob. Remember, Abraham had two sons. The older son was known as Ishmael. Ishmael was not part of the covenant with god and Isaac's family of direct heirs. Ishmael had a different mother than Isaac, whose mom was Sarah. Sarah was old and thought she could not conceive. She did and Isaac was the gift from god it was thought in those times.

Ishmael was banished to the desert; however, it was written that god did promise Ishmael that he, like Isaac the ancestor of the Hebrew nation, would build a great nation too. Ishmael was the son from Abraham that is the source of the Islamic connection of their nation from the Hibiru-Hebrew god Enlil. They called Israel of their family's roots of Earth soil.

The Hebrew (Hibirus) as they were called from the olden order under Enlil's supervision became a tribe. This tribe was numerous. Marduk escaped Babylon and moved back to Egypt. Now in command of Earth as the Ram (RA), he rebuilt society under his order. He created his newest version of priest and the ruling class of Egypt. He then conquered the Hebrews and brought them to Egypt to be the domesticated slaves of his ruling class. I am repeating myself, but with reason. I want you to see the picture.

The stories of the Hebrew old life, before Egypt, in the land of good and plenty across the Red Sea, are told to the young, who were a few hundred Earth years old. The Hibirus wanted their land back, just like the old Good & Plenty commercials I used to see as a child.

The Hebrews prayed for their god to save them. Enlil did not disappoint. Now ready to go back to Nibiru, Enlil picked Moses as his captain and proceeded to set the Hibirus-Hebrews free once again from Marduk. We know the story as the Passover event. Only the Egyptians got the diseases that Enlil was creating using his weapons of death. The same weapons, I must remind you, that were used to poison Inanna back in her Gemini role by her sister who became the first witch of African folklore.

Then Enlil instructed Moses to bring the flock of escapees to Sinai. And I do believe Enlil used the ME powers to part the sea for the Hibirus to get across the Red Sea into Sinai.

This was Enlil making his final appearance on Earth. He needed the Hibirus-Hebrews as his chess pawns to protect his land we call Sinai from intrusions by other beings looking to steal the weapons and secret machines of Nibiru while Enlil was packing up to leave Earth.

Enlil does two things during this era of time.

The first is he gives Moses the Ten Commandments. These commandments are how the beings of Nibiru lived their lives on Nibiru. It was not how they lived their lives in the jungle they made creating mankind. The Nefilim themselves broke all their rules on Earth.

The rules are simple and easy to follow only if everyone has their necessities they need to live. This requires a community of equals where everyone gets those necessities of life as a community asset, not a third-party asset.

These rules are the goal to achieve in any society. The rules are commands of what one should do and not do. These ten rules are the following:

1) You shall have no other Nefilim (gods) before me.
2) You shall make no idols.
3) You shall not take the name of your lord, your Nefilim (god), in vain.
4) Remember the Sabbath day to keep it holy.
5) Honor your father and mother.
6) You shall not murder.
7) You shall not commit adultery.
8) You shall not steal.
9) You shall not bear false witness against your neighbor.
10) You shall not covet.

I am only sharing with you all the story. I will not tell you what these mean to anyone today. I now ask you see what it meant back in those days of the Nefilim rules for mankind and how they fell apart and why.

The Nefilim made our lives on an urban jungle. The Nefilim on Earth had freedom from the Nibiru rules, and they played in my eyes rock n' roll gods without order or controls until King Anu and the Elders of Nibiru had to intercede and stop the children's games.

Now I must introduce you to another thought I have left out. We know that the Nefilim had to burn the gold to get it into liquid form to bring back to Nibiru. This was done in the Sinai Peninsula. This is what Enlil was also protecting in his post. The manufacturing of gold in his temple in Sinai.

Remember, the Hibiru slaves stole gold from their owners as they were leaving. Ask yourselves why.

You will say gold had value. The Nefilim wanted gold, so to gain favor, the Hibirus would give their god the gold. Good answer.

But the Nefilim did not need more gold as they were leaving Earth. Their temple on the Sinai Peninsula was to manufacture gold, and while Moses was up on the mountain top with Enlil in the clouds for those forty days and forty nights, his troops were downstairs waiting and watching for Moses to come down.

Aaron, who was second in command, got the gold into this temple factory and converted some of the token goods into an idol. The idol was a bull. The bull was the symbol of Enlil. The Hibirus under Aaron's command did exactly what the second commandment said not to do. They made an idol. Moses lost it and broke the cuneiform tablet that had Enlil's written-down commandments.

And yes, Moses went back up to Mount Sinai and got the second version. He wrote this version.

I ask you all now to take a breather and ask yourselves why we have an obsession with gold. There are other metals that can do what gold does for us today. Why are we obsessed with gold?

It's in our DNA. We still hoard it for the Nefilim. We hoard it so when they come back for the gold, we have it ready for them.

That is the answer. We were created as a physical species to get the gold.

One more thing about this trip to Mount Sinai of Moses to meet Enlil.

A deal was brokered. Enlil told Moses how the Hibirus could reach him now that Enlil was going home to become the next king of Nibiru. This is the real Ark of the Covenant.

Now what is the Ark of the Covenant? If one looks today, one can find readily available the information I am about to share. The covenant is the promise that when Enlil leaves, if you use this device, I,

Enlil, am instructing you to build, you can always reach me while I am away from Earth living as the future or current king of Nibiru (Heaven).

I submit for all mankind to understand and believe that this ark was nothing, neither more nor less than a communication radio and maybe FaceTime device—a device that allowed for communications between two beings who are on planets or spaceships inside our universe. A device so the chosen few of Enlil could reach their god, Enlil, and get Enlil the commandments as to what to do and how to do it when Marduk's followers would mess with Enlil's he-brews.

We learned before in this story how Alalu spoke to the fellow Nefilim when he reached Earth back on Nibiru. The Nefilim had the technology to do this communication. So Enlil taught Moses how to communicate with him, Enlil. Enlil helped Moses make the first Earthling home radio-telephone device.

When you read in the tablets found in the sands of fallen empires of this time period, you will see how the ark was to be constructed. You read and see what these few were told to do by Enlil (god) in the tablets. The instructions of how to build and what to build are translated into our English language: "I will meet with you there above the mercy seat, between the two Cherubim that are over the Ark of the Testimony, I will speak with you from there about all that I command you regarding the Israelites."

The ark was made up of different parts. Those parts are the cherubim, poles, and gold as well as special wood. Why? Let's examine why as I share with you the usage of each part.

The cherubim were really headphones I believe and see as I write this to you. The two poles were the antennae to send and receive messages. Not carrying poles. Why the gold? Gold is a very powerful metal, and it does more than glitter and shine to blind your mind. "Balance the cost of the soul you lost with the dreams you lightly sold.

Are you under the power of gold?" Creatures of habit and we run like rabbits for a possession that constantly needs physical protection. That is the physical truth of gold. Not the metaphysical truth, which we have yet to learn let alone understand. The power of gold.

The metaphysical use of gold was for more than just one purpose of fixing the atmospheric leak on Nibiru. I will now share. Gold was needed, and when found on Earth, used to fix the leaking atmosphere of the planet of Nibiru, we learned. Yes, but know that gold helps us run our technical world of creature necessities of transport and communication. The Nefilim obviously knew that gold was one of the metals that could be put to use to communicate with others by a current that is able to pick up messages sent into the universe matrix of Earth's existence. It was not just our solar system one could communicate with using the gold.

So, from where does this desire today and back then to have gold stem from? The Nefilim, whom we can now call the gods, wanted gold for many reasons, and these gods told their Earth creations called man, whom they used as slaves, that gold was the possession of the gods. As a reward, the gods would let their favorite Earth caste system slaves have gold. It was a status symbol for mankind, but it was a necessity to get for the Nefilim, who needed it to plug the holes in Nibiru's atmosphere.

The naked truth about gold today in our world's order is the following: gold as both a physical and chemical metal is unique among the other metal groups. Gold does not react with oxygen, meaning it does not rust or tarnish. Think of the mask of gold that man found in the tomb of Tutankhamen. This was found by the explorers of Egypt dirt and tombs in 1932. When found, it probably had the same shine it did back in 1300 BC when it was first placed in the tomb where it was found.

Why the gold in the tombs? In case it was needed one day or to prove here lies a body who once had power. On Earth the Nefilim, we have learned, used, yes used, it to send electronic messages to their posts out in other locations as well as outside our planet. It was used to transmit signals here, there, and everywhere.

Gold is the metal that can convey messages called electric currents on Earth and beyond where temperatures range from -55°C to 200°C. It is indestructible and can and did withstand nuclear attacks. Outside our atmosphere, there is no temperature. We need molecules of some sort to bounce around to create heat. It is said that the temperature of outer space is 2.7 Kelvin, which translates into -270.454°C and -454.810°Fl.

Ever ask yourself when we started calculating temperatures? How do we know what the temperature was on Earth in our previous years? Interesting read for you to undertake. If we can figure that out, why could no one tell you the truth about Earth's gods and end the hate that religion causes by worshiping the physical makers of mankind?

The ark of Enlil's covenant's need for gold is so signals can be sent and received. The instructions to build the ark, which are written so we can all read, require gold to be used in the structure of the ark itself. As it is written, use the gold inside and outside the acacia wood and then make a molding of the gold to cover the wood.

The structure, as demanded, required gold rings to be placed each side of the poles. The poles, themselves made of acacia wood, were also to be covered with gold. The poles needed to be part of the ark and not removed.

Then we read that the commandments, as it is written, the tablets of the testimony that I will give, must now be placed inside the ark. This ark was to be protected and became the place where the head priest's role, which was then Moses, would be to communicate with Enlil (god).

The written tablets that Moses got are what we today call the Ten Commandments. These commandments are how Enlil told his Hibiru tribe of the way they must live and build a society in the lands that Enlil, their god, was going to give to them to live in peace and have prosperity under the ruling order of Enlil, the He-brew god.

Problem was that the people of Egypt, now set free from the overlord of Ra, Marduk's golden rule, did not follow the rules. They were human and they broke each and every rule of these Ten Commandments while waiting for their promised land to be taken over. We do break these rules to this day.

We live in a society that calls itself capitalism. What is capitalism? Is it really nothing more than (1) accumulating for the few to own and control (2) what others have created, and (3) are told to create so (4) the few in control can own this material and (5) figure out how to distribute what is needed (6) to share with others so this system of the few controlling society can be perpetuated forever and ever more.

Yes, and this game of capitalism in truth teaches you how to kill and lie and steal and cheat and covet what is not yours for your own personal use. The system teaches you to worship possessions, which is now the god of material, and for whom we break all the rules instead of living with and for our One God. And just think, you then go and speak to a third party who tells you that god is okay with the wrong behavior you in your heart knew you did. Nope, our Christ with prayers and donations, our god as the only god has forgiven your sins as his son Jesus died so god would forgive your current sins. And the big point is we believe this?

Then mankind, in times of war, goes to church and asks the god to protect our armies. Our armies that steal and kill as well as maim others for you over other gods' creations. Why? Because your god in your big church is meaner and better than the other side's god? Needed to release to all my thoughts at this moment.

Is this not just a game where some get to join the ruling few with the dreams that they too can own the gold of this society if they follow the golden rules that society commands you to follow? If not like Jesus before you, you too will be thrown on the cross so society can see what happens to those who gain a following by questioning the rules of others that do not serve the community equally as a whole.

Time for a change. This us versus them mindset only leads to premature death and destruction. It is pure animal survival when you are taught that the basic necessities of life are scarce, and only these few can figure out what crumbs you get as they eat and control the pie of living life.

I have now brought you up to the creation of the Hibirus-Hebrews and their wish for occupancy of specific lands and waiting for Enlil, their one god, to come back to and rule over them in living physical form.

The Hebrews, like mankind, created an us versus them so the power of absolute rule could be established. See, in our physical form, we need an *us* and a *them* to be the right choice. We live in a world of two choices—you are either with us, or you are one of them. That is the tug-of-war. Whose side are you on?

I must now share what is going on in my head as I finish this section on Moses. One, Moses took his flock to the Sinai Peninsula. Why there? This was Enlil's sacred and soft spot. Enlil was able to protect them in this location with his weapons, as we saw, there in Sinai.

They stay there under Enlil's (god's) protection and rule until Enlil can secure safe protection and success in the coming invasion of the lands inhabited by the Canaanites, another Semite tribe not yet identified as loyal to Enlil. This was a land grab for Enlil to re-create his utopian society that obediently followed his Ten Golden Rules of building a just society in the Edin region. Enlil is the Hebrew god, and we get mixed up learning history because the other tribes had many Nefilim gods. Not the one Nefilim (god) as required by Enlil.

Act Seven
The Era of Aries

Marduk in Control and Earthlings Creating New Societies on Earth
Act Seven, Scene One: Israel and Judea

The Hibirus had a rough life trying to be the chosen ones. The anointed few is what they believed they were, who speak to the only one god. The other Earthling tribes did not agree with this proposition and caused them many problems. And Enlil did not reappear.

How do they get Enlil back was their question. They needed his help as the protector. What did they do? They decided when David, their anointed King, took control to build the temple to make the gold, so Enlil came back to Earth. This took place around 1000 BC. Still the Age of Aries and now run by the unseen Nefilim god, Marduk.

The ark was made around seven hundred Earth years ago from David's succession to being King of Israel and Judah. Who knows where the original ark is. Did the Hibirus alive then even know what it was? A lot of tugs-of-war went on in this region of Earth. Possessions got lost or stolen.

David wanted to become the king of the Hebrews. David must beat the current boss of the Hebrews as a lion would do to rule the lion's jungle. David decreed that he was the new boss, and it was the way it must be. David got the right to his crown by winning his match with Goliath, just like Anu got his kingship of Nibiru by fighting the then-ruler Alalu.

To prove that he was king of the Hebrews by his physical strength and wit, David grabbed the talisman of a lion, as that was the most ferocious animal fighter of Earth. So David is remembered as the man who killed the one-eyed ferocious fighter of the Philistines. Who were the Philistines? They were the descendants of the Igigi's current creations of mankind going back to when the Watchers fell to Earth. The Watchers, if you remember, were also known as the Igigi. And they were in this era of Earth time the roadblocks to Marduk's paradise, Egypt. Egypt of this era also included today's Giza and the myths or stories of Samson.

Now David, in control of Israel and Judah, was succeeded by the son, one of many sons David sired, named Solomon. This son was created with David's best friend's wife, whom he killed to sleep with Solomon's mother named Bathsheba.

Bathsheba was a daughter of Elian and was probably of part-Nefilim pedigree by birth. She was married to a Hittite named Uriah, who was a friend of David whom David killed to get his noble son by DNA Nefilim creation, Solomon.

Now Solomon fulfilled David's promise to god-Enlil and built a temple at Mount Moriah. It was built where they believed the Nefilim created Adam and Eve. Which version? I now ask. Not the primitive worker named Lulu.

This temple stored what the Hibirus believed was the Ark of the Covenant as well as the place to melt gold. And this is where the concept of manna from Heaven first appeared, as the gold in gas form liquified and fell back to Earth. The Hibirus believed this alchemizing gold would bring Enlil back to Earth.

Act Seven, Scene Two: The Aryans and the Creation of the Hindu Religion

The world outside Edin heading east toward Asia is now in focus. The Ice Age was receding. More land of Earth could now be lived on. Mankind was spreading out. As man spreads out man, does take its stories with him on his journey. Each region gets their own myths based on the Nefilim and their games they played loosely, and not under the control of Anu the King of Nibiru. Here is a quick review of what went on here in this region of Earth during this Age of Aries.

Between 1500–1000 BC, the Aryans, the Indo-Iranian tribesmen from the Steppes of Central Asia, moved into the Indus Valley. We know this area today as Pakistan and Northern India. Somehow the poems and hymns of what we today call the Big Veda (knowledge) are now put down in written form.

This is really the bible of Hinduism. The Vedas are the body of the thought process we call Hinduism that tries to trap you into believing this past as the reason you live. So, you continue your life with this philosophy of life and love and death as prescribed not by man but by the warring Nefilim (gods) who control your fate and dictate your living caste system by birth.

Now these stories are called *Sruti*, which means in our English tongue, "what is heard." Other so-called religious texts are called *Smriti*, which means "what is remembered."

So, are these the texts dictated to mankind by Inanna and her priests before she departed Earth on her return to Nibiru with her dad, Enlil? I believe they are.

The Hindus have different interpretations of these texts, so different schools between Orthodox and Reform like today's Jews or the divided Christian religions of the East separated from the West are created, all claiming to be the real truth. Islam, which is coming soon in our Earth timeline, did the same division game of having an Us versus Them. This is the current religious war of today's Middle East Sunnis and Shiites. Division of the faith being divided into two faiths being the theme.

The Vedas for the Orthodox are revelations seen by ancient sages after intense meditation and then preserved by these sages. While meditating, a question I must ask is were they communicating with Inanna (Isis) and her crew?

The epic tale of Mahabharata, one of the two ancient Sanskrit texts of the Aryans, narrates the struggle between two groups of cousins in their war of their world called the Kurukshetra. The war determined the fate of the Kaurava and the Pandava princesses and their successors. The writer of this tale is Brahma, the creator god. Could this be our Enki?

The Vedas were credited as coming from Vyasa. He was called Veda Vyasa or Krishna Dvaipayana, which refers to his dark complexion and where he started life this time on Earth. Krishna means dark and is the name of a Hindu god who reincarnated from the god Vishnu. Vishnu is the god responsible for the upkeep of the world. This is one of the three gods of the Hindu world belief system. Then we have Brahma, the creator of all. The third god is Shiva the destroyer who destroys the old so the new can come in. The circle and really the rotation of all Earth life. We are created, we live and co-create, and we die. So, the new creations can live and repeat the cycle of life.

Just see what happens when the season of your existence extends three or four and maybe more lifelines of generations of beings called your family. It will cause a ruckus as what are all of you to do on planet Earth? You will become the problem and not the solution. Why are we here on Earth? To serve whom and what for?

The Ramayana is the second text of the Hindus. This is the story that is claimed to have been written by Rishi Valmiki. The story is oral in its beginning and narrates in verse, a rap song of an earlier era so others could remember. Remember what?

Remember the tale of Rama on his fourteen-year exile in the forest by his father King Dasharatha at the request of his stepmother, Kaikeyi. The story tells you the listener, as it was oral and then many eons later written down, about how Rama did what he did to come back to power. Sounds like Marduk, does it not?

Rama's wife was kidnapped by Ravana, the so-called great king of Lanka. Now we have the Homer story of Troy. We know Lanka as Sri Lanka. Rama and Ravana went to war with their people, and Rama won. With victory, Rama got his kingdom back and was now the king of Ayodhya. This city is found today in Uttar Pradesh, India. It is called the mystical city today because of this folktale. The epic has been written and rewritten over centuries of time.

These two tales Ramayana and Mahabharata are the twin towers of the Hindu faith called the Hindu Itihasa. *Itihasa* means "history" in Sanskrit. The writer of the story must witness the story for it to be history in this world. And it is, for it is *his*-story.

These two stories preserve the tradition of the Lunar Dynasty and Solar Dynasty. The Lunar Dynasty is said to be descended from moon-related deities. We know these deities as the Igigi. The Igigi were under the control of Marduk. This dynasty made up the warrior ruling caste system.

The Lunar Dynasty's founder was Pururavas. Later, this man is described as the son of Buddha. His mother was the gender-switching deity known as Ita, who was born as the daughter of Manu, the first man in Hindu tradition.

The Solar Dynasty in Puranic literature was founded by the legend we know as King Ikshaku. This king came to human form from Manu, his father. This is the dynasty that gave us Prince Siddhartha. This is, in my mind, the Enlil family tree.

Prince Siddhartha, in my mind, was Gautama Buddha. The one who lived to give the teachings of how to live with others, as Moses gave his people the commandments of what a society must do to live in peace in Earth's earlier time as dictated by Enlil before Enlil left Earth. The Buddha lived sometime on Earth between 600-400 BC. This we will learn in the second book of this series, *Taking Jesus Off the Cross* in Act Nine.

It is important to understand that if the Nefilim (gods) left Earth, one definitely did not. Marduk was forbidden to go home, so he stayed. Marduk was not one of Nefilim (god) of celebrations. Marduk was always hidden. He did not like people. He liked to be the big and controlling boss. The people were left at a loss. Marduk acted like we will learn Zeus acted. The ancient Earth beings were used to royal visits and royal gatherings to celebrate life. The people needed to be told what to do. We Earthlings were created to be slaves or servants. Remember that.

Now we are left alone with a Marduk, a Nefilim (god), who loves conflict and war. All so everyone could worship him to resolve differences without totally wiping out the other side. The enemy needed to survive so Marduk could play again. Also, the weapons and the ME left with Enlil were nowhere to be found. Weapons were now what man could make on Earth. The wars now were hand-to-hand combat.

Mankind's knowledge would evolve, and we would in Earth time have our own weapons of mass destruction. We just needed to evolve and remember as well as understand the hidden information in our DNA. Hidden with the key to unlock requiring you to not have fear nor let hate run your life. Hate and fear and ignorance so we do not know how to work together as one team of mankind.

If you study those who are called geniuses, these few are the ones who tap into the higher powers that are not physically seen. These powers are all around us as our guides to end or maybe continue the game of the slave and servant of all mankind, except the chosen few. Who chooses them? And why them and not you, you ask? Ask yourself if you are open to receive. You must be willing to live outside the book of conventional dogmatic religion. When you reverse the dogs, we have become for the few you start to live with the supreme force of all creations.

The sheep-people needed stories and leaders they called prophets to lead and show them the way and meaning of life. All of a sudden, the Buddha started to appear. Could these few really be the Nefilim (gods) visiting Earth and giving the info to the chosen few? I believe it could be so. Something is getting me to do this. I pray it is to open us up to have on Earth the heaven we could become if we learn where we are from and how we got here. With this knowledge we can come together as a team and change our world.

Act Seven, Scene Three: China and Their Mandate from Heaven

The Chinese have a fascination with dragons. Why? Fire-breathing flying serpents? Could these dragon images of the Chinese culture be the flying fighting machines of those who colonized Earth? Were the Nefilim the only ones? Did they have a battle in this region to gain control of Earth? Was China a region that was colonized by another alien race who lived on Earth before being wiped away by the Nefilim?

Do the Chinese have our same DNA code? There is some panda, not just gorilla, in their appearance. Are they a combination? What did Enki do?

These are my thoughts, which can just run wild. Something is not right here. They do not have the same goals we here with Edin genes believe our purpose is to exist.

My goal now is to show us all where our current worldwide system of land ownership and government control and imperial religions start. And why mankind works like a dog for the few as slaves and servants, not equals.

Now when did the Chinese world of empire begin? Same time as the Indus River and the empires of Babylon and the Assyrians. Empires became a worldwide phenomenon.

The first Chinese dynasty we can read about is called the Shang dynasty. This started around 1600 BC. The time right after Moses and his Ten Commandments.

This dynasty is given credit by today's historians as the beginning of Chinese civilization. This civilization is known for its writing system as well as the practice of the worship of gods, walled cities, bronze technology, and use of horse-drawn chariots to carry the bosses of the sheep-people around.

In Act Nine of this series, I go heavily into this civilization. The Chinese are a civilization, they are not a race of people. We can reproduce with them, us Westerners, but they do not think like us. They work for the good of all.

Act Seven, Scene Four: Zoroaster

Around mankind's timeline 1200 BC, a new prophet appeared in the region we know today as Iran. The prophet is known as Zoroaster. Zoroaster had visions of the first supreme god he saw manifest in front of him calling himself in human form Ahura Mazda.

Ahura Mazda is the Lord of Wisdom. This was the newest pet rock religion that swept through the Asia of the Assyrians and Persians before Christianity and Islam. These lands were wrapped up and called Media, which was in conflict with Persia for top dog back then. Media the land mass was located in today's northwestern Iran and the regions of today's Azerbaijan, Kurdistan, and parts of Kermanshah.

Zoroastrianism is a monotheistic pre-Islamic religion that said life is about the battle between good and evil. The religion had its cast of characters of angels, demons, and saviors. All similar ideas that can still be found in the todays Jewish, Christian, and Islamic faiths.

Their book/bible is called Avesta. The Avesta contains hymns and rituals and spells to stop evil. The descendants of this faith who survived the conquering killers for Islam are today known as Parsees. Their home or sacred ground is our Iran. In the killing Saudi minds, Iran is a fake Muslim. So, we are taught to hate the Iranians as they are not pure Muslims let alone the instigators of the fake lie that split Islam. Split it between the Shiite (Iran) and Sunni (Saudi). Now add the Saudi's

Wahhabi interpretation of their god. This gives these killing Saudis permission to wipe out all nonbelievers with death, not conversion, wisdom, or love.

We will go into this sect in detail in Book of Earth Two.

Act Seven, Scene Five: Marduk's Egypt (The Ra, Now the Amun)

Sit back and let me dial you in on the tugs-of-war between Egypt and Babylon during these coming years. Watch the globe of Earth now in your minds. See the Middle East and read this crazy story of mankind.

Around 1000 BC, Marduk's Egypt lost its grip and control of the region then called Meroe. See today's Egypt and Sudan. Those current lands have the same issues with issues today from those yesteryears. Meroe became an independent kingdom. This kingdom lasted until 350 AD.

In 727 BC, Meroite King Pye invaded Egypt. As new king and exclusive ruler, Pye began the twenty-fifth dynasty ruling Egypt with an anointed pharaoh. But did he have Marduk's family seal of approval? Probably not. This dynasty was short lived and ended on Earth after seventy-four years. A truly dysfunctional territory, Egypt was awaiting a new ruler of absolute authority.

Now let's flash to the Red Sea. Yemen is the nation today.

There was a dam built by someone, not Earthlings, called Marib Dam. One can find this archeological wonder in today's Yemen. This area still has the biblical wars of the past occurring as if it were only yesterday. The Saudis are trying to eliminate freedoms in religions in this region at the same time they are fighting with Iran over who shall rule Islam.

Books claim this dam was built around 800 BC. I doubt that estimation. This dam was redone for the people and their trade around 800 BC. With that assessment I agree. There is a series of ancient dams in Yemen that hopefully the Saudis will not take out. These dams are definitely, in my mind, the dams the Nefilim built to control the waterways of their landing spaceships when their colonization began here on Earth.

This dam in this era of 800 BC is important for it was to protect the burgeoning trade route of frankincense and spice trade of the new kingdoms that suddenly appeared using Sinai in that past forbidden space under Enlil's control spaceport. I say this here and now because the Hebrew god would never allow this region to have Earthlings run free and not under their pet owner's control. Too much to risk if things under the Anunnaki era were still in existence.

The dam was fixed by Earthlings so they could navigate the desert and have their trade. There are many great stories of the travelers crossing this region in those days before AD began. This was for trade with the land then known as Abyssinia, today's Ethiopia.

ACT SEVEN, SCENE SIX: THE ASSYRIANS AND PERSIANS AND BABYLONIANS

Now flash to our land that we today call Iraq.

In 744 BC the Assyrian Empire was formed in the old Babylon of Marduk's rule. This Empire last until 609 BC. The empire had a capital, Nineveh, on the banks of the river Tigris, which is in today's northern Iraq. Inside these old ruins were found many of the original and subsequent tablets that help me investigate and write this tome to mankind.

The empire was the stomping grounds of Marduk and his savage killing tribes on the loose during the star rising called the Aries Era. Iraq, we will learn, was a nation created by the writings of the UK and France when they divided the spoils of the First World War villain the Ottoman Turk Empire. The British made a mess creating new nations when once there was one. Plus, to perpetuate their imperial rule, the British gave this empire as the spoils of war and created the following nations that we know as Iraq, Syria, Jordan, Lebanon, Israel, and Saudi king rule.

In 722 BC Assyria conquered Israel and the ten tribes. This left the two tribes of Judea out as these tribes were very close to Sinai.

In 626 BC Babylon was back as a powerhouse. This tribe conquered Assyria. Did Marduk cause this to happen? Maybe as now the story of the creation of Earth, which we read here, in the beginning is changed in this Babylon area's version of history to Marduk being the god that created Earth in its fight with the dark god called Tiamat.

This new his-story was required reading in public on New Year's Day back in Babylon. New Year's Day was around our March 15; it coincided with the coming of the Northern Hemisphere Equinox of the first moon after daylight and darkness lasted twelve hours each that special day. This passage of the Sun's and the moon's positions is also how Passover and by necessity Easter is chosen each new calendar year. Never the same day the next following year.

The story in Babylon's world order is now a new reign of god, with Marduk creating Earth who was called Enuma Elish. These written tablets, also known as the Seven Tablets of Creation, were found in the library of Nineveh. In this version Enki, Marduk's father, is credited as being the creator of humans.

Under Babylonian rule we learn of the new captivity of the Hebrews' Abraham and Moses's people. The people whose males are circumcised to show they believe in the god Enlil. Their protector, Enlil, who had disappeared for around 1,200 Earth years. This goes on in our timeline of 587 BC and ends in 537 BC. The captivity started in the city of Babylon. In 587 BC Babylonia conquered Judah and moved the Enlil followers to serve Marduk's regime in Babylonia. These conquests took place under Nebuchadnezzar. And these marauders destroyed the first temple to Enlil. Legend says that the Ark of the Covent was stolen during this invasion. They never found it, and many legends were created to give this story the energy to stay alive.

Nebuchadnezzar was king of this ruthless killing regime. His father Nabopolassar, who set his stage to royalty, was an official of the Neo-Assyrian Empire who rebelled again their exclusive regional rule in 620 BC to create his new version of the old kingdom of Babylon.

The Assyrians had a relationship with Egypt, whose relationship Nabopolassar ended when his king of Assyria died by teaming up with the king of Meorite, who we learned about earlier. My point here is under Marduk, influence this region was in a state of tugs-of-war with new alliances made so the biggest ego among the few living in this region could control the chessboard of living pawns and their urban empires. Same theory Napoleon used to rule Europe from 1799–1815. That is until he got his Waterloo Sunset defeat.

This tug-of-war never ends well. For the universal soldier of Marduk's killing philosophy who does not understand LOVE and the one Supreme Source of Energy but kills for their Nefilim remaining Earth-god is the real problem. If we can learn to live love and love life without rules of order for the few who make the rules we believe to be true and get the rest of us to serve, the game of Marduk ends.

But maybe the DNA we were given has roadblocks that make us live to serve the few who control the fears they create to control all of us. The back line of Marduk's chessboard requires the religion and their priests with walled-in castles of the urban people with armies working for the king and queen. When you lose your king to another team, the game ends and long live the new king—same reasoning as the displaced king. If you lose your queen, you just use your pawns and find the next queen.

The game of life without love but with many competing servants for their god and that god's chosen rulers of kings and priests with their own made-up rules for their order and their control.

So, what happened to Babylon? Babylon in 540 BC fell to the Persian king we know as Cyrus. Cyrus is different from Marduk's crew. Cyrus tried to rule the people with wisdom and understanding. Not love, but that concept is coming shortly with the Age of Pisces. And soon we will learn of the essences and the games these people played with metaphysical energies from here on Earth and the Sun and the beyond. That is Book Two, *Taking Jesus off the Cross*.

Cyrus, a Persian, allowed the Hebrews, if they chose to do so, to return back to Judea. Many did, but not all. And those who did built a second temple to Enlil to replace Solomon's.

Act Seven, Scene Seven: Speculation of the Neanderthal

This is speculation as the Book of Enki does not detail what I am now writing about. I am now putting together this section by examining what mankind does know and how it marries the actions of what we know the Nefilim did during their stay here on Earth.

We learn about a species called the Neanderthal by our politically correct scientists. It is written that they first appeared out of nowhere around two hundred thousand years ago in Eurasia. There was an Ice Age in those regions. They also lived in Eastern Africa. They lived in caves in these regions. They are called Neanderthal as the first fossils were found in the caves of the Neander Valley in Germany around 1876.

Who were the Neanderthals? I believe they were the second grouping of Enki's creation who were supposed to be domestics for the Nefilim in their urban regions of Edin and East Africa. The timeline matches. These Neanderthals were discarded by the Anunnaki when model three of mankind came into existence. They were set free to roam, and roam they did. In tribes they ended up in southwest Europe by crossing the Strait of Gibraltar, which before the Great Flood may have been connected to Europe. The bones from this species are found in the caves of Spain and France and are dated to this era. They migrated to Central Europe and Asia.

Regarding the Neanderthal bones found in Eastern Africa, we know that the Nefilim built a society there of model two human beings. That is the exact timing of the Neanderthal bones found in these eastern African regions.

Now if you take a moment and just see society of a superior race with humans as their pets who were created to be the beasts of the Nefilim burdens, once you have what you need, you either give the excess up for adoption or you just let them go and roam free. They died out around forty thousand Earth years ago. Why?

These Neanderthals did not have the ability to socially organize as they were not taught these skills by the Nefilim. These skills were reserved for mankind classes three and four, which began around forty thousand years ago.

Mankind models three and four did overproduce as the Neanderthal prototype did, but they were taught skills that were not just DNA-related but social skills such as using tools. Speaking and writing organized community languages, not just drawing what they did or needed to do, which is how mankind types one and two were used as slaves and servants for the Abzu and Edin Nefilim societies before the Great Flood.

The excess of mankind types three and four did leave the nest of the urban societies of these ancient times. As we have read, they created the tribes that moved with the Nefilim royal blue-blooded families and the Demi-Nefilim (gods).

Societies were built around those tribes as they moved east of Edin, and after the flood, north.

Going north, they first went to today's Turkey once Greece and next the Balkans region as well as what today we call the steppe territories of the lands that once made up the USSR. Lands of early nomads who acquired no national identity and where the grounds of absolute war and destruction, be it Genghis Khan's ancestors, which includes the Scythians.

Act Seven, Scene Eight: The Balkans

In the cuneiform texts of Assyrians kings of the eighth and seventh centuries BC, we discover the concept of invaders from the steppes who rode horses on lands of today's northern Iran and Kurdistan, Afghanistan, and Pakistan as well as the other lands of these mountainous regions. They are referred to as barbarians in the history books of Herodotus, maybe civilized man's first historian around 412 BC.

Here is where the Greek Schools of Sacred Knowledge begin the Greek culture. A culture that definitely had models three and four of mankind. This group escaped Edin. They were taught in the arts by the Nefilim as well as in the sciences.

I also believe that Marduk followed them and set up his kingdom of twelve gods with him the king of this new royal court. Marduk called himself Zeus, and it is where I now take you to as we learn the reason we today study the Greeks.

And one last thought I must share. Mountains in the Olympus range did not exist in the form they do today when the Nefilim came and invaded Earth. These mountains were created by the sheet of ice that covered Europe. The mountains were freed of ice when the Great Flood hit this region, and the heat of those seas helped peel away the ice that once covered these mountains.

Mount Olympus is on today's Macedonia and Thessaly. This is the home of what we call the myths of Greeks. Supposedly just mankind's imagination trying to explain what they were seeing happening in their full view and just could not understand. That's what we were told and taught. I will now open our eyes to an alternative view.

These gods did exist.

The people of the Balkans even built their version of the pyramids in the land that we can now see called Bosnia. We see them today as the Bosnian pyramids. I was there with my son in 2011.

These lands were tilled to create a visual as if they were the rocks used in Egypt. Look up the Bosnian pyramids and let me know your thoughts. As I just said, I was there, and it fascinated me. The pyramids were not discovered until we, mankind, started seeing Earth from above. What a wonderful world of new discoveries we have seeing Earth from above.

Everyone, when we discover who we are, looks for eternal life. Rumors then said the pyramids to the sky would attract the gods, who can make it happen for us. No one understood the game as to why and how others have what you do not.

The people of the southern Balkan regions knew well the stories of kings and rules by god and god's court of twelve. These local people created their own myths, their own gods. Or did they? They created their own governments. Or did they? Governments with no king just the people who cared telling others what to do. They created the first people governments.

This new concept created the Greek city-states. They did not have a king from Nefilim appointment. They were experimenting with people community rule. But were they? Again, they had a Zeus, who many swore was real, and Zeus had his family of eleven, and those twelve had their families of the next twelve. Was Zeus Marduk when he was traveling the world as the only living Nefilim royalty still on Earth?

This Greek civilization experimentation gives us the concept of republic and democracy. But the truth is, it is all imperial haves on one side of the coin and the slaves and servants on the other. Those slaves and servants were never part of the republic nor democracy. The slaves fought the wars.

The southern Balkans were the first to unite under a king. To unite, the king must be a Demi-Nefilim (god) if not a Nefilim full-bloodied god, and so my friends, I will now share my story of Alexander, the son of Zeus.

Act Seven, Scene Nine: Alexander

The time was when this book was being researched by my quest for life so I could write this book with my son, Barron Alexander Machat.

Barron and I went to Egypt together in August of 2010 to learn and discover truths. I had gone earlier to set the second trip up. I knew the answers were hidden in plain view. East fighting West to have one ruler replace the old ruler. Meeting the new boss, the same as the old boss. We always get fooled again.

Barron and I went to Egypt to discover Alexander. I knew this story has mankind fascinated, and therefore the truth can be seen uncovering the metaphysical truths of this man and his energy while alive.

I knew some people in Egypt who I met the previous winter in my first trip to Cairo. They worked in a perfumery near the sphinx. They told me they had worked for the KGB and the American Secret Service, showing both sides the ins and outs of Egypt's spiritual and sacred, now-secret, past. I could not resist wanting to know more.

They took me around Egypt. They took me to a few Memphis pyramids, which are in plain sight but not part of the politically correct circuit, so they go unnoticed. These pyramids were structures created to unload and then load the small Nefilim spaceships when those ships came to Earth from Mars when Mars was the main warehouse for the gold before departing to Nibiru. They are older than the other famous Memphis pyramids.

I stood on the cylinders that we folk believe were built by common man. They were not built by man. They were Nefilim built, as I just inferred. I, back in that timeline, knew of the Nefilim and their space travelers, Nefilim-Anunnaki, and I read plenty of books that said they were from the planet Nibiru.

On this trip I started seeing cuneiforms sharing the knowledge not yet publicly taught. Now the rumors I thought contained in those books took on an awareness where I started to understand they were truths that we poopoo.

We became friends as they needed my info, which I really did not understand, but hey, I thought why not continue. I needed their knowledge and its resulting awareness. They said come back. I did.

I was so excited to know these folks. I did research again on the Nefilim-Anunnaki tales. I actually did a lot of research over the next six months as the quest became my life, and I was living in London where the information was available to discover with people who believe something is wrong with our interpretation of man's life on Earth. I knew where to begin, and I knew what I was looking for. I wanted more. But I wanted my son to learn and become aware with me. Barron, my son, and I went and skipped out of our business running an independent record label, Hippos in Tanks, for a couple of weeks. We went that September of 2010 on a magical, mystical tour with these folks of Egypt.

Today they are all dead, as they helped cause the public stir that overthrew Marduk's ruling order of Egypt for that moment in time we call the Arab Spring uprising of January 25, 2011. Truth that uprising did not last.

Our first destination was an oasis known as Siwa. Siwa is the Egyptian oasis on the northwestern desert of Egypt's lands. Why there, you ask? Because I wanted to feel and try to understand without lies firsthand why Alexander went to Siwa instead of finishing off the Assyrian's ruling order.

I needed to understand the metaphysical energies that ruled Alexander. I knew there was something more that was left out of the history books. I gave my son the name Barron Alexander for I dream wanting to believe it was his destiny to lead us to the freedom of our minds and souls.

I write now using the wisdom and the teachings of Zecharia Sitchin as my spiritual light putting together the true metaphysical story of what Alexander was after when Alexander left his home and went off to conquer the known world, which he was taught by Aristotle existed.

Questions that run through my head are the following: What was he doing in Egypt? Why the detour instead of just finishing off the war against the Persians who succeeded the Assyrians and Babylonians? Who was this god Enuma Elish who ran these armies killing armies, and of whom it was said could transform his body into another being?

Who was Alexander?

Alexander was the son of the Macedonian king, Philip. Philip was the latest king of the Argead family dynasty. This family ruled over Macedonia since 700 AD when someone known as King Caranus, claiming descent from Heracles, combined this region with his kingship Argos and created the new family dynasty kingdom called Macedonia. This region is where the Greek mythology began in the peninsula called Peloponnesus in today's southern Greece.

This is where mythology of the Greek gods borders on truth as we examine the metaphysical elements that exist in the ethers as well as on the ground putting together where these Greek god myths began and why these myths are so important to us today.

The myths are based on truth, and these myths helped keep us locked inside the Nefilim imperial energies of our matrix called Earth inside this glass called a solar system. The light of metaphysical truths I will now share. What we are taught are the Greek gods are cartoon mythological characters and may really be Marduk living as Zeus and controlling his half-breed troops of Demi-Nefilim living on Earth and becoming Marduk/Zeus royal gods of this Balkan region.

Alexander's mother was Olympias. Was that her real name? Think about it. The name is a feminine version of the Greek word Olympia. That was the name of the plain in the ancient area known as Elis in western Peloponnesus. This was the region sacred to the Greek gods of the beginning of Greek civilization and was where the gods ruled the runaway human beings now populating this region of Earth.

Look at the name Peloponnesus. Think about what it signifies in these past ages of our existence in this region of Earth. Let's be life gazers and see the stars, which I see as stars of previous thoughts used when naming an object such as a child as well as a land. Examine the meaning of that word to those who used that word when they labeled an object with that name. The energies buried inside that word, which are a talisman hiding the truths for those in the know to see and begin to understand what was going on in that time period.

So again, the home of the Greek gods was Olympia. Olympia was the name the mother and father gave their daughter Olympias. Who was she? Is she Inanna, who is also known in her energy form as Isis? Is Isis not extremely important in the development of Greek mythology when we examine the similarities of that mythology to Egypt with Horus and Osiris and Isis?

All the mythologies in our world today circulating around are based, I believe, on tales spun explaining the games and frontiers of the Nefilim here on Earth creating new Earthling societies. These stories are explaining in reality what these Nefilim energies did while they were bored and waiting for the "okay" to return to Nibiru. Or are these stories really based on what happened when the other Nefilim left Earth and Marduk and demigod family and friends needed something to do to fill their days being the gods of this plateau?

Philip, Alexander's supposed father, was the latest hereditary king of his Greek region. He had Nefilim demigod blood in his DNA. Philip wanted out of his marriage to his queen, we can read in our history books, who was the required blood partner of creating next-generation leadership in the Greek gods' game of life chess. You married to keep the bloodline going for your heirs. That blood line was your family's ticket to living on Earth where Earthlings were raised to serve you and your family.

Philip, bored being just a king, found a new queen he believed he loved. And to get out of this hereditary rules marriage, he called Olympia a whore. This unfaithful act meant she was unfaithful and therefore had to be dethroned. Philip found a new wife and started a new life, which produced a male offspring, who he wanted to have this throne of his when he departed Earth form.

Olympia was having none of this crap. She would not go away. She set out to have her cake called a kingdom and be the only one who would eat it. Olympia had a teacher for Alexander named Aristotle to teach him the Sacred Knowledge of Earthlings.

Aristotle was the third major guru in the educated line of knowledge from the Elysian Schools of Sacred Knowledge. Socrates, the first guru of these schools and who is my spiritual guide, knew the Nefilim-Anunnaki game of ownership and control of Earthling lives under the Nefilim rules of order. The Nefilim lived by controlling the order of lives and watched the solar system and the galaxies to discover when a supernatural event would shake up the predictable life one had while living on a living planet that could not escape the metaphysical elements that came into its place in space from time to time.

Pluto, guru number two, was placed in this position to perpetuate the system of absolute boss with the priests who authenticated absolute rule by the few. Aristotle was just one who did as he was told to do.

However, Marduk was not part of that Socrates or Pluto game. Marduk was bipolar, and he liked stirring the pot of predictable lives, which would lead to war. Marduk's game plan of control was to divide the masses. Make people kill for their version of god.

Socrates's teachings were simple. Do not blindly follow the old rules. Bury fear. Teach people to question rules and resulting order. Who does the order work for? The We the people or the Me the new god of life.

Socrates was a rebel. Socrates was a disruptive philosopher who would not perpetuate the matrix metaphysical understanding of what the Nefilim wished you to see in your thoughts called dreams. Socrates was put to death for teaching his students to reason on their own. His successors Pluto and Aristotle started their teaching by making students live in the matrix of Nefilim rules and resulting order, which is why Alexander got Aristotle to be his teacher. He would be taught that he was immortal and would have everlasting life here on Earth. How? We are able to learn the game played.

Philip dumping his royal queen placed doubt on the crown prince line of succession in this kingdom. Philip married a woman of Macedonian nobility. This nobility was human nobility and outside the Greek Parthenon line of gods. Mankind did not have eternal life, but one accepted by the gods to rule the lands on their behalf.

Aristotle, as required by Olympia, put the true news of who Alexander's birth father was in truth into the lad's head. Alexander, Aristotle said, was the son of an Egyptian pharaoh who the Greeks named Nectanebus. Nectanebus had visited Macedonia and was rumored to have seduced Olympias and was in fact the royal father of Alexander. A thought to share: Was he?

Alexander loved hearing this version of his creation. He wanted to be in reality everlasting royalty.

Phillip was mysteriously assassinated. Alexander was now twenty, so it is written. The boy was now king of Macedonia, and as the new prince from wife two, could not fight for his title regime. Olympias had way too much control. So, with Olympias as his mother queen, he went to unite the Greek municipalities finally as one fighting force to end the battles once and for all by the maundering Persians and their new king and following kings. These kings wished to use war to keep the people's minds under their rule occupied on physical safety, not spiritual awareness.

It was rumored from this story of his real dad now placed in Alexander's head, who the Greeks called Nectanebus, who was none other than the god in disguise, Amon. Alexander was at least a Demi-Nefilim (god). Hearing and wanting to believe this, Alexander now had to confirm this truth. Yes, his mother slept with more than one man. But Alexander did not care as this made him true royalty.

Alexander was now in charge of the Greek army team of local municipalities called states. He was to lead the charge into Asia minor, today's Turkey, then today's Syria into today's Iran and put an end to the war and evil rule of the Persians and their version of king for an Anunnaki day.

Before departing for the overseas Asia Minor war, Alexander stopped at the Greek port of Delphi, a sacred site in the south of Greece.

This is where the then rich and famous would go to consult the Oracle living inside the temple dedicated to the god Apollo, a.k.a., Mercury. Mercury is the name given to share the metaphysical energy messenger for our universe and the Sun's rules and resulting matrix running order.

There in Delphi, according to written legend, the living physical Oracle named Sibyl would go into a trance, and speaking for the regional Nefilim (god), would answer the question asked by communicating with the local or regional or head god.

Thought to share with you. Was this just another telecommunication center like Enlil built in Moses's era? A communication line to keep the civilians in line by orchestrating truth so the god who answers can control destiny and stop others from having their own fate?

Sure, it could be. The site at Delphi, which means "womb" in Greek, was said to have been the one chosen by Zeus, head of the twelve Greek gods, to house the information. Zeus picked this site according to legend because he set two pigeons in flight, and this is where they met. The pigeons carried the message of where the top god wanted the Oracle to be stored and for others in the know to get the information.

Zeus declared the site to be the navel of Earth. And this Zeus placed an oval-shaped stone called an Omphalus, Greek for "navel," as the place for this Whispering Stone.

Alexander asked the Oracle if he was a demigod of Nefilim or a full-blooded God and would he thus gain immortality. The stones, the Alexa reply of that era, were as always subject to interpretation. You heard what you wanted to hear. But this much is true as he was told to go and visit the Egyptian Oracle in Siwa.

Siwa, again an oasis in the western desert of the lands today called Egypt, which is three hundred miles west of the Nile Delta, was also chosen by the flights of two birds. These birds were black, and the god Amon Zeus (Marduk) set these birds in flight. Amon again was considered by the Greeks to be their Zeus.

Siwa in Egyptian means "palm land." The region today is famous for dates and olive oil products as well as basketry, which are exported around our world. This is also the region for the seat of the Oracle temple of Amon-Zeus (Marduk) and was written about in earlier times by Herodotus (alleged sacred teacher of history, in this case the wars of the Greeks and Persians).

Now in history we learn that a few very famous characters visited this Oracle in Delphi. One of the two I will now mention is first, none other Hercules. Hercules, the man who myth said beat the twelve labors to win his destiny and change his fate set forth by the other gods. Here at this site, it was told that Hercules was the son of Zeus.

The other visitor to the Oracle was also a son of Zeus. This son was Perseus. The son of a god. This warrior managed to destroy Medusa without turning into stone, as Medusa was able to do to her victims.

Alexander was told he maybe was the son of Amon-Zeus, the unseen god, by the Oracle in Delphi. The Oracle told him to go to Siwa. Zeus, as we learned, was the name the Greeks had for this Amon god. Makes sense if you realize that when Marduk disappeared from Egypt, he probably went to the other territories not built under Nefilim supervision. Both Rome and Greece built their mythology on their second round of gods after their Zeus or Jupiter, a.k.a., Marduk. The next generation twelve. Both Greece and Rome had very similar gods with names changed to fool the innocent as well as ignorant.

Alexander was told to go to Siwa, Egypt, as fate dictated to him by the Oracle at Delphi. He should have ended the Persians once and for all as they retreaded eastward. Alexander and his troops should have continued on to Asia Minor and continued the war and get the Persians to stop their murdering runs on other societies. But his fate or his destiny gave him a different course.

Alexander, instead of doing what generals would do to win a war, put his search in front of his troops and turned the army south and then went west. He followed the Delphi Oracle's suggestion. He went to Siwa. On this trip to Siwa, he did free the Egyptians of a rule by the Persians that the Persians could not control. Alexander freed Egypt, so it now fell under his Hellenic rule.

Alexander's march to Siwa was met with little resistance except in the region of today's Tyre. Alexander's troops had to march alongside the Mediterranean Sea. There they encountered the tribe we call the Phoenicians. This tribe was loyal to the Persians. The Persians used the Phoenicians' navy to fight the Greek armies. They lost as Alexander destroyed the navy and those sailors and soldiers.

Now on the African continent in Egypt, the Persian armed forces stationed to keep Persian rules surrendered without a fight. Alexander was the liberator. Liberator of the Egyptians from Persian rules and order.

In Memphis, the capital then of Egypt, the priests knew of the rumored divine rule of Alexander. Word was spreading, as the troops marched on, that Alexander was the new divine ruler due to his parentage to the god Amon—remember, the unseen god.

The Egyptian caste of priests tried to get Alexander to go to Thebes, todays Karnak, and the Luxor region, what was then called Upper Egypt. The priests looking to be the ruling order again wanted Alexander to be crowned a pharaoh. This would bring back Amon rule was their thought.

Again, understand that Amon and Zeus as well as Ra and the Enuma Elish god of Babylon's story of creation under the god called Marduk are all the same energy. Divided to control the living people so they could not unite and understand why they are living here as a consciousness on Earth. This division using imperil religions and imperial governments is still going on today.

Alexander wanted the info from the Siwa Oracle. So instead, he took some troops west and went to Siwa by traveling along the northern coast of Egypt till he then headed south and went to Siwa. My son and I in 2010 took this same path to the Oracle in Siwa. I was also told this trip west was the same path and resulting battle lines the Nazis used to take over the Mediterranean region trying to create the Aryan Igigi energy order in the 1940s Nazi battles conquering and then losing their North Africa tug-of-war.

But what did Alexander hear from the Oracle in Siwa? History says he was told that he was not immortal, but a Demi-Nefilim god, and he must continue his quest to find Marduk in any form living on Earth. Remember, to be immortal one needed a 100-percent-Nefilim bloodline, and to rule, one must be born on Nibiru.

Alexander was told he was in fact the son of Zeus. It is said that Alexander then made silver coins with his head on the face. A tradition we still do now with our leaders to make them remembered forever by society under either control or order. These coins of Alexander had the horns, so he paid homage to the horn god, the ram god, Amon, a.k.a., Marduk. I am trying to show you that all three gods and their myths all emanated from Marduk and his rules on Earth during his Aries-Ram rule.

The stories of Alexander now are many. One even goes so far as to say that he was told to seek out a certain mountain with subterranean passages in the Sinai Peninsula. Here in these passages, one would find the angelic encounters that Alexander needed to hear so he could change destiny and fulfill his Great Fate. His fate, he was told, was to unite the worlds of Enlil and Marduk, the fighting gods. The Nefilim energy was trying to get him to be the uniter as opposed to the divider. Mankind has never united and operated as one planet of one government order. Nibiru, as we learned, did have only one king.

After it was confirmed that he was the son of Amon, Alexander, still looking for eternal life and following in the footsteps of Gilgamesh, was told he must then go and conquer Babylon. He must get the territory back to unite the lands under the ruling order of the Ram horn god, Marduk. He would be crowned the Great at the Temple to Marduk, which survived the nuclear assault of the Nefilim gods back in the time of the nuclear bombing of Sodom and Gomorrah.

This all ties together. Even today we are fighting the two Earth-based Nefilim gods' ruling order. Alexander, now with knowledge that he believed he knew who he was, set out to conquer the Olden World and went to Babylon. Darius III, the current king of Persia, rushed to stop Alexander's march near the city once known as Nineveh, which today is the contested Kurdish region in Northern Iraq. Iraq is a twentieth century nation created by the British after World War I. This is also, as I have said before, the site where Earth digs recently uncovered many of the scriptures that we can read to put together the story I share now.

After the defeat of Darius III, Alexander marched on to Babylon. There in this olden city built for the god Amon, a.k.a., Marduk, he received a hero's welcome. The priests wanted him to rule so they could have a reason to be. That reason was to have their jobs back of Marduk rules and regulations. That simple.

Alexander went to Marduk's temple and discovered that Marduk was dead lying in wake inside a golden coffin. This shocked Alexander into human reality, for his divine father was himself not immortal but subject to the physical living realities of life and physical death, not just here on Earth, but inside our solar system regardless of birth planet.

Alexander, like Gilgamesh, learned that life has its seasons here on Earth.

So, what does Alexander decide to do? Well, he said he would rebuild the Golden Empire.

Alexander made it clear that Babylon would be the new capital of his great empire. Resources were spent rebuilding the old for the new order of Alexander. As the building began, Alexander went to take over the Indus Valley, the land of Inanna (Isis), once upon an Earth time the goddess of Earth's living order.

Alexander saw he was taking on too much. So, he retreated and went back to Babylon.

Alexander, on his return to Babylon the following year, believed he had taken over the Nefilim-Anunnaki three divisions of the Olden World. Now set to reenter Babylon and get his crown and scepter, Alexander was told by the priests of this region not to enter Babylon just yet. If he did, he surely would die, so the priests say the omens from the sky told them and asked the priest to make Alexander aware of this truth.

The stories are written that Alexander did not reenter the Arch of Babylon. However, he got a fever from what today we would call a biological disease. Who gave him this death elixir we do not know, but I believe it was murder. He died as a result at the gates of the thrones of beings named the rulers of the Nefilim-Anunnaki once-golden order.

Back to my trip to Siwa. I went to the temple of the Oracle. It was in ruins but still was majestically standing. I was with Barron and tried to get him to meditate with me so we could get the messages. Barron did not sit still. It is hard for any twenty-three-year-old, including me when I was that young, to be still. I had a blast with Barron on this journey.

I did start to reflect on what went on while writing this book. I remembered I had heard whispers in my ear back then that I was not ready for the whole story of mankind's creation and the significance of Siwa's role here on Earth.

As I began to write this story, I heard, "Reflect on Egypt. Write your noted reliving your days back then with Barron." Then I heard, "Now carry on."

I asked, "Who is this?"

I heard, "Your Thoth. You are ready." Shivers went up my spine.

Act Seven, Scene Ten: The Aftermath of Alexander the Great. The End of the Age of Aries

Marduk is dead. There are no living Nefilim, we are lead to assume, now on Earth. But remember, assume has three letters to begin the word: ass. Those who assume are fools. Assume nothing; investigate. So, let me take us all somewhere. Somewhere we all wish to believe exists. We now had a world without the Nefilim. We were created to be pets of the Nefilim. We had work to do. We had to get the gold. We had to serve the royalty who created us beings. We still are not ready to live on our own and create a world of love as opposed to servitude.

Those living then were looking for the messenger from god. The messenger from god is known as the Messiah in Samaritan languages. In Greek, it is Kristos. It Latin, it is Christ. Christ meaning the messenger from the god. It does not mean God until 325 AD, when the Roman Emperor Constantine had a convention with the priests of those years of the lands of Edin and their surrounding regions. These priests voted in the concept of Christ, once man and now the God. Constantine created one religion to work hand-in-hand with the one empire of man.

Constantine tried to merge the imperial religions with his imperial government.

But in this time right after Alexander's empire was in charge of this region, the prophets were running wild. They were everywhere.

They claimed they spoke with god, and they became the prophets of different regions of our past. They were not thought to be crazy. No, not at all. Why? Because those living then knew the oral stories of the gods and that the special ones chosen to represent them were based on truth.

It's time for me to bring this Book One of Earth series to a pregnant pause. The next book, *Taking Jesus off the Cross*, will delve into our systems created to rule us on Earth without the Nefilim. The God was missing from Earth. But we never learned what god is other than those who created us to serve them and their burdens.

But right now, a quick spin of the Middle Eastern globe back through Earth time we call 300 BC—to Jesus.

Look at the area we today call Syria. No local rulers. Just first the Greek-Hellenistic controls, which ended around 31 BC with the Battle of Actium. After this battle, the Roman Empire controlled this region and the trade by using the Roman legion army.

Where is the Nefilim god? Gone, but not forgotten.

So, the people looking for more than just sunrise and sunset days becoming nights with no purpose but to exist start to castrate themselves in the city streets. Why? The reason was to become priests and devotees of Atargatis. Atargatis was their local goddess of love and war. She was the goddess of fertility and also virginity. This is really the confusing order of Inanna, or Isis as she was known in these parts.

Now let's look to the Sea of Galilee during the Jesus era. This region was forced to become Hebrews just one hundred years earlier. They were forced to either be a Hebrew or die. So now a Hebrew choosing Enlil as your new Nefilim god meant the inducted, regardless of age, were circumcised so the woman would know who was chosen to be the tribe of the one god, Enlil's, mankind. Woman had no say in those times as they were a breeding asset, and that oven that I call a womb was the only way to make your kind win the battle of numbers. Hence the lofty position given women to live and not be involved in the choruses of life, except keeping the household and raising the children so they can do the same in the human cycle of existence here on Earth.

However, not everyone bought this line. The Essenes were created. Equity was the theme. But not all would join. Just like Moses versus Aaron with the golden bull, people need to believe in a god and need an image to follow to become the flock. A spiritual image I call a shepherd to take human form. And for a new sensation to follow, the people first needed to be led astray and reconnect in the new field of understanding and awareness. A new living sensation. A new image to follow. Who would become this celebrity of mankind?

Why? Simple. We create images for the people to give their energy to and worship because we are all looking for that father image, god. Sad because we are not taught in any form of understanding that we are all part of the consciousness energy force that is the Supreme, the force of everything and more.

So now there is an unannounced contest to see who was the celebrity-messiah for the coming new order. The Age of Pisces. The man-fish who can swim all the lands and seas free or locked up in a contained thought region of air and water. This area becomes loaded with the next contestants for being the messenger from god. Jesus won this contest three hundred Earth years after he died, anointed the Christ in death form. So here I am just sharing those who came in second or third place back in this Earth era.

Hanina Ben Dosa is a name we should now know. Dosa lived in Galilee at the time of Jesus. That moment when BC meets AD.

Dosa was a holy man. A Hasidim. Not just a tribe as we are taught today of Orthodox Hebrew religious orders. The talisman holy man means "who taught how to reach god." This is the literal Greco-Roman translation.

Dosa addressed his prayers to "his" father in Heaven. We now know this father as Enlil, and Heaven was Nibiru.

But in the metaphysical sense of Hebrew and Aramaic languages, this meant being a child of god. Know that truth as we learn the story of Jesus as we take the man Jesus off the cross in the next book, *Taking Jesus off the Cross*.

Dosa lived a life in total poverty. Pretty much what the physical Buddha had become in his region of Earth. Dosa upset his wife when he gave up property for the love of love. Dosa did not succeed.

There were many messiahs all from this region. They spoke for the one god.

But others had many gods, not just one big man as god, who was always presented as an older man. Hence the word *pagan,* as the pagans worshiped the gods of wind and fire and the water as well as the land. The cross of human life. The messiah had the message from the one God, not the gods who also had to worship the metaphysical truths of the winds and fires created on the lands and the seas by events outside their Earth control. That is why they worshiped the stars in the sky to see where the next hurricane of universe energy would toss and turn their Earth with floods or fire coming down from elements like meteorites to make a new balance here on Earth.

These people of the non-urban cities believed in healing powers of a prophet to get rid of the evil, both physical and mental, that causes diseases. Not just the physical. Someone who spoke to the God. Not the local disappearing god who ruled.

The religious people of Enlil, living in Judea, a city of its time, then hated the pagans of Galilee. They were considered to be living in the backwaters of time. There was no absolute rule. There was resulting same order. With order in control, you lived in your caste of birth.

Imagine the scene when Jesus came to a town called Jerusalem by a donkey ride to show he was born free. Jesus took on the priests of the Nefilim god Enlil. He also took on their king assigned by Rome to rule and perpetuate Roman colonization.

Jesus also took on the rules and order of the Pharisees. The ones who worshipped Enlil, who left the building called Earth. Jesus was the people's representative. He kept it that way on purpose.

Jesus had a real competitor for the new way of life. Living life being free. This competitor was known as Apollonius.

Who, you ask, is this competitor? Actually, in the time of Jesus, this man was more known than Jesus. He was called the son of Zeus, and Zeus was the Hellenistic god of our universe, Enlil's competition, Marduk, for the only Earth god. They did not know the sacred story of Alexander and his dad, Marduk, who was not dead.

The Greeks burrowed their way into the Middle East with Alexander's exploits. They brought with them their gods of nature. And then these gods of nature did not stop one from learning philosophy and using awareness to explain one's reasons. They created Sacred Schools to teach people how we physically die so you know your life does not end on physical death as you, your living eternal energy of being called consciousness, just leaves your physical body.

The Egyptian schools were different from the Greek, in which you would get all geared to go to Heaven if you were one of the chosen few. Chosen by the Egyptian Nefilim (god), if he looked down on you with favor. Really a trip to Nibiru where you could get the water and food for eternal life and sit next to your Nefilim god forever and ever more.

One was never told that no one but 100 percent Nefilim could live on Nibiru, as stated in their charter, which authorized the creations called human beings. Marduk, the Egyptian Nefilim God, needed the Earthlings to believe in his Book of the Dead. This was his control. Those Egyptian schools were based on lies beyond any human control.

The Helen of Troy Greek Schools of Philosophy of Alexandria were closed down and outlawed in Egypt by Pharaoh Ptolemy VII . The pharaoh called Psychon had expelled all the Greek scholars back in 170 BC. The Ptolemy was the Greek dynasty that took over Egypt after Alexander and lasted until around 30 BC when the Romans got their rule. The schools had to be closed because the philosophy was against any individual god, not just the coming Christ.

Apollonius's manager was a Sophist we know as Philostratus. Today the teaching methods of a Sophist are considered by many, if they question imperial rule, wrong behavior. They were considered wisemen. Does not work well if you question, as Socrates did, why the few rule over all of you.

Philostratus taught how Apollonius, when living, inspired universal goodness, and had exorcisms to get rid of evil too. And, of course, performed miracles like Jesus is said to have performed.

It was said that Apollonius abstained from women and wine and wore nothing on his skin made from any animal. Dressed in white linen and never cut his hair nor his beard.

His teaching centered on the one supreme god of all. The immortality of the soul and in reincarnation were his themes. We come back till we get it right and then rejoin god as one no longer an ego that edges god out with a want or a need.

Very similar to the mystery cults of the mystics, as we call them now, when they were really mystic cults. The difference is mystery means "an imagination gone wild." Mystic means "is in touch with spirit."

Apollonius's wish was, we are told, to purify the many cults of the Roman Empire. Apollonius did not wish to create a new community. He was not an Essene, meaning of the people.

The Apollonius energy was hanging out with royalty and their priests, wishing to change them, and fighting a system that was dead. Dead for it no longer had the living god of ownership and control.

Looking for answers as to what this game of physical life is all about?

One answer. One purpose. One word in all languages describes it all.

LOVE

The game is to learn what it means and how to live it as an individual as well as a member in a community of equals.

So now to the next book as I come to the end of the Age of Pisces.

The book is *Taking Jesus off the Cross*.

STEVEN MACHAT

TOLL THE BELLS

To reveal the future
Hell we'll endure
Just gaze into the past
Toll the bells

War theatres may change
With weapons more deadly
The endgame the same
Toll the bells

This world is rife
With hatred abound
Load up the artillery
Toll the bells

Believe in your gods
And pray as you might
They cannot save you
Toll the bells

A new path is upon us
Tho the bridge is asway
Either make love your option
Or Toll the bells

— Debbie Veltri Machat

Made in the USA
Columbia, SC
23 January 2024

fe3cf58d-ec29-4838-9b47-fa4c94d02455R01